BOHEMIAN GLASS

BOHEMIAN GLASS

1400-1989

Edited by Sylva Petrová and Jean-Luc Olivié
Photographs by Gabriel Urbanek

Harry N. Abrams, Inc., Publishers, New York

Editorial note: All dimensions are given in centimeters.
One inch equals 2.54 centimeters.

Designer: Pierre Dusser, Paris

Translated from the French by Lysa Hochroth

Library of Congress Cataloging-in-Publication Data

Verres de Bohême. English.
Bohemian glass: 1400-1989 / edited by Sylva Petrová and Jean-Luc Olivié.
p. cm.
Translation of: Verres de Bohême.
Includes bibliographical references.
ISBN 0-8109-1241-4
1. Glassware--Czechoslovakia--History. I. Petrová, Sylva.
II. Olivié, Jean-Luc. III. Title.
NK5171.C9V4713 1990
748.2937'1--dc20
90-32731
CIP

Published in 1990 by Harry N. Abrams, Incorporated, New York
A Times Mirror Company

Printed and bound in France

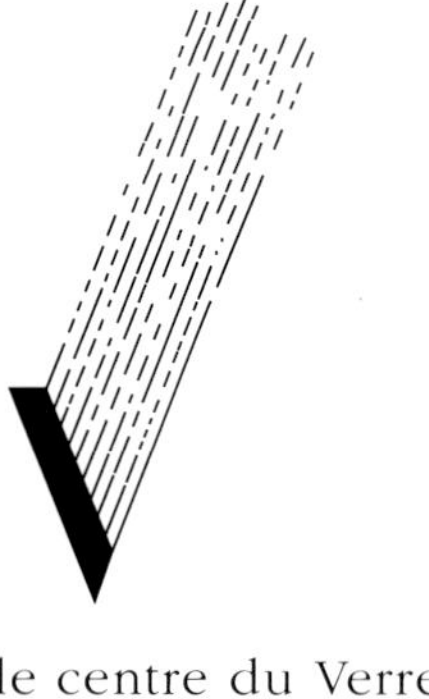

Contents

ACKNOWLEDGEMENTS

This book was published on the occasion of the Exhibition
Verres de Bohême, 1400-1989,
Chefs d'œeuvre des Musées de Tchécoslovaquie,
organized in Paris by the Musée des Arts décoratifs and the Museum of Decorative Arts of Prague (October 1989-January 1990) with the assistance of the Ministère des Affaires Etrangères, the Secrétariat d'Etat aux Relations culturelles and internationales, the Association française d'action artistique, and the support of the Ministère de la Culture, de la Communication, des Grands Travaux et du Bicentenaire, and the Centre national des Arts plastiques.

We would like to express our gratitude to all the artists who lent their work for this publication. We owe a special debt to Michel Louyot, Yves Mabin and Pavel Spiroch who were at the origins of this project, and to the following institutions for their generous assistance:

Moravian Gallery, Brno
Hluboka Castle
Museum of Glass and Jewellery, Jablonec nad Nisou
Glass Museum, Kaminecký Šenov
Regional Museum, Liberec
Sumava Museum, Kašperské Hory
Glass Museum, Nový Bor
National Gallery, Prague
Museum of Decorative Arts, Prague
Museum of Western Bohemia, Plzeň

9

Bohemian Glass Lodged for centuries in the heart of Europe

Glass objects appeared around 1500 BC; and, through all the remarkable wealth of creations arising from this bewitching material since then, the evolution of knowledge and the vagaries of taste, three names, three places, three periods have had a mythic value: Egypt, Venice and Bohemia.

Egypt and the Middle East resounded with creation myths, temple secrets and the colourful pageantry of Alexandria. In Venice, enriched by the Orient, Renaissance glass-makers attained an unsurpassed purity and lightness of material and form, and then discovered the prodigious achievements of Mannerism. In Bohemia, glass, despite its fragility, discovered a strength and vitality that flourished in the atmosphere of the Baroque.

Among all the scientific, literary and artistic works that Bohemia gave to the history of Europe, few were as widely celebrated and internationally known as its glasswork. The seventeenth century, despite the ravages of the Thirty Years' War, and the eighteenth century formed a kind of golden age of Bohemian glass, but other periods also provided masterpieces, technical inventions, forms and colours, all linked to the particular genius of the people and the land of Bohemia.

Bohemia lies in the heart of Europe, amid mineral-rich mountains. (The silver mines of Kutna Hora were one of the sources of its medieval wealth.) It has been linked throughout its history to Moravia, either as an independent state or under the foreign domination of the Hapbsurgs. In addition, from the fourteenth century until 1742, Silesia—today in Poland—was attached to the Bohemian crown. Since the creation of the Czechoslovakian Republic in 1918, Bohemia, Moravia and Slovakia have formed one state.

It has been difficult to date the first use of glass and glasswork in

Bohemia from archaeological findings and present historical knowledge, but the first original forms of local production appeared during the fourteenth century. Even before the excesses of the Baroque, a certain exuberance already appeared in the large fluted glasses used during the time of Charles IV—King of Bohemia, Holy Roman Emperor, founder of the University of Prague, and father of the nation. These glasses evoked the wealth of the country at that time.

A new force was given to glass when, instead of Venetian fluidity, the Czechs invested it with a mineral quality. It was in the workshops of the stone and crystal-cutters attached to the court of the Hapsburg Emperor Rudolph II that the modern western version of engraving and glass-cutting was born.

Unlike rock crystal, or crystallized quartz, glass is not a natural material but a fabricated, composed, proportioned mixture of fluxes, oxide of silicium, and stabilizers melted at high temperatures. It had always enabled man to imitate precious stones, but in Bohemia, at the end of the seventeenth century, glassmaker discovered a compound particularly well adapted to imitate rock crystal. But glass did not become a sort of "poor man's rock crystal". At a time when European sites could no longer provide blocks of such quality and size as those of the Renaissance, Bohemian glass came to the fore and assumed rock crystal's composite image of purity, force and rarity. Diamonds, rock crystal and glass were at that time the only transparent solids known. Rock crystal, an extract of nature, was succeeded by glass a product of human industry.

Bohemian glass had the quality of stone—the philosopher's stone. It was born in the crucible of the alchemists—who, as we know, were favoured by Rudolph II. The famous reddish-gold colour, developed in Germany but spread by Bohemian glass-makers throughout the world, was an alchemist's creation and long was believed to possess magical virtues. Prague is a magical city, awash with the rabbinical secrets of the Middle Ages and modern science-fiction. Two words were born here: Golem and Robot. Glass in Prague, more than anywhere else, hangs suspended between magic and science, illusion and rigour.

Nevertheless, as in Egypt and Venice, it was also an export network that made the concept of Bohemian glass known. Its commercial success dates back to the eighteenth century, when Bohemian-glass syndicates extended from Hamburg and Constantinople to New York and Mexico. In North Bohemia at this time, glass-makers, who often alternated between periods of production and commercialization, could learn more than ten foreign languages.

Well before glass production and textiles helped to enrich Bohemia, Medieval glassworks played an equally important role. As they were often in the forefront of clearing the forests—wood was used for combustion, and its ashes for flux—they opened up new territories for agriculture and colonization. Later, the exploitation of hydraulic power furnished by the numerous rivers of North Bohemia and Silesia—part of Bohemia until 1742—permitted the extraordinary flourishing of engraving and cutting techniques.

In addition to the individual characteristics of the workshops, regions and periods, is the difference between German and Bohemian glasswork. The entire history of Central Europe unfolds here because Bohemia, lying at the cross-roads of European trade routes, was a land of transit and one of the favourite terrains for the battle between Slavism and Germanism.

Engravers and glassmakers travelled a great deal. (Like Caspar Lehmann, the first to adapt wheel-engraving for glass, who was active in Munich, Dresden, and Prague, and whose students founded the workshops at Nuremberg.) If Bohemia, therefore, played an important role in the history of glass in Central Europe, Dresden, Berlin and Nuremberg also had their hours of glory.

In Bohemia, the glass industry was well-enough established to survive severe periods of crisis and to rise again from its ashes. Unlike other centres of the Baroque, it found new geniuses and new investigators during the nineteenth and twentieth centuries.

In weathering the difficulties of industrialization, glass-making continued to attract new generations of creators, who first founded the modern school of Bohemian, then later of Czechoslovakian, glass. The engraver Dominik Biemann provided the first milestone in this modernity. Like all engravers before him, he interpreted models from paintings, prints, and medals, but he was also the first to create original portraits, intimate psychological studies hollowed out in the transparency of glass.

The country that gave us the great humanist Jan Amos Komenský, known as Comenius (1592-1670), who founded modern pedagogy, also created glass-making schools in the nineteenth century in which pluridisciplinarity prodominated, along with both technical and artistic instruction. These schools were the basis for the creative expansion that began at the end of the nineteenth century and continued into the twentieth.

Art Nouveau in Bohemia was linked to the Viennese centre, which continued to influence creators even after the independence of Czechoslovakia in 1918. Students of the Viennese architect Otto Wagner, like Jan Kotěra (professor at the School of Decorative Arts in Prague) or Pavel Janák (director of the Artěl group), played a vital role in including glass in the Czech Cubist movement. Lobmeyr house, at once profoundly Viennese and Bohemian since the nineteenth century, saw the birth of the most extradordinary creations of the twenties, like the engraved glasses of the sculptor Jaroslav Horejc, which eerily combined neo-Classical rigor and Expressionist feeling. The success of these glass manufacturers in Paris in 1925 was followed by those of Functionalist tendencies, as attests the Grand Prix received by Ludvika Smrcková at the 1937 International Exposition.

The history of Bohemian glass displayed a rare continuity after the Second World War. The deck had been re-shuffled; Czechoslovakia reaffirmed its glass-making tradition and began a spectacular development with an original, two-tiered teaching system. Solid technical training in experimental workshops allied with different glass manufacturers led to plastic creation at the Academy of Applied Arts in Prague, under first-rate instructors. By the end of the 1950s, the success of young Czech artists at international shows—the Triennales in Milan, the Universal Exposition of 1958 in Brussels—gave them the confidence and determination to glaze new trails.

Glass-making in Czechoslovakia at this time bore certain resemblances to Finland's. Each country anchored its renaissance in a secular tradition expressing a unique cultural identity, and each harkened back to a heritage of the thirties that had affirmed its national orientations. The practice of Finnish designer Tapio Wirkkala, for example, in the Iittala Glassworks at the end of the forties, displays a subtle understanding of technique and knowledge in the elaboration of a work.

Educational programmes in Czechoslovakia generally call for factory experience. The linking of creation and technique, or more generally of art and industry, was taken to exemplary heights in the relationship between René Roubiček and master glass-maker J. Rozinek at Nový Bor. The young generation of glass-makers, educated in this rigorous but open post-war system, was lucky to have professors who could lead them from the simple practice of making glass to a unique plastic expression in glass. Josef Kaplický opened the way for those who would teach the next generations, especially Stanislav Libenský.

Stanislav Libenský was both pedagogue and creator. He taught in Nový Bor before taking over first the Železný Brod workshop, then, in 1963, the glass workshop at the Academy of Applied Arts in Prague, which he ran until 1987. Libenský shepherded several generations of artists-in-glass in an atmosphere of mutual exchange and enrichment; and at Železný Brod he met Jaroslava Brychtová, who, before exploring glass's optical properties, worked in molten glass, or pâte-de-verre—an echo of eighteenth-century Bohemian practice, and charged with some of the same myths attaching to rock crystal. Libenský and Brychtová achieved great dramatic effects with this technique, which would soon become synonymous with Czechoslovakian glass.

The Libenský/Brychtová team helped introduce contemporary Czech glass throughout the world, and later brought it to international exhibitions, like those organized by the Corning Museum of Glass in 1959 and 1979. The latter exhibition was shown at the Musée des Arts Décoratifs in Paris in 1982, which also revealed a new generation of French glass-makers.

Libenský represented Czechoslovakia on the International Council of the University of Glass in Pilchuck, in Washington State, where young glass-makers from five continents gathered with older artists from all over the world. In the United States they found an educational system integrated into the university, the origins of the Studio Glass Movement —glass-making executed in workshops independent of factories. We should note with interest the determining role of education in both these countries—the two places of choice for contemporary glass.

The dynamism of the Libenský/Brychtová tandem was crucial to glass in Czechoslovakia. They never reached the end of one road without immediately starting down another.

Václav Cigler, a man of discretion, played a decisive role in breaking with the past, releasing from blocks of glass the effect and movement of light. Cigler's works capture both the whimsical beauty of optical games and philosophical musings about the spatial metamorphoses of glass's reflecting surfaces. Whatever their dimensions, they are monumental. Contemporary Czech glass is allied with architecture, which uses it extensively. It is utilitarian or useless, in the forefront of plastic movements and nonetheless independent, and always informed by a multi-secular heritage.

Although the art of glass-making has always been rooted in an industry with a remarkable commercial network, this book is not a history of the glass industry, but rather of seven centuries of creation. Bohemian Glass is a co-production of two decorative arts museums, those of Paris and Prague, whose evolutions are very similar. They were founded in the wake of the universal expositions of the second half of the nineteenth century, and their collections were formed according to the "products of industry" honoured in Paris in 1878, 1889, and 1900. They have both based their activities on exhibitions and collections, but also on teaching. Bohemia's rich glass-making tradition explains the high quality of the collections of the Museum of Decorative Arts in Prague. This very important patrimony is regularly enriched by contemporary works, which are all the more numerous as the years following World War II—and up until today—constitute a new golden age of Bohemian glass.

YVONNE BRUNHAMMER AND JEAN-LUC OLIVIÉ

The Museum of Decorative Arts, Prague.
Photo Gilles de Chabaneix.

The Prague Museum of Arts and its glass Collection

The museum

In 1881, the "Arkadie" Association organized an exhibition of antique *objets d'art* at the Town Hall in the Old City of Prague. This was the first exhibition of its kind, and from it sprang the idea of creating a museum of decorative arts in Prague, similar in spirit to the Victoria and Albert Museum in London. Several years went by, however, before the project was realized.

As early as 1868, the Prague Chamber of Commerce, in collaboration with the Austrian Museum of Decorative Arts, had organized an exhibition assembling objects purchased by the Viennese museum the preceding year at the Universal Exposition in Paris, as well as a group of antique *objets d'art* whose source was, for the most part, the seminal collection of Vojtěch Lanna. The success of this exhibition confirmed the need to create a permanent collection in Prague. The Prague Chamber of Commerce followed through on this project and renewed its funding each year. It gradually constituted a small collection, whose first pieces were acquired in Paris at the Universal Exposition of 1878.

In 1885, the Museum of Decorative Arts became a completely separate institution. As it had not acquired its own buildings, its permanent collections were housed in rooms at the Rudolfinum (today the Artists' House), which had just opened its doors. The collection was augmented by objects borrowed from the Vojtěch Lanna holdings, but the museum needed an independent building. One was built between 1897 and 1900 in neo-Renaissance style, designed by architect Josef Schulz. Now the museum could develop and house its collections properly.

During the first fifty years of its existence, the museum dedicated itself to the acquisition and display of new objects, and to the organization of lectures. It also offered training sessions designed for professors and artisans. The museum collaborated with various specialized schools and organized competitions in which numerous artists and artisans participated. During the thirties, the museum expanded its activities to work with enterprises involved in the production of objets d'art. This co-operation both improved the artistic quality of common objects and educated the public taste. In addition, the museum offered scholarships for young artists to participate directly in this production.

In the years following World War II, the collections grew significantly because of the new property laws, which enhanced in particular the museum's holdings in ceramics, furniture and textiles. In 1949, the museum was nationalized and placed under the Ministry of Culture; it became a specialized institution of national importance, and its prestige increased. Its budget was augmented, which allowed the planning of acquisitions. New horizons opened: the museum assured its status as a research institute, participated in international shows like the XIth Triennale in Milan and the 1958 Universal Exposition in Brussels, and worked in close co-operation with production enterprises, especially in the glass and ceramics fields.

In the 1960s, the museum recruited a considerable number of specialists, and six specialized departments were created in 1970. The photography collection in the Applied Graphics department became world famous, thanks to several exhibitions abroad. The very rich collection of twentieth century applied art grew every year through new acquisitions. The contemporary pieces were shown abroad on numerous occasions.

The glass collection

Funds were allocated to the future museum in 1873, and some were used in 1878, during the Universal Exposition, to acquire what became its first collection. This included a large number of glass objects.

From its very creation, and under extremely favourable circumstances, the Museum of Decorative Arts worked to expand its holdings in glass. In 1886, Sir Vojtěch Lanna—a passionate collector and patron of the arts, industrialist and member of the museum's administrative council—lent his collection of over a thousand pieces, and then donated it in 1906. Lanna's magnificent bequest included a great variety of glass objects spanning antiquity to the nineteenth century. It provided a solid basis for the development of new collections, and even today represents one of the most priceless ensembles in the field of enamelled Renaissance glass, Venetian glass from the sixteenth and seventeenth centuries, Spanish glass from the seventeenth and eighteenth centuries, and cut and engraved Baroque Czech glass. In 1913 the collection of double-walled glass (Zwischengoldglas) was completed through a gift from the collector A. Potuček; and in 1925, after the death of Leon Bondy (a distinguished member of the museum's administrative council), the Minister of Finance donated his collection.

The most important donation (in 1932) was that of Gustav E. Pazaurek, the great Czech glass specialist, former director of the Liberec Museum (Reichenberg), and director of the Museum of Industry in Stuttgart. This collection of almost two thousand glass pieces, dating principally from the nineteenth century, constituted, along with the Lanna donation, the cornerstone of the museum. After its nationalization, the museum acquired the glass object collections, shown in 1957 and 1960 at the Triennales in Milan. Thus it completed its contemporary holdings.

Nevertheless, the collection was not exclusively built through gifts and transfers. The nationalization of the museum permitted a more aggressive purchasing policy, and the collections were extended to twentieth-century creations (Art Nouveau and Functionalism) and to the works of contemporary glass-makers. Six thousand new pieces were added to the museum's holdings.

The glass collection at the Museum of Decorative Arts in Prague illustrates the development of glass-making from the Roman period to the present day, through pieces of both Czech and foreign origin. It includes approximately twenty-five thousand objects, and represents one of the greatest and most prestigious collections of glass in the world.

Dagmar Hejdová

BERLIN
Potsdam
POLAND
G.D.R.
See enlargement of North Bohemia
Wroclaw
Dresden
Silesia
METALLIFEROUS MOUNTAINS
Teplice
Košťany
Most
Klodzko
ORLICKÉ HORY
Hradec Králové
Elbe
Karlovy Vary
Cheb
PRAGUE
Pardubice
Kutná Hora
Škrdlovice
Plzeň
Vltava
Bohemia
Moravia
Anín
Klášterský Mlýn
Adolfov
Vimperk
Lenora
České Budějovice
Nové Hrady
Stříbrný Vrch
Brno
F.R.G.
ŠUMAVA MOUNTAINS
Danube
VIENNA
Munich
AUSTRIA
N
Scale
0
50
100 km
Capital
City
Glass production sites

Enlargement of North Bohemia
G . D . R .
POLAND
JIZERSKÉ HORY
Jelenia Góra
Cieplice
Sklarzska Poręba
Chřibská
Falknov
Kamenický Šenov
Nový Bor
Česká Lípa
Dolní Polubný
Nový Svět
Harrachov
Liberec
Jablonec nad Nisou
Železný Brod
GIANT MOUNTAINS
CZECHOSLOVAKIA
Elbe
Opava
Ostrava
Olomouc
Slovakia
U.S.S.R.
Morava
Košice
CZECHOSLOVAKIA
HUNGARY
Bratislava
Danube
BUDAPEST

The Middle Ages and The Renaissance

The Middle Ages. Slavic civilization first blossomed in the Czech countries between the eighth and tenth centuries, during the time of the Great Moravian state. Jewellery was notable among the objets d'art of this period, especially glass pearls—stretched, compressed into moulds, blown or strung. The fall of Great Moravia at the beginning of the tenth century did not end glass-making in Bohemia, and from the thirteenth century onwards, this industry fluorished in Central Europe. It developed both the technique for hollow glass (for objects) and sheet glass for architectural use. In the fourteenth century, large-scale construction work in the city of Prague, undertaken by Charles IV of Luxembourg (1346-1378), King of Bohemia and Holy Roman Emperor, once again stimulated production. Stained-glass windows, for either historical or ornamental decoration, are among the most valuable artworks of this period. Few have come down to us, since most of them disappeared during the Hussite revolution in the fifteenth century, or during the reconstruction of Gothic churches in Baroque style in the seventeenth and eighteenth centuries. The glass mosaic representing the Last Judgment, which decorates the south façade of the Prague cathedral, constitutes a work unique north of the Alps. Italian masters no doubt took part in its creation in 1370-71, but the style of composition, and chemical analysis of the glass pieces, attest to Bohemian origin. The construction of cities, churches and monasteries spurred the fabrication of the coloured glass used for windows. These commonly-used objects —simple flat glass and hollow glass— emanated from small itinerant glass-makers, who were often among the first to colonize the vast forested regions along the borders of the country. Our knowledge of medieval table glass is founded partly on archeological discoveries and partly on iconographical documents, especially the illuminated manuscripts of the second half of the fourteenth century. Archival texts, place names and the results of digs testify to the activities of twenty-five glass-makers in Bohemia between the thirteenth and fifteenth centuries.

.6.

The Renaissance. The changes occurring all over Europe on the economic, political and spiritual fronts reached the Czech countries around 1500, an important turning point in their history. In the sixteenth century, the abundance of precious metals coming from America led to a drop in the price of silver in Bohemia, which encouraged the feudal lords to exploit more efficiently the natural resources of their dominions. In the second half of the sixteenth century, glass production in the mountainous and wooded regions evolved considerably, thanks to the perfecting of new technical procedures used for the construction of furnaces, for fusion, for purification, and

.2.

for the colouration and de-colouration of pastes. The adoption of forms and decoration influenced by Venetian Renaissance glass, and by the Venetian style common north of the Alps, also contributed. Many great glass-making families deserve credit for this progress, among them the Friedrichs, founders of a glassworks still active in Chřisbská (Kreibitz) in North Bohemia; the Schürers, responsible for twenty or so factories, the first of them the celebrated glassworks of Falknov (Falkenau), in 1530; the Wanders, in the Jablonec region (Gablonz); and the Preusslers, active everywhere to some extent in Bohemia, Silesia and Bavaria. The main glassworks in the south of the country was the Wilhelmsberg, in the Rožmberk domain. The Rožmberks were the most powerful lords of Bohemia.

Despite improvements in the paste, the potash-lime glass of Bohemia remained less malleable and less transparent than the soda glass coming from Venice. The production of wine goblets based on Venetian models was of little importance. More numerous were the *Willkomm*, enamelled glasses of one to two litres, used for making toasts during the banquets of the nobility. Enamelled decoration existed in Bohemia from around 1560 on, although, at first, it was probably the Schürer and Friedrich glassworks alone who used it. It became more common during the 1590s, as the significant number of pieces conserved will attest. The size of the *Willkomm* offered a considerable surface for painting, and the choice of subject depended on the piece's destination. Heraldic decorations exalted the prestige of the host; satirical subjects and episodes taken from fables amused the guests; allegories and scenes from biblical history constituted a wise reminder. From the end of the sixteenth century, the various trades and their emblems were also evoked, which suggests that these glasses were used in the artisan's entourage and during guild meetings.

.5.

Linear engraving by diamond point, used in conjunction with cold-painting, was another technique of decoration inspired by Venice. Examples date from the seventeenth century, from the Nové Hrady (Gratzen) Glassworks, on the Rožmberk properties in South Bohemia. This ornamentation was also practised in Chřibská. These tall glasses usually depict allegories of the Virtues inspired by the engravings of Jost Amman (1539-1591), but we also possess pieces in cobalt blue glass or manganese violet with purely ornamental engravings. The white filigree decoration, also borrowed from Venice, was used in Nové Hrady and Chřibská, most often on characteristically Bohemian shapes.

Only at the end of the Renaissance was wheel-engraving applied to glass-making. This technique, which would make the reputation of Bohemian glass, owed its revival to the passionate devotees of rock crystal and precious stones at the end of the sixteenth century. Italian artists, and particularly Annibale Fontana and the brothers Saracchi and Miseroni, cut and engraved works of immense value in these materials for the reigning families of Munich, Madrid, Paris and Prague. In Munich, Caspar Lehmann (deceased in 1622) learned the art of semi-precious stone-cutting and glass-engraving. From the end of the 1580s on, he worked in Prague in the service of the Emperor Rudolph II. For a short period, he was also active in Dresden. Lehmann is the only glass-engraver of his time whose works have come down to us in significant numbers; their identification relies upon affinities with the only work signed by him, a glass with allegorical decoration from 1605. Lehmann also engraved on glass plaques: sometimes allegorical and mythological scenes, sometimes portraits (Christian II, Elector of Saxony; Rudolph II; and other personalities and their entourages). The influence of the celebrated Miseroni workshop can be seen in the spread of glyptics throughout Bohemia. The Miseronis worked in Prague for Rudolph II and his successors, and their technique for engraving precious stones was flawlessly assimilated not only by cutters and engravers of semi-precious stones in Prague, but also by provincial artisans, especially in the north, at the foot of the Giant and Jizerské hory mountains. In the seventeenth century, regional glass-engravers would benefit from this tradition.

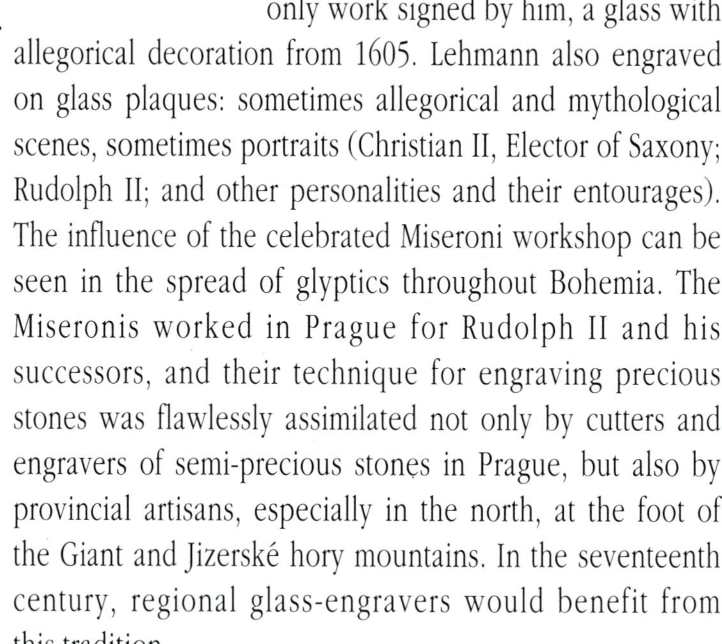

Olga Drahotová

Blown glass in the Middle Ages

Fluted or club-shaped forms with applied beads of glass (prunts), sometimes ornamented with various threads—pincered, soldered, vertical, wraithlike—were most common in Bohemia in the fourteenth century and the first half of the fifteenth. Archeological digs in urban zones have uncovered numerous fragments of these glasses in Prague, Plzeň, Olomouc, Kutná Hora, Hradec Králové, Opava, Most and Cheb. Rarely are they found outside of Bohemia. Larger prunts decorate the cylindrical and keg-shaped goblets frequently unearthed in Bohemian digs. They follow the model known in the tenth and eleventh centuries in Corinthium, and later in the Balkans, Italy and Germany. We should also mention various larger glasses, decorated with applied drops under a bottle neck, then stretched to create thin ribs down the sides. Objects of this type, common from the end of the thirteenth to the middle of the fifteenth centuries, are more or less characteristic of Bohemia. Bottles of different sizes—either a simple cylindrical body with a bulge under the rim, or a tight neck and a spherical body, usually ornamented with optical sides or applied threads—constitute a considerable portion of the production of hollow glass. The *Kuttrolf*, beakers with spherical bodies and necks formed out of three to six interlaced tubes, appeared as early as the fourteenth century. Their manufacture continued through the first half of the seventeenth century.

1. Fluted glass, second half of the 14th century. Yellow-green glass with heat-applied droplets. H. 42 cm. Discovered at the dig in the Saint-Peter's quarter in Prague. Center for the Protection of Monuments and Natural Sites, Prague.

2. **Glass bearing the imperial eagle and coat of arms, dated 1644.**
Enamelled glass.
H. 30 cm.
North Bohemia, probably Chřibská.
Museum of Decorative Arts, Prague
(Inv. 9 898).

Enamelled decoration

Enamelled decoration was widespread throughout Central Europe in the middle of the fourteenth century. This technique, originated in Italy, lent itself to various styles and subjects. The tall welcome glasses, or *Willkomm*, depicted coats of arms, religious allegories and satirical scenes, as well as the imperial eagle, symbol of the union of Central European states in the Holy Roman Empire. Because the Hapsburg emperors were also kings of Bohemia, most of the glasses coming from the Czech countries included this decoration by the middle of the fourteenth century. In the seventeenth century, a candidate for Master of Glass-painting in the Chřibská corporation, in North Bohemia, had to execute the effigy of the imperial eagle, among other things.

3. Pitcher, scene from the fable of the fox and the geese, dated 1595.
Cobalt glass painted with enamel.
H. 20 cm.
North Bohemia, probably Falknov.
Museum of Decorative Arts, Prague
(Inv. 9 894).

Cobalt blue glass

The striking colours of enamelled decoration show up particularly well on dark blue glass, coloured with cobalt oxide. In Bohemia, blue glass was manufactured in the fourteenth century, tinted with a mixture of cobalt and copper; but in order to obtain a deep blue, one had to await Christopher Schürer's discovery. In his glassworks at Eulenhütte, in the heart of the metalliferous mountains at the Czech-Saxon border, he added cobalt to paste in fusion. Cobalt glass was produced in Bohemia and Saxony from the 1570s to the first third of the seventeenth century.

Enamelled window glass

Window glass represented an important part of glass production in the sixteenth century. It was made either by the crown method—making a parison of glass spin until a flat disk was obtained—or by blowing, through a sort of cylinder or sleeve, cutting the two tops, splitting them lengthwise, and then laying them out. This last process, called the "Bohemian process" abroad and used as early as the Middle Ages, was known in the Czech countries until the nineteenth century. During the Renaissance, it was customary to integrate enamelled glass pieces, representing shields or the patron saint of the owner, into the windows of newly constructed houses.

4. Roundel window representing Saint Catherine, dated 1591. Glass painted with enamel. D. 8.5 cm. Museum of Decorative Arts, Prague (Inv. 10 379).

Cold-painting

Cold-painting, in laquer or oil paints, made a brief appearance during the second quarter of the sixteenth century in Venice. This technique, which evokes easel-painting, does not have the resistance of enamelled decoration, solidified by firing. In the last quarter of the sixteenth century, cold-painting was adopted in the Tyrol. In Bohemia, it was practised by the end of that century, first in the Wilhelmsberg Glassworks on the Rožmberk properties in South Bohemia, then in other workshops. More often than not, cold-painting was used in conjunction with diamond-point engraving.

5. Glass, two dancing couples, dated 1621. Glass decorated with cold-painting. H. 39 cm. Probably South Bohemia. Museum of Decorative Arts, Prague (Inv. 10 041).

6. Tankard, beginning of the 17th century. Pea green glass with filigree decoration. H. 27.5 cm. Museum of Decorative Arts, Prague (Inv. 2915).

Venetian technique

By the end of the Middle Ages, Venetian soda glass was considered the most perfect and the most luxurious. It embellished the tables of great lords and, mounted in silver and gold, it was conserved among their treasures. In the sixteenth century, different glassworks attempted to imitate Venetian glass, first by employing Italian immigrants, and later by employing themselves. With the potassium composition used in Central Europe, however, it was not easy to obtain glass comparable in its purity to that of Venice, nor to imitate the light forms and transalpine decorations applied on the surface or included in the mass. Nevertheless, archeological digs reveal that a certain number of works of this type were created in Bohemia. The filigree was found on traditional glass shapes, like quadrangular bottles, cylindrical glasses, or conical tankards.

THE PREUSSLER GLASSWORKS

In the sixteenth and seventeenth centuries, the Preusslers possessed several important glassworks on the Saxon side of metalliferous mountains, their native region. The members of this great family were mentioned in different workshops in Bohemia as early as the middle of the sixteenth century, where they worked as master glass-makers or glass-painters. In 1617, the Preusslers founded a glassworks in Sklarzska Poreba (Schreiberhau), the most important on the Silesian side of the Giant Mountains. Later, they were credited with the creation of other centres, both in Silesia and in Klodzko (Glatz). Before World War II, there were three glasses extant with painted decorations bearing different dates, all the work of members of the Silesian branch of the Preussler family. Only one of them, dating from 1680, has come down to us. This view of the Zeilberg Glassworks is an important iconographical document, attesting to the evolution of the furnace in the second half of the seventeenth century.

7. GLASS, VIEW OF THE ZEILBERG GLASSWORKS, dated 1680. Glass painted in enamel. Silesia. Museum of Decorative Arts, Prague (Inv. 9 818).

The Baroque Period

The Thirty Years' War, from 1618 to 1648, paralyzed all activity in Central Europe. It was not until the last third of the seventeenth century that an economic recovery, a necessary condition for cultural revival, occurred in Bohemia. However, the disaster more or less spared the glass factories established in the middle of the forests of the mountainous regions, which continued the work undertaken during the reign of Rudolph II.

.15.

In the second half of the seventeenth century, various noble clients desired brilliant and perfectly transparent glass, comparable in quality to rock crystal. This encouraged new creations, and the making of "Bohemian crystal" was mentioned for the first time around 1670. Credit for this technical perfection was mainly due to two factories in South Bohemia: the Buquoy Glassworks,in the manor of Nové Hrady, and the Michael Müller Glassworks in Helmbach, near Vimperk (Winterberg). Although the tableware glasses, in the beginning, were similar in character to the very elaborate works in Venetian style made in the Netherlands, by the end of the 1680s they had evolved towards a simplicity of geometric inspiration. The baluster-stemmed glasses and the conical goblets (or tumblers) constituted the most common models. The thick walls of these pieces lent themselves particularly well to engraving and, later, to cutting. Decoration was masterfully practised in North Bohemia, land of the glassworks founded during the Renaissance: Falknov, Chřibská (then Česká Lípa), Jablonec and their surrounding areas. Guilds of glass decorators also formed in these regions: Chřibská in 1661, Polevko (Blottendorf) in 1683, Kamenický Šenov (Steinschönau) in 1694, Jablonec in 1720.

Towards the end of the seventeenth century, Česká Lípa also became a great commercial centre. Glass exportation in Bohemia exploded after the peace treaty of Rastatt in 1714, which ended the War of Succession in Spain between Austria and France. Beginning in the 1680s, merchants of the region, originally members of glass-making families or engravers themselves, undertook trips to faraway places: Transylvania, Valachy, Northern Germany, the Hanseatic towns in the Baltics, Lithuania, Sweden, Russia, the Netherlands, England, France, Portugal, Spain, Italy, and Turkey. In the eighteenth century, their most important outlet was Spain, which did not begin to produce glass comparable to that of Bohemia until around 1750. A few years later, the Czech merchants extended their business as far as Egypt and America, but during this period, rich companies had already succeeded the modest pedlars of earlier days.

.15.

The North Bohemian companies transported their merchandise by car or boat, established show-rooms in foreign countries, and monitored the demands of the different markets. These merchants bought blanks, or rough forms, from different glassworks throughout the whole of Bohemia, had them decorated locally, and sold them off by their own means. In this way Bohemian glass acquired its worldwide reputation, and it was the glass-making industry, after the textile industries, that most contributed to developing the country's exports.

Bohemian Baroque glass was admired as much for the quality of its material (based on potash-lime) as for the beauty of its engraving. The rather rustic decorations of the elaborate pieces of the end of the seventeenth century gave way to deeply engraved mythological or allegorical scenes toward 1700, the most beautiful of which were, without doubt, the work of anonymous artists in the towns. The foliated scroll and ribbon themes, combined with elements of the grotesque, appeared during the early 1700s, around 1710. This light decoration, borrowed from Jean Bérain and his followers, was practised in Bohemia until the middle of the century. It inspired the geometrical forms of the faceted pieces and underscored the link between glasswork in the Baroque period and the crystal-rock work of the Renaissance.

Another centre for glass decoration developed in Silesia, under Bohemian rule until 1742, on the northern side of the Giant mountains, in the Jelenia Góra (Hirschberg) valley, where Friedrich Winter (deceased before 1711) figured among the greatest glass engravers of the region. His works, in which an energetic engraving in relief blended with a carving of great complication, announced the kind of decoration that came to characterize Silesian glass of the eighteenth century: a sumptuous cut, relief engraving, and an intermingling of engraved motifs in intaglio. The subjects depended on the destination of the pieces, and included portraits of the sovereign, city views, allegorical themes and amatory scenes in the Rococo taste. They were sold everywhere, especially as souvenirs to the patients of the health spa at Cieplice (Warmbrunn), where Silesian glass engravers had established themselves in the 1740s. (The separation of their province from Bohemia had closed export routes to them.) They were also offered by the Silesian merchants to their foreign partners. In the last quarter of the eighteenth century, the work of the isolated Silesian engravers sharply declined.

.19.

In Bohemia, luxury production remained extremely varied. Double-walled glass of the second quarter of the eighteenth century represented a particular expression of it from the technical and artistic point of view: a sheet of gold or silver engraved with religious, hunting or amatory scenes was inserted between two cut elements, exactly fixed by cooling and glued. All evidence suggests that works of this type were issued by a workshop active for two generations and employing a small number of engravers. This workshop probably collaborated with a glass factory that also practised cutting and delivered forms to it. Given the present state of research in this area, one can hazard a guess that it was the glassworks of Nový Svět (Neuwelt), in the manor of the Counts of Harrach.

In the first half of the eighteenth century, painting on glass went through a period of stagnation. The black enamelled glass of Ignaz Preissler (1676-1741) formed the sole exception to the rule. As a painter on porcelain and glass directly inspired by the Nuremberg model, he worked for years in Wroclaw (Breslau), then returned to his native village in Northeastern Bohemia, where he worked for the Count of Kolowrat. After 1750, glass ornamented with polychrome enamels came back in fashion. This decoration, of Rococo taste and influenced by porcelain makers, was most notable in the table services made at Harrach. In the 1760s, Harrach produced another of its great sucesses, opaque milk-white glass painted with bright colours and imitating porcelain. In the first quarter of the eighteenth century, the array of products for export was enriched by crystal chandeliers with multiple branches and cut pendants, copied from the older French chandeliers of rock crystal pendants and sold, among other places, in France. The making of pendants added to the coffers of numerous glass manufacturers; they were often exported, to be hung on the spot of the chandelier fitting. Important as well was the production of mirrors (encouraged by the Count of Kinský), with cut and Venetian-style engraved frames. According to documents available today, some forty glass factories existed in Bohemia before the Thirty Years' War, about fifty in the first half of the eighteenth century, and sixty-four around 1800. During periods of crisis, the glass-makers, cutters and engravers looked for work abroad, and thereby helped propagate the technique and style of Bohemian glass throughout Europe.

OLGA DRAHOTOVÁ

.21.

RUBY RED AND RUBY FILIGREE

8. COVERED GLASS, end of the 17th century.
Cut glass with ruby filigrees.
H. 19 cm.
Bohemia, probably the Müller Glassworks in the Vimperk region.
The Glass Museum, Jablonec nad Nisou (Inv. S. 6658).

9. COVERED GLASS IN FLUTE FORM, c. 1720.
Cut glass.
H. 37 cm.
North Bohemia.
Museum of Decorative Arts, Prague (Inv. 10 270).

10. COVERED GLASS, end of the 17th century.
Ruby cut glass.
H. 30.5 cm.
Bohemia, probably the Müller Glassworks in the Vimperk region.
Museum of Decorative Arts, Prague (Inv. 78 001).

The discovery of ruby glass coloured in gold originated from alchemical experiments of the sixteenth century. Johann Kunckel (1630?-1703) was the first to make this kind of glass on a large scale, during the 1670s in Potsdam. He used pure gold dissolved in aqua regia, then precipitated with tin. The secret of this process was known in Bohemia by the end of the1680s, where Christoph Fiedler of Munich briefly made ruby glass for Duke Jules Francis of Saxon-Lauenburg, in a laboratory in his château in Zákupy (Reichstadt) in North Bohemia. Another producer of ruby glass, Michael Müller (deceased in 1709), made his reputation in the Helmbach Glassworks, in South Bohemia. He was responsible for the filigree, with ruby threads and gold melted into the mass, found during the first half of the eighteenth century on the feet of Bohemian Baroque glasses.

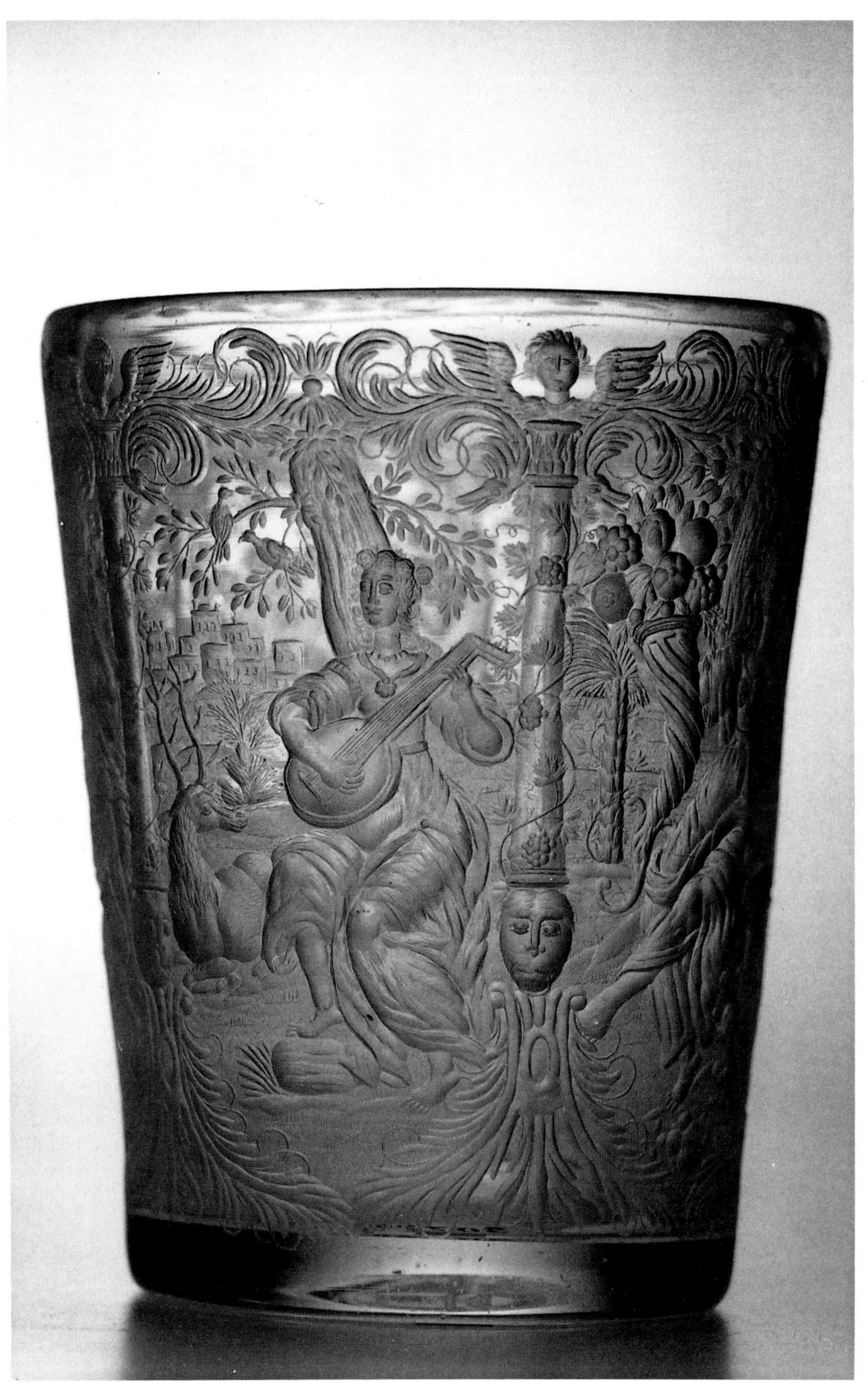

11. Beaker, allegory of the five senses, c. 1685-1690. Polished and engraved glass. H. 13 cm. Silesia, Jelenia Góra Valley. Museum of Decorative Arts, Prague (Inv. 30 720).
Page right: details of fig. 11.

Engraved decoration with figures

Decoration with figures was the most difficult of all genres, requiring great artistic maturity on the part of the engraver and great technical skill. Only the true masters practised it, for the preliminary drawing supposed a certain knowledge of anatomy, perspective and composition. They used engravings as models: contemporary and antique, and especially those of the late Renaissance. Themes corresponded to the tastes of aristocratic society: episodes from mythology and the history of the saints, allegories, emblems, scenes of hunting or gallantry. These were also found during this period in the decoration of silver and ivory objects. Compositions with multiple figures were much more frequent on Silesian than Bohemian glass, where religious subjects predominated. A goblet conserved in Prague at the Museum of Decorative Arts was part of an original group of works from the Jelenia Góra region at the end of the seventeenth century. It reproduced the allegory of the five senses of Martin de Vos, engraved by A. Collaert at the end of the sixteenth.

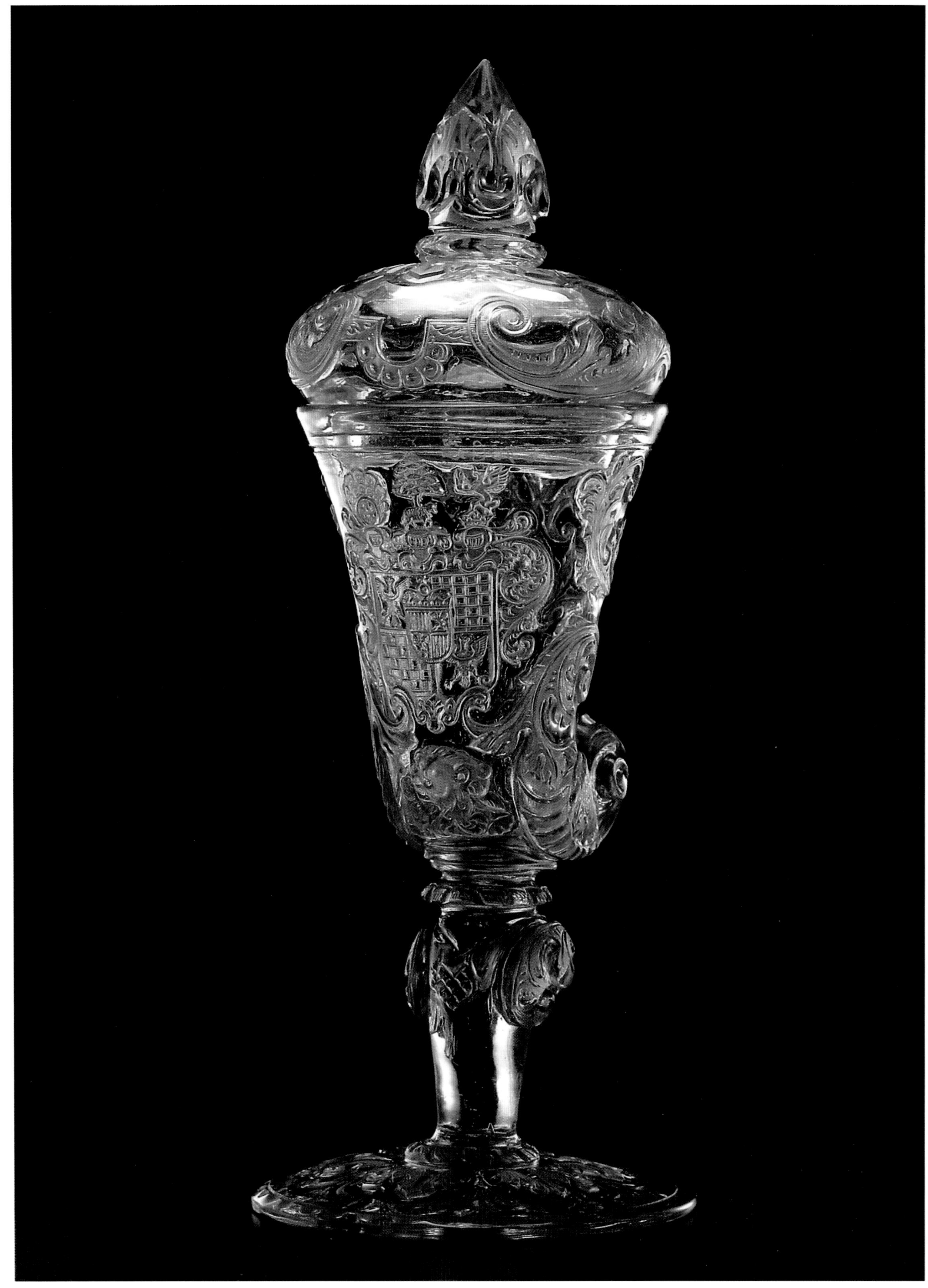

Silesian relief cutting

By the 1670s, glass engraving was flourishing in the Giant Mountains, in the domain of the Counts of Schaffgotsch, in Jelenia Góra. This art attained a high level of perfection with Friedrich Winter (deceased before 1712), native of Silesia and intendant of the Kynast château, who was given a title of privilege in 1687. He introduced relief cutting in Silesia and practised it in a glassworks that used a water-driven machine, constructed in 1690-1691 in Hermsdorf, province of Piechowice (Petersdorf). The covered glass with a volute from the end of the seventeenth

Preceding double-page, left:
12. Covered goblet with volute, bearing the Schaffgotsch coat of arms, c. 1700.
Relief-cut glass.
H. 21 cm.
Silesia, Hermdorf, F. Winter.
Museum of Decorative Arts, Prague (Inv. 10 178).

Preceding double-page, right:
13. Goblet with volute, floral decoration, 1710-1715.
Relief-cut and intaglio-engraved.
H. 22 cm.
Silesia, Hermsdorf, F. Winter workshop.
Museum of Decorative Arts, Prague (Inv. 4453).
Above: Details of fig. 13.

century, bearing the Schaffgotsch coat of arms, was one of Winter's finest works. Engraving in relief was related in Silesia with the last style of the Miseroni workshop, the celebrated cutters of semi-precious stones in Prague, and developed in Baroque ornamental taste: compositions with large acanthous leaves and wide bands mixing birds, grotesque masks and volutes. As of 1700, small landscapes, ribbons, flowers and intaglio-engraved *putti* were used in combination with relief engravings. The latter, usually of ornamental character, coexisted on Silesian glass with hollowed engraving up to the 1740s.

Portraits

The official portrait of the sovereign has occupied an important place in the iconography of engraved glass since the renewal of this technique in the modern period. During the seventeenth and eighteenth centuries, effigies of the Hapsburgs—emperors, but also kings of Bohemia—often figured on glasses made in the country. (The portrait of Rudolph II engraved by Caspar Lehmann preceded the portraits of Ferdinand III, Leopold I, Joseph I, Charles VI, Marie-Thérèse and François de Lorraine.) In most cases, engravers chose medallions or coins as models: they had the advantage of being directly reproducible. The sovereign's portrait on glass attested to the nobility's devotion to the reigning family; it appeared in Baroque-glass decoration not only in Bohemia, but also in Silesia and Germany. After the reuniting of Silesia with Prussia in 1742, portraits of Frederick the Great began to appear on Silesian glass as well.

14. Engraved goblet, portrait of Leopold I, end of the 17th century.
Cut and engraved glass.
H. 20.5 cm.
Engraving executed in Silesia on Bohemian glass.
Museum of Decorative Arts, Prague (Inv. 52 039).

Cutting and engraving in the seventeenth and eighteenth centuries

The artists of the court of Rudolph II (1576-1612) established the cutting and engraving profession in Bohemia in the villages and towns at the feet of the Jizerské hory and Giant Mountains, which are rich in semi-precious stones. The tradition was interrupted by the Thirty Years' War, and resumed after the peace of Westphalia. Like Caspar Lehmann at the turn of the sixteenth and seventeenth centuries, regional artisans applied cutting and engraving techniques to glasswork which, thanks to the improvement in pastes throughout the seventeenth century, came closer and closer to the qualities of rock crystal. Cut and engraved Bohemian glass reached its zenith during the first half of the eighteenth century. Crystal fashioned with a refined sense of proportions, and brought back to geometric forms by cutting in facets that multiplied the streams of light, provided an ideal support for engraved decoration. As in the other branches of the decorative arts, glass-engravers often followed the models furnished by ornamentalists, especially those influenced by Jean Bérain. Re-embracing the themes of the grotesque, Bérain decoration once again underscored the link between Baroque engraved glass and the works in rock crystal from the late Renaissance. Cutting favoured the play of light and enhanced the lustre of the material by multiplying the facets and motifs in the form of olives or stars.

15. Covered goblet and grotesque decoration in the Bérain style, 1715-1720.
Cut and engraved glass.
H. 37.5 cm.
Northern Bohemia, probably the area of Česká Lípa.
Museum of Decorative Arts, Prague (Inv. 33 346).

City views

As of the seventeenth century, views of great European cities—either engraved, as in Nuremberg and Potsdam, or painted in grisaille—became a frequent theme in glass decoration. Throughout the eighteenth century, and even at the end of the seventeenth, the *vedute* appeared on Silesian glass. Wroclaw was represented most often, but Oels, Schmiedberg and Liebenthal, as well as views of the Giant Mountains, were also common. Glasses with views of Amsterdam, Harlem, Leipzig, Hamburg, London and Constantinople were probably intended as gifts by the Silesian cloth merchants to their foreign clients.

16. Engraved goblet, view of Wroclaw, c. 1730. Cut and engraved glass. H. 28.2 cm. Silesia, Jelenia Góra. Museum of Decorative Arts, Prague (Inv. 10 417).

17. ENGRAVED GOBLET, VIEW OF THE HAMBURG STOCK EXCHANGE, c. 1750- 1760.
Cut and engraved glass, gold threads.
H. 20.3 cm.
Silesia, Cieplice.
Museum of Decorative Arts, Prague
(Inv. 10 184).

18. Goblet and sweet-meat bowl, bearing the coat of arms of Ph. G. Schaffgotsch, bishop of Wroclaw (1747-1795), c. 1750-1760. Cut and engraved glass, trimmed in gold. H. 25.5 cm.; H. 12.5 cm. Silesia, Cieplice. Museum of Decorative Arts, Prague (Inv. 16 838 and B I 42).

Rococo engraving in Silesia

Dozens of independent glass engravers were established in the eighteenth century in the Jelenia Góra Valley, close to the Sklarzska Poreba Glassworks and to the thermal spa in Cieplice. Their compositions, for the most part unique and brilliant works, ornamented the pieces intended to be offered as gifts. The thematic repertoire varied: allegories of Friendship, Health, Faith, Hope, Victory, Commerce; portraits of sovereigns; landscapes of the Giant Mountains; amatory dalliances inspired by Watteau; equestrian scenes. Figures emerged from among putti and animals, surrounded by decorative motifs—wide ribbons, and later rockeries—liberally interpreting the ornamental compositions taken from the collections of contemporary models. Christian Gottfried Schneider (1710-1770) was the most famous engraver of the period.

Double-walled glass

Double-walled glass (*Zwischengoldglas*, or gold between glass), with engraved gold leaf and decorations painted with transparent laquer, was characteristic of Bohemia in the first half of the eighteenth century. It carried forward the process described by Johann Kunckel in 1679 in his *Ars vitraria experimentalis*, which recommended placing an oil-painted decoration imitating precious stones between the two walls of the piece. Similarly, Bohemian glassmakers used gold leaf engraved with coats of arms, saints, or large compositions surrounded by ornamental motifs. These glasses and goblets —representing religious scenes, hunts, battles, games, or chamber music concerts— were often given as gifts on births, birthdays, graduations, ennoblements, or the taking of religious orders.

19. Glass with a scene of society life, c. 1730. Double-walled cut glass with engraved gold leaf. H. 16.7 cm. Probably North Bohemia. Museum of Decorative Arts, Prague (Inv. 13 168).

20. Glass bearing the coat of arms of the abbot of Vyšši Brod Quirin Michel (1747-1767), after 1747. Double-walled cut glass engraved with gold and silver leaves. Decoration painted in transparent laquer. H. 9.7 cm. Probably North Bohemia. Museum of Decorative Arts, Prague (Inv. 64 468).

Ignaz Preissler (1676-1741)

Ignaz Preissler is the only independent painter-decorator of Bohemia about whose existence we have any real information. The profession fluorished in the second half of the seventeenth century in Nuremberg, where Johann Schaper (1621-1670) was the first in a line of artisans who ornamented pieces of pottery, porcelain imported from China and glass with grisaille painting. Ignaz Preissler, son of the glass painter Daniel Preissler, of Bedřichov (Friedrichswalde) on the Czech-Silesian border, perfectly asssimilated their lessons. He spent time in Nuremberg, where he practised the art of applying very fine painting on glass. Afterwards, he worked in Wroclaw before returning to Bohemia around 1729 to establish himself in Kunštát in the Orlické hory Mountains, on the property of the Kolowrat family. At the beginning of his career, Preissler treated mythological subjects and city views in a style close to that of Nuremberg painters. Later, he developed decorative themes characteristic of the period, like ribbons or foliated scrolls, surrounded by hunting scenes, mythological subjects or chinoiseries.

21. Covered goblet, figure of Diane, c. 1730.
Cut glass, painted in grisaille.
H. 42 cm.
Ignaz Preissler, Kunštát.
Hluboká Château
(Inv. 6 867).

Glass with enamelled decoration from the second half of the eighteenth century

Enamelled decoration reached its peak during the Renaissance, and by the second half of the seventeenth century it had taken a more rustic turn. From then on, it was intended for current sale or for export. Luxury glasswork, trying to imitate rock crystal, used engraving and cutting as decorative techniques in this period. Enamel on glass reappeared with the boom in the manufacture of porcelain in Europe from the middle of the eighteenth century, but now it was influenced by the porcelain-makers' style. Credit for adapting enamel to the Rococo taste goes to the Nový Svět Glassworks, on the domains of the Counts of Harrach. Glasses with amatory scenes set amid rock gardens enlivened feasting tables with their colours. Painting on white opaque glass imitating porcelain was even more popular. The possibilities of this kind of glass (Milchglas), known in Bohemia by the sixteenth century, were not fully developed until the second half of the eighteenth century. Thematic variations of enamelled decoration on milk glass were rich: coats of arms, amatory scenes, biblical history and allegories of divine virtues, seasons and months of the year, and sundry parts of the world. Floral compositions in conventional neo-classical style alternate with subjects treated in a very personal manner.

22. Tankard, allegory of Africa, c. 1770.
Opaque milk glass painted in enamel.
H. 14.5 cm.
Probably the Harrach Glassworks in Nový Svět.
Museum of Decorative Arts, Prague
(Inv. 10 090).

FROM NEO-CLASSICAL TASTE TO HISTORICISM

At the transition from the eighteenth to the nineteenth century, Bohemian glass suffered intensely from customs barriers, wars, and the continental blockade. Exports dropped significantly. This decline also resulted from modifications in European social structures and competition from English and Irish glass. This glass from across the Channel, transparent with cut decoration in the Neo-Classical style, was a powerful source of inspiration in Czech countries. Bohemian glass manufacturers began by imitating the English cut and very quickly exploited all of its possibilities. Diamond-cutting, of star-or fan-shaped motifs on rounded shapes, joined with engraved decoration by the middle of the 1820s. The most beautiful pieces came from the Harrach Glassworks in Nový Svět, the greatest of all the Bohemian and Austrian factories at that time. Next came the Buquoy Glassworks in the manor of Nové Hrady in South Bohemia, known for its perfectly transparent works and, beginning in the 1820s, for its black or red opaque Hyaliths, evoking the exquisite stoneware of Josiah Wedgwood. The Meyer Glassworks in the Vimperk region was also notable.

.27.

North Bohemia—Kamenický Šenov, Mistrovice (Meistersdorf) and the region of Nový Bor (Haïda then Bor)—saw the rebirth of fine engraving and painting techniques, in which Friedrich Egermann (1777-1864) played so distinguished a part. Egermann, after having worked at the Meissen factory, invented Lithyalin—glass with a marbled surface imitating precious stones. This discovery, patented in 1828, involved perfecting the process of staining in yellow and red transparent decoration on coloured glass, by utilizing silver sulfate (for yellow) or copper sulfate (for red). Silver staining for glass and porcelain was known before Egermann, but copper staining was one of his inventions. As of the 1830s, staining, like shiny decoration, brightened the colourful array of Bohemian glass in the Empire and Rococo Revival styles. The making of coloured glass was pursued with great success, not only in Nový Svět but also in the Šumava Mountains of South Bohemia. Its effects proliferated through the superposition of numerous layers of paste, and by cutting and engraving.

Wheel-engraving reached new heights, particularly in the ancient North Bohemian centres of Jablonec and Česká Lípa, and in Karlovy Vary, where it benefitted from the experience of semi-precious stone-cutters of the eighteenth century. Two original artists in particular stand out: Dominik Biemann, celebrated portraitist and a disciple of Franz Pohl of Nový Svět; and Karl Pfohl of Kamenický Šenov, who played superbly with the tints of doubled or tripled glass. Several engravers headed the great workshops in the 1830s: F.A. Pelikan of Oldřichov (Ullersdorf) near Mistrovice, A. Simm of Jablonec, A.H. Pfeiffer of Karlovy Vary.

.43.

Bohemian glass-making attained its apogee between 1835 and 1850, and its complicated cutting, painted decoration and vivid colours were imitated in France, Belgium and England. Eighty different glass manufacturers made pieces endowed with a genuine unity of style, despite the differences in quality and price; but by the middle of the century, Bohemian glass, though still lucrative, was beginning to fade. The tendencies taking shape in the decorative arts in England—the study of antiquity and the fight against the mass-produced object—found few echoes in Bohemia. Shortly thereafter, however, the return to Italian Renaissance and Bohemian models of the seventeenth and eighteenth centuries marked a turning point. Luxury pieces conceived by well-known Viennese artists, or by teachers from the glass-making schools in Bor and in Kamenický Šenov (whose execution was entrusted to Czech masters), lay at the heart of a renewal in engraved and painted decoration. The Lobmeyr firm of Vienna was the main link between creators and production. An Oriental series by František Schmoranz was among several models created for Lobmeyr in Bohemia. The 1891 Anniversary Exposition of Prague, which witnessed the success of glasses by the architect H. Koula, brought out components that harkened back, in the eclectic spirit of the epoque, to the great Czech traditions.

OLGA DRAHOTOVÁ

.40.

23. Engraved beaker with portraits of Napoleon I and Marie-Louise, after 1810. Engraved glass, bearing the inscription: *Napoléon Ier. Empereur des Français et Roi d'Italie. Né le 15 août 1769. Marie-Louise. Impératrice des Français et Reine d'Italie. Née le 12 décembre 1791.* H. 11.5 cm. North Bohemia, probably Kamenický Šenov. The Glass Museum, Kamenický Šenov (Inv. KS 1820).

A revival of engraving

By the 1810s, modest engraving in low relief on thin-walled glass was replaced by a much more elaborate and affected decoration, whether ornamental or historical. Cutting and engraving sought to return to their original expressiveness, which led to diamond-cutting with finely engraved decorative motifs, or even inserted portraits (Kugel-graveur arbeiten). Glasses thus worked came from Kamenický Šenov, but were probably also made in Nový Svět and perhaps even on the Silesian side of the Giant Mountains. Indeed, the glassworks of the Counts of Harrach, in Nový Svět, were among the most respected centres of engraving; the most famous engraver of the nineteenth century, Dominik Biemann, began his career there. The technique was practised with equal distinction in Jablonec, home of Anton Simm and many other masters, noted in particular for their treatment of religious subjects. In Karlovy Vary, three glass-engravers benefitted from the experience of semi-precious stone-cutters: A.H. Mattoni, A.H. Pfeiffer and E. Hofmann.

In the first half of the nineteenth century, travel and thermal cures were the rage. The spas in West Bohemia and Teplice (in North Bohemia) attracted a rich clientele from all over Europe. Many engravers from Kamenický Šenov and Bor established themselves in such spas for the season. Among the artists we know by name were F.A. Pelikan (1786-1858), Moriz Oppitz (active in the 1840s) and August Böhm (1812-1890). Franz Hansel (1802-1883) and Karl Pfohl (1826-1894) were associated with France: the first worked at Baccarat in his youth, the second lived in Paris during the 1850s and 1860s.

24. BEAKER, c. 1815-1820.
Cut and engraved glass, bearing the inscription: *Joseph Graf Wratislaw von Mitrowitz.*
H. 13.3 cm.
North Bohemia, Kamenický Šenov.
The Glass Museum, Kamenický Šenov
(Inv. KS 81).

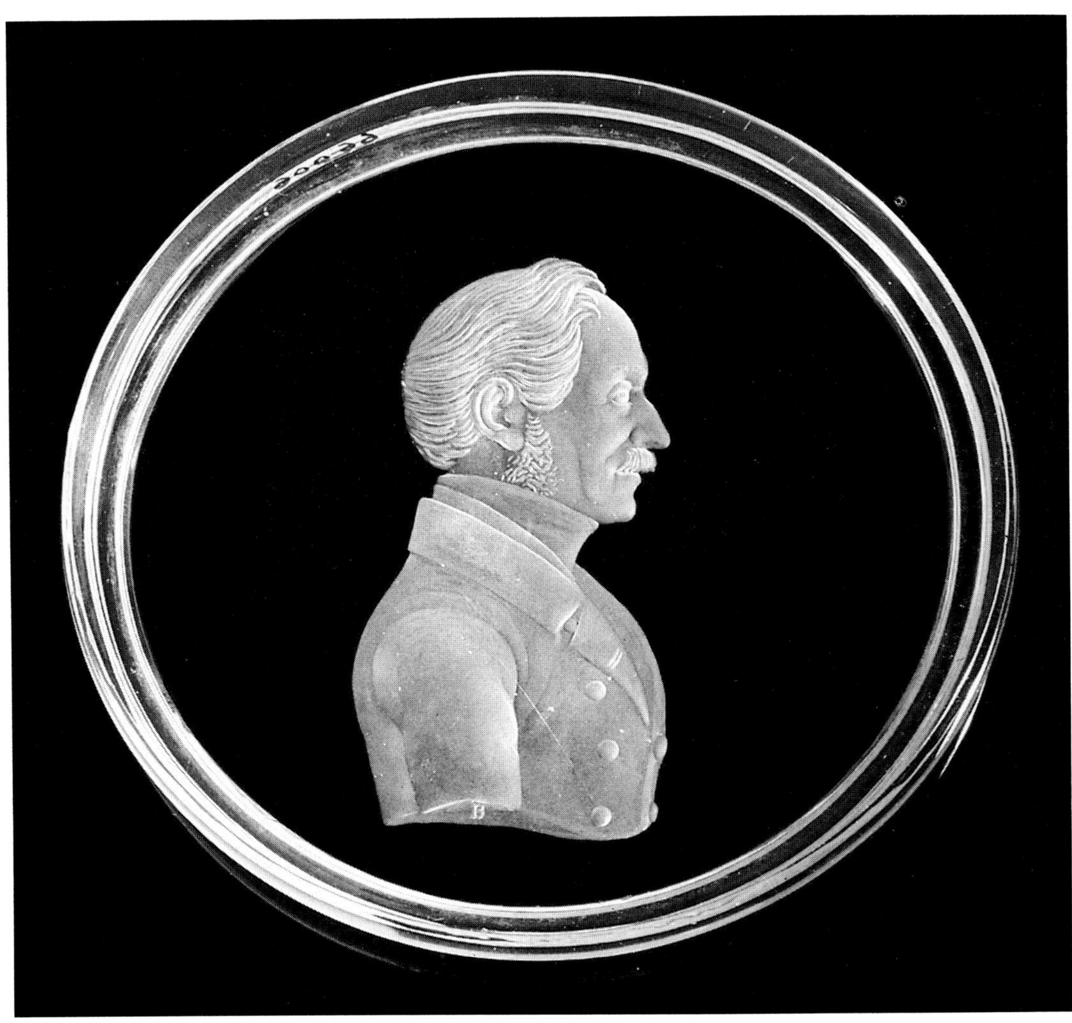

Dominik Biemann (1800-1857)

Dominik Biemann, born in Nový Svět in the Giant Mountains, was probably the greatest Bohemian glass engraver of the nineteenth century. He studied under Franz Pohl, a master of the technique and owner of a workshop in Nový Svět, which the Harrach Glassworks used to execute high-level works. Franz's brother Johann, director of this factory, quickly recognized Biemann's talent, and offered him the position of first engraver. Biemann, although he did not accept the offer, remained very attached to the Harrach Glassworks: he never engraved on anything but material coming from their ovens. It was doubtless the Count of Harrach who suggested that he study at the Academy of Painting in Prague and who furnished the necessary means. In 1827, Biemann definitively established himself in the capital, and showed two years later at the Academy exhibition in 1829. He twice obtained the silver medal in the Prague Industrial Exhibition, in 1829 and 1831. Biemann spent the summer months in Františkovy Lázně, returning to Prague in the winter; he also visited Hurky, in the Šumava Mountains, where he directed the engraving workshop of a mirror factory. His works are remarkable for the delicate modelling of details and, in portraiture, the search for psychological truth. Biemann signed with his full name, the initials DB, or with the single letter B. His art occasioned general admiration well beyond the borders of the Czech countries, but his followers, particularly in North Bohemia, did not attain his mastery.

25. Medallion, portrait of Prince Alfred de Windischgratz, 1849. Deep-cut and engraved glass, signed B. H. 9.7 cm. Františkovy Lázně, Dominik Biemann. Museum of Decorative Arts, Prague (Inv. 66 006).

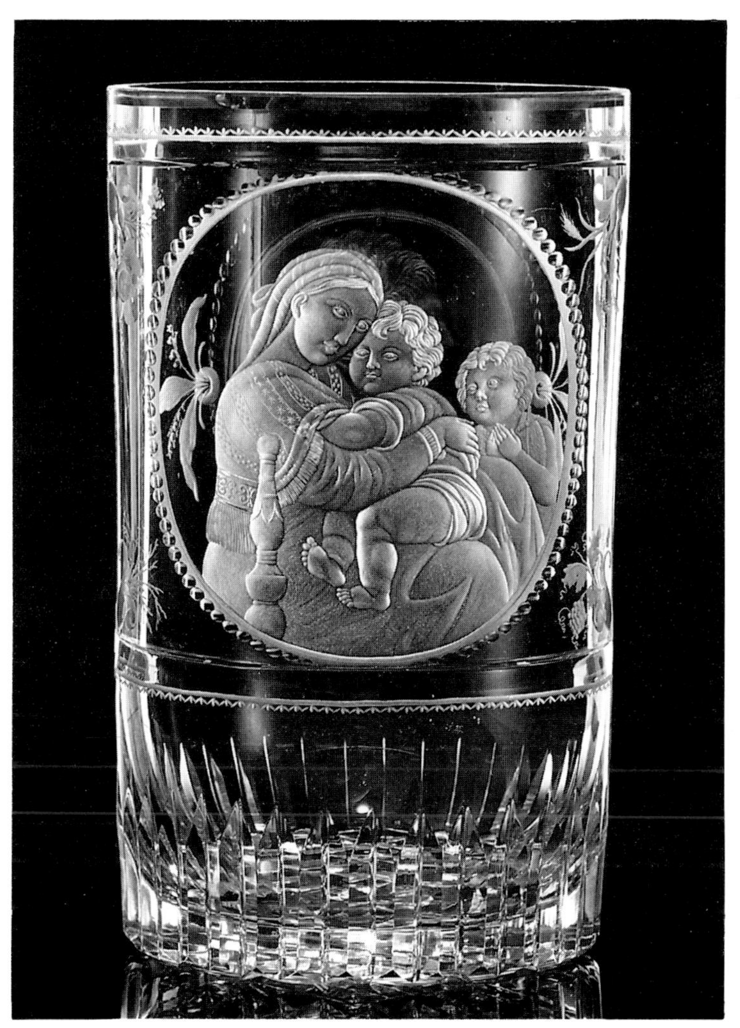

26. **Beaker,**
Engraving after *Madonna della Sedia*
by Raphael and portrait
of an unknown man, c. 1826.
Cut and engraved glass.
H. 15.5 cm.
Nový Svět, Dominik Biemann.
The Glass and Jewellery Museum,
Jablonec nad Nisou (Inv. S 2569).

27. COVERED GLASS, Allegory of Art and Science, c. 1840.
Cut and engraved glass.
H. 24 cm.
Nový Svět, Dominik Biemann.
Museum of Decorative Arts, Prague
(Inv. 34 197).

Cutting

When they adopted diamond-cutting around 1800, glassmakers of the Czech countries joined a current coming from England and France. Bohemian cutters reasserted their Baroque tradition during the 1870s. They wanted to perfect the form of the piece and animate the surfaces, and they achieved a great diversity of motifs by using moulds with various profiles. Numerous glasses—coloured, colourless, with one or more layers—were employed in the abundant production of the 1830s and 1840s, which makes it extremely difficult to distinguish the work of different glass manufacturers and other decoration workshops. The cutting technique used in the Harrach Glassworks in Nový Svět, however, is relatively easy to identify: its archives conserve drawings of luxury pieces furnished to distinguished clients. A vase executed in 1832 for the Telzer brothers of Brno, commercial partners in the enterprise for many years, illustrates the mastery of the Nový Svět artisans. Elaborately cut decorations also survive from the Kamenický Šenov region, especially Práchen, but also Adolfov and Lenora, in the Šumava Mountains. Bohemian decoration characteristically blended motifs in relief (olives and pearls) with a hollow cut, using cornered or convex moulds. It was practised on coloured, colourless and cased glass, and was soon imitated in Belgium, France and England.

28. Vase, 1831.
Cut and engraved glass.
Inscription presenting the arms of the Münch-Bellinghausen and reading:
Vom brünner k.k. Kreisamte, 1831
***Aus Liebe und Hochverehrung*,**
along with the names of the employees who offered the vase as a souvenir.
H. 34.8 cm.
Nový Svět.
Moravian Gallery, Brno
(Inv. MG 12 074).

29. Tumblers with portraits of Francis I, emperor of Austria, and his wife Caroline, 1831.
Cut glass with yellow staining, painted with translucent enamels.
H. 10.8 cm.
Polevsko, near Bor, workshop of Friedrich Egermann.
Museum of Decorative Arts, Prague (Inv. 24 695 and 24 696).

Painting on glass in the first half of the nineteenth century

As the supply of heating wood in the Northern Bohemian forests gradually disappeared, glass manufacturers in and around Bor died out one after the other. Families that had existed on this industry had to content themselves with finishing touches alone. During the first half of the nineteenth century, however, the region became an important centre for glass painting. This kind of decoration was especially developed by Friedrich Egermann and the artists of his entourage. Samuel Mohn of Dresden and Anton Kothgasser of Vienna inspired painting with translucent enamels. Most of the decorations using this technique came from the Egermann workshop: portraits of the reigning family, *vedute*, multicoloured flowers and Oriental subjects. Some artisans, based in Okrouhlá and in Skalice, not far from Bor, specialized in gold painting, especially on coloured hyalith glass.

By 1835, the return to eighteenth century models led to the use of new shades in the colouring of glass and the resurgence of decorative motifs like rocaille and flower seedlings, painted in gold or silver with coloured enamels, mostly on cased opal glass. During this period, another centre of glass-painting arose in Southwest Bohemia around the glassworks of Adolfov, Lenora and Anín. An independent painting studio was established in Vimperk in the 1840s.

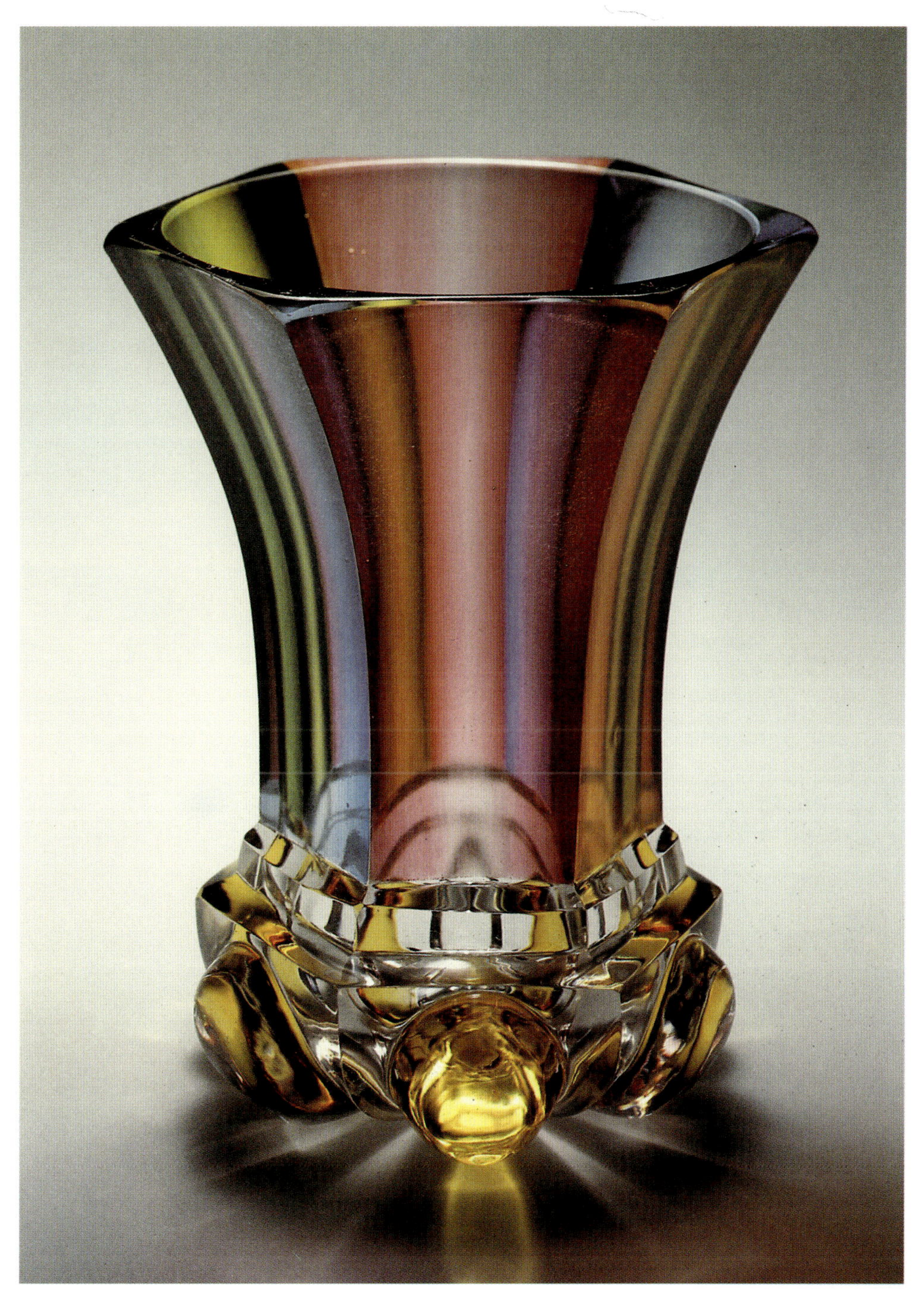

30. TUMBLER, c. 1835-1840.
Cut glass with yellow staining
and coloured lustres.
H. 14.3 cm.
North Bohemia, Bor.
Museum of Decorative Arts, Prague
(Inv. 37 841).

31. Tumbler, c. 1825.
Cut and engraved black Hyalith.
H. 10.3 cm.
South Bohemia, Georgenthal.
Museum of Decorative Arts, Prague
(Inv. B I 416 a).

The Buquoy glassworks

Count François Buquoy de Longueval, descendant of an Imperial Army general during the Thirty Years' War, owned several glass factories on his property in South Bohemia renowned for the quality of their production. The Georgenthal and Silberberg glassworks made Hyalith glass. (François Buquoy, encouraged by the enormous success of black and red fine stoneware, Josiah Wedgwood's basalte and rosso antico, discovered the recipe in 1816.) Hyalith was used for making a great variety of objects, from bottles and pharmaceutical containers to luxury merchandise like coffee and tea services, vases, decanters, tumblers and paperweights. At first, Hyalith glass was cut and engraved. Later, gold-painted chinoiseries were the preferred decoration: characters, dragons, pavilions, rocks, insects. Since no tradition of painting existed in South Bohemia at this time, these pieces were ornamented in the north of the country, in Okrouhlá. The finished products were transported to Prague, Karlovy Vary, Vienna, Budapest and other European cities.

32. TUMBLER, c. 1830.
Gold-painted black Hyalith.
H. 11.2 cm.
South Bohemia, Georgenthal or Silberberg.
Painted decoration executed in Okrouhlá,
near Bor.
Museum of Decorative Arts, Prague
(Inv. 75 317).

Friedrich Egermann (1777-1864)

Friedrich Egermann occupied a very special place among Bohemian glass-makers. As painter, technician, and diligent worker of great artistic sensitivity, he gathered and developed the essential aspects of research done in other countries. Egermann learned the craft of glass painting in Chřibská, then was employed by a porcelain manufacturer in Meissen. In order to discover the secret of the preparation of its colours, he infiltrated the workshop pretending to be a deaf mute. By the beginning of the nineteenth century, he had added considerably to the array of glass production. His Polevsko workshop near Bor made vases in forms inspired by the ancients, in white milk glass or other colours, recalling the fine tastes of Josiah Wedgwood. At the beginning of his career, Egermann covered unpolished glass with kaoline, polychrome enamels and opaque white enamel (nacre), applied in relief. Above all, however, the name of Friedrich Egermann evokes the use of yellow cementation (with silver) from 1816, and the discovery of red staining (with copper) in 1832. Staining consists of covering the piece with metallic oxides, applied by brush, which, when fired, form a coloured and transparent layer on the surface of the glass. Egermann used staining to decorate works in Lithyalin, a glass imitating different precious stones. In order to create his first Lithyalins, he used black and red Hyalith or opaque blue glass, made by the Buquoy and Harrach Glassworks. In the 1830s, he used uncoloured glass cased with ruby and transparent green glass. Around 1840, when lithyalins were being replaced by glass with painted and engraved decoration in Rococo Revival style, Egermann was the only maker of glass ornamented by red staining. Realizing the importance of this discovery, several glass-makers broke into Egermann's workshop, now in Bor, stole the manufacturing secret, and left North Bohemia for France. The technique was sold to the Saint-Louis crystal-manufactory, and then spread rapidly to Europe and America.

33. Tumbler with view of the Saint Stephen cathedral in Vienna, c. 1835.
Lithyalin (dark green glass, coloured by staining) cut and painted in gold.
H. 11 cm.
Bor, Friedrich Egermann workshop.
Museum of Decorative Arts, Prague (Inv. 18 113).

34. Bottle with stopper, c. 1830.
Lithyalin (red Hyalith glass, coloured by staining) cut and painted in gold.
H. 13 cm.
Polevsko, near Bor,
Friedrich Egermann workshop.
Museum of Decorative Arts, Prague
(Inv. 70 899).

35. Two-piece bottle, c. 1830.
Lithyalin (blue glass, coloured by staining) cut and painted in gold.
H. 26 cm.
Polevsko, near Bor,
Friedrich Egermann workshop.
Museum of Decorative Arts, Prague
(Inv. 58 200).

36. Bottle with stopper, c. 1830.
Lithyalin (red Hyalith glass, coloured by staining) cut and painted in gold.
H. 10 cm.
Polevsko, near Bor,
Friedrich Egermann workshop.
Museum of Decorative Arts, Prague
(Inv. 18 072).

37. Service bearing the coat of arms of the counts of Desfours-Walderode, c. 1840.
Uranium glass (Annagelb),
cut and ornamented with incrustations.
Carafes H. 31 and 28.5 cm.;
Goblet H. 13.5 cm.;
Sugar bowl H. 1.5 cm.;
Plate 46 x 28.5 cm.
Nový Svět.
Museum of Decorative Arts, Prague
(Inv. 66 122 to 66 126).

Coloured glass

In the first quarter of the nineteenth century, colourless glass still represented a major part of Bohemian production. By the 1830s, however, it began to decline in favour of coloured glass. Colours used in the past returned first: ruby red, opaque red, transparent or opalized violet, blue and green. Hyaliths and Lithyalins imitating basalt and gems also appeared. Later on, colour even invaded colourless glass itself, due to the technique of staining. Colourless glass could also be covered by glazes or cased with a coloured layer (cased glass).

Opalines had been fashionable in France in the 1820s; by 1835, in Bohemia, the Buquoy Glassworks was creating agatines, or marbled opaque glass. Glass in colder colours, evoking opal in its appearance and called alabaster, emerged as well. The coloured array of glass responded to the constantly-evolving demands of fashion; its richness resulted from progress in glass techniques and the industrial production of metal oxides used as colouring agents. No glass factory managed to keep the secret of its colours for long; yellow and gold uranium glass was introduced both in the Riedel and Harrach Glassworks in Northern Bohemia, and in the Šumava Mountains in Southern Bohemia, almost simultaneously.

38. Covered goblet, 1849.
Colourless glass, cased with rosaline glass and covered with white enamel, cut and painted with vibrant enamels and gold.
The inscription reads: *Zur Erinnerung an den Fasching 1849 für unseren verehrten Herrn Protektor Johann Waniček.*
H. 47.5 cm.
Adolfov or Lenora.
Museum of Decorative Arts, Prague
(Inv. 11 674).

Karl Pfohl (1826-1894)

The work of Karl Pfohl, inspired by the Biedermeier style, bespeaks the high artistic value of Bohemian engraving in the second half of the nineteenth century. After finishing his apprenticeship as an engraver, Pfohl worked under Friedrich Egermann in Bor, then in Wiesbaden and finally in his brother's workshop in Kamenický Šenov. He left Northern Bohemia twice to live in Paris, in 1858-1864 and in 1866-1872. During this second stay, he worked for a merchant of *objets d'art* in the Palais Royal. His Parisian experience obviously influenced Pfohl's art, especially in his choice of subjects. He engraved hunting scenes and large compositions with historical or mythological themes after Rubens, Guido Reni, and Murillo. The influence of Courbet and Daumier was also evident. His style continued in the work of numerous North Bohemian engravers: Karl Günther, Eduard Pelikan, Karl Pietsch, Josef and Anton Sacher. In Bavaria, the Czech engraver Franz Zach followed Pfohl's example.

39. Covered goblet depicting the Good Samaritan, before 1858.
Colourless glass cased in blue cobalt, with cut and deeply engraved decoration, signed C. Pfohl.
Engraving by Karl Pfohl of Kamenický Šenov on glass from Nový Svět.
Museum of Decorative Arts, Prague (Inv. 30 997).

40. Covered glass, c. 1880.
Colourless glass, cut and deeply engraved signed K.P.
H. 40 cm.
The Glass Museum, Nový Bor (Inv. NB 237).

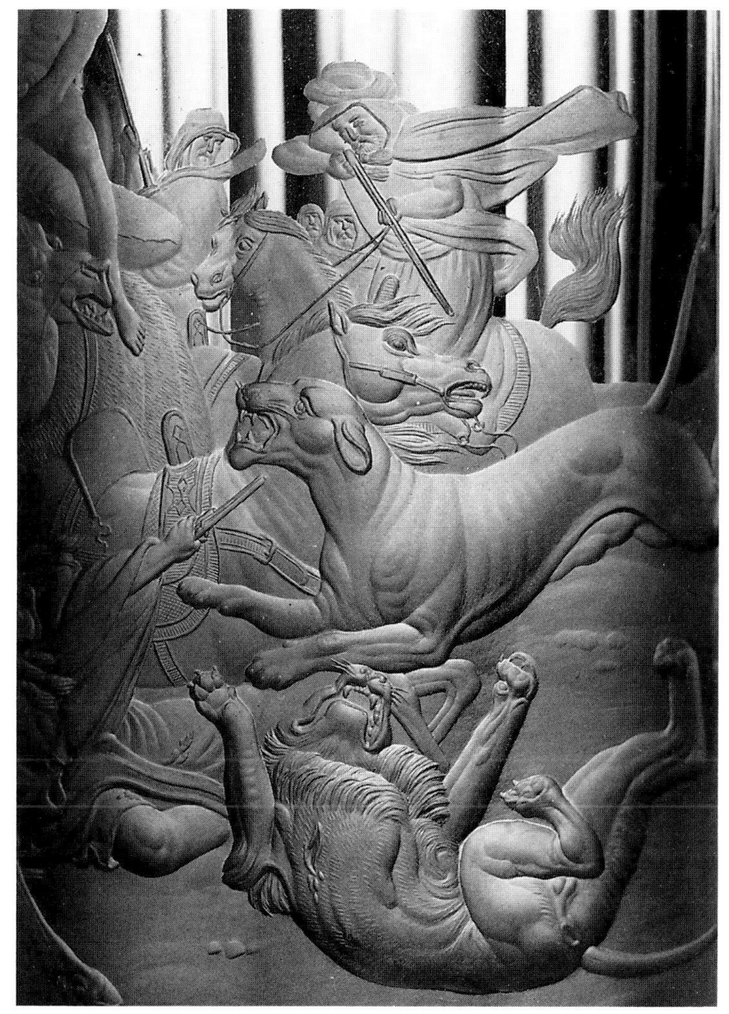

The Lobmeyr firm

At the Viennese Industrial Exhibition in 1835, the Lobmeyr house, created in Vienna in 1823, made contacts with Bohemian glass manufacturers. A regular collaboration began after 1864, when the firm came into the hands of Ludwig Lobmeyr, one of the patrons of the Museum of Art and Industry (founded the same year in Vienna) and friend of the great architects of the period. The decorative arts were then turning to past European styles for inspiration. The Universal Exposition of 1878 in Paris also revealed the influence of the Near East. In South Bohemia, the Meyer Glassworks realized models created in an Italian and German Renaissance flavour by the Viennese architects Theophil Hansen, Friedrich Schmidt, Josef Storck, Moritz Knab and A. Eisenmenger. The cutting and engraving were entrusted to two different workshops in Kamenický Šenov and the surrounding area. The pieces of the Arab and Persian series launched by Lobmeyr were made in Adolfov, in South Bohemia, from drawings by František Schmoranz (1845-1892), future founder and first director of the Prague School of Decorative Arts.

41. Ewer, c. 1889.
Colourless crystal, cut and engraved, marked *fa Lobmeyr* on the handle.
H. 28 cm.
J. & L. Lobmeyr House, Vienna.
Model by Moritz Knab and A. Eisenmenger; executed by Karl Pietsch, Peter Eisert and Franz Ullmann, Kamenický Šenov.
Museum of Decorative Arts, Prague
(Inv. 75 559).

42. Arab style vase, 1878.
Colourless glass painted in enamel and gold, bearing the mark of the Lobmeyr house.
H. 20.5 cm.
Lobmeyr House, Vienna. Model by Machytka and Schmoranz, dated 5 November 1877.
Execution by the Meyer Glassworks, decoration by the Vimperk painting studio.
Museum of Western Bohemia, Plzeň
(Inv. UP 10 052).

**43. Ewer, after 1880.
Cut and engraved glass.
H. 34 cm.
Kamenický Šenov,
Specialized School of Glassmaking.
Museum of Kamenický Šenov
(Inv. S 6168).**

The first professional schools

After 1850, the art of glass underwent a certain decline in Bohemia from an excessive attachment to the decorative techniques and aesthetic criteria of the Biedermeier period and the Rococo Revival. Exports declined appreciably. The will to renovate production and to reconquer its place on European markets led to the foundation, in 1856, of the Specialized School of Glassmaking in Kamenický Šenov, directed by the painter Jan Dvořák, the first establishment of its kind, not only in Bohemia but in the entire world. The school also offered training in painting. In 1870, a second school was created in Bor. In 1920, the Czechoslovakian School of Glassmaking was opened in Železný Brod, intended to train specialists in the glass-making and jewellery industries of the Jablonec region.

In 1880, the Kamenický Šenov school created an engraving class taught by artists of the J.& L. Lobmeyr firm: Karl Pietsch (1880-1883), Franz Ullmann (1883-1887) and Otto Pietsch (1888-1919). As of 1886, its director was the Viennese architect Leo Chilla. The school collaborated closely with the Kamenický Šenov Glassworks, whose production it influenced, and thus contributed to its European reputation. Former students of the establishment—painters, engravers, commercial agents—worked in all the glass-making centres of Bohemia, but their fame grew beyond its borders, in various cities of Europe and America.

44. SMALL VASE, c. 1890.
Engraved glass.
H. 12.2 cm.
Mistrovice, Franz Fritsche.
Kamenický Šenov Museum
(Inv. KS 907).

From Art Nouveau to the End of the 1930s

Bohemian Art Nouveau glass was an original phenomenon whose distinction resided in its diversity of techniques, materials and artistic approaches. No single personality in Bohemia compared to Emile Gallé, whose genius dominated an entire period in France. In Bohemia, many glassworks participated in elaborating the new style by following parallel but different paths. A will to innovate manifested itself by the last years of the nineteenth century in conceptions, materials, colours, forms and decoration. The procedures, not always original, initially revealed the influence of Tiffany and Gallé, and different glassworks concentrated on their specialities. Large factories in Southern Bohemia, like the Lötz Glassworks in Klášterský Mlýn, experimented with new materials and sought out new possibilities for working with heat; North Bohemian masters asserted the modern style in engraved, cut and painted decorations—techniques in which they possessed a centuries-old tradition; and some manufacturers, like the Harrach Glassworks in Nový Svět, successfully explored both domains. Czech Art Nouveau glass took two forms: one inspired by floral models, the other by geometric shapes. Floral decoration with supple and undulating lines, characterized by a nuanced colouring in which cold shades dominated, held sway between 1898 and 1908. It ornamented pieces of every type but found its purest expression in iridescent flame-blown glass made especially by the Lötz Glassworks. The Harrach Glassworks used elegant floral themes, in engraved form, for vases and crystal drinking glasses. Another very gracious style, of linear engraved decoration, was inspired by the Belgian architect Henry Van de Velde. In South Bohemia, floral themes were developed in the painted decoration of drinking glass services by the Meyer Nephew factory in Adolfov.

.50.

Sober geometric forms appeared in Bohemian Art Nouveau glass around the beginning of the century; the Rindskopf or Riedel glassworks turned to it in order to exalt chromatic qualities and the texture of the material. As of 1908, geometric stylization predominated in North Bohemia, as the decoration of glass was then under a strong Viennese influence, particularly that of the artists gathered at the heart of the Wiener Werkstätte. The professional school in Bor became the principal centre for the Viennese style in Bohemia; works from this establishment authentically captured its spirit. Before 1914, elements of the Art Deco aesthetic flourished in the Expressionist current that determined the character of North Bohemian production between the wars. Works

.56.

executed from artists' models often remained unique pieces or extremely small series without major influence on factory productions. This was true of the Lötz Glassworks; of Marie Kirschner and Leopold Bauer; of Carl Lederle (the Harrach Glassworks); and of Anton Hanel, teacher at the Bor school. Jan Kotěra, professor at the School of Decorative Arts in Prague, was the sole exception to this rule. His 1904 punch service, through the architectonic structure of its volumes and its emphasis on the optical qualities of the material, marked a stage in the evolution of this art. Kotěra's work established a standard for Prague artists between the wars.

The architectural conceptions of Kotěra provided the starting point for the artists of the Artěl, founded in 1908 in Prague. The group evolved towards Cubism in the beginning, as in the models for glasses of Josef Rosipal. Immediately after the war, the Artěl rallied to the national decorative style, a not always brilliant variant of Art Deco, that mixed Cubist forms with ornamental elements and chromatism borrowed from Czech folklore. František Kysela and V.H. Brunner, both professors at the Prague School of Decorative Arts, were the main representatives of this current.

.71.

In the 1920's, however, the major figures in the art of glass were the sculptors Jaroslav Horejc and Josef Drahonovsky, who revived the tradition of glass-engraving, which they considered an authentic national technique. Drahoňovský, formed in glyptics, deeply adhered to neo-classicism; he created an important body of work, imbued with patriotic spirit, aided by his disciples and collaborators—for the most part former students of his workshop at the School of Decorative Arts in Prague. Among them were the eminent engraver Ladislav Přenosil, who later taught at the glass-making school of Železný Brod, and Oswald Lippert, future professor at the glass-making school of Kamenický Šenov. Their varied production is truly authentic. Jaroslav Horejc surpasses even the Drahoňovský school in the originality of his engraved glasses. The precious vases with antique subjects engraved from his drawings by the workshop of the Lobmeyr firm reveal his talent for exploiting all the optical resources of the surface of the piece, and his mastery of varied composition and expressive detail. His work dominated Czech glass-making between the two wars.

Functionalism, which had already asserted itself in architecture and interior decoration, affected glass art at the end of the 1920's. The young generation's interest was directed to the utilitarian object, giving it a simple form adapted to its function. High-level glass-making also began to conform to the aesthetic canons of the Bauhaus by working with elementary geometrical figures: the rectangle, circle, cube, pyramid, sphere. The work of Ludvika Smrčková, Ladislav Sutnar and Alois Metelák demonstrates pointedly the variety of applications of Functionalism to glass. Much of their work was intended for the "Krásná Jizba" firm, which at the time guaranteed the circulation of quality interior decorations. Throughout the 1920s, creators participated directly in the stylistic elaboration of Czech glass. This was not true of the period before.

ALENA ADLEROVÁ

.52.

45. WINE GLASS, 1885-1890.
Partially cased glass inlaid with flowered branch made of coloured glass. Details engraved by cutting wheel and acid, motifs painted in gold.
H. 19 cm.
Lötz Glassworks, Klášterský Mlyn.
Museum of Decorative Arts, Prague
(Inv. 70 212).

WIDOW OF JAN LÖTZ GLASSWORKS, KLAŠTERSKÝ MLÝN (KLOSTERMÜHLE)

Founded in 1836 by J.B. Eisner of Eisenstein, the factory came into the hands of Zuzana Lötz, widow of the glass industrialist Jan Lötz, in 1850. Lötz's grandson, Max Ritter von Spaun, who owned the enterprise from 1879 to 1908, made it one of the greatest glassworks not only in Bohemia, but in all of Central Europe. In the 1880's, Lötz was known for its marbled glasses and decorations (Intarsia or Octopus). In 1897, the glassworks began to produce iridescent glass, ornamented with heat-applied threads, in the Tiffany style, but it rapidly emphasized its own variants of shapes and decorations. The Universal Expositions in Chicago (1893), Paris (1889 and 1900) and Saint Louis (1904) awarded their Grand Prizes to Lötz and brought him international recognition. Adolf Beckert was artistic director in 1909-1911. Many creators, Viennese in particular, entrusted the glassworks with the execution of their models. (Marie Kirschner was one of the manufacturer's most appreciated collaborators.) The Lötz Glassworks closed its doors in 1947, but in 1989 the Düsseldorf, Frankfurt and Prague Museums dedicated an important exhibition to the whole of its production.

46. VASE, 1901.
Colourless glass cased with opal glass. Heat-applied threading and iridescent decoration.
Engraved signature: Lœtz Austria.
H. 16.2 cm.
Lötz Glassworks, Klášterský Mlyn.
The Glass Museum, Nový Bor
(Inv. NB 88).

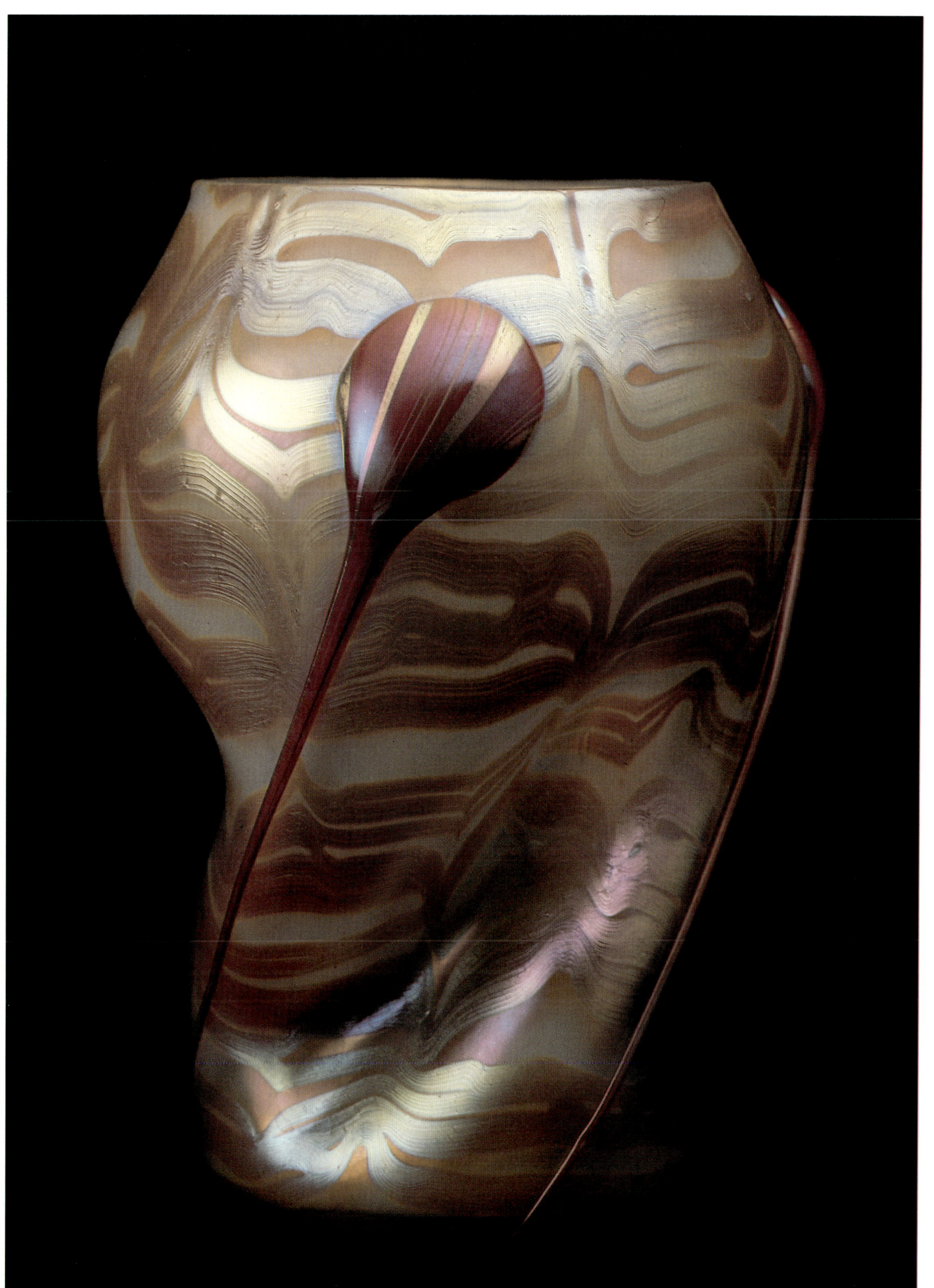

Lötz Glassworks, Klášterský Mlýn.
47. VASE WITH FOUR HANDLES, 1902.
Large-splotched Iris decoration.
Engraved signature: Loetz Austria.
H. 12 cm.
Regional Museum, Hradec Králové
(Inv. S 454).

Leopold Bauer

Krnov 1872 - Vienna 1938.
Studied at the Academy of Beaux-Arts of Vienna, O. Wagner workshop.
As of 1900, architect in Vienna.

Bauer discovered the potential of glass at the Lötz factory when he arrived in Klásterský Mlýn at the beginning of the century as the villa architect of the proprietor, Max Ritter von Spaun. He created more than sixty models, remarkable for the purity of their forms and the rich texture of their material.

48. Vase, 1902.
***Butterfly iris* decoration**
and heat-applied threading.
H. 37 cm.
Lötz Glassworks, Klášterský Mlýn.
Šumava Museum, Kašperské Hory
(Inv. S 1529).

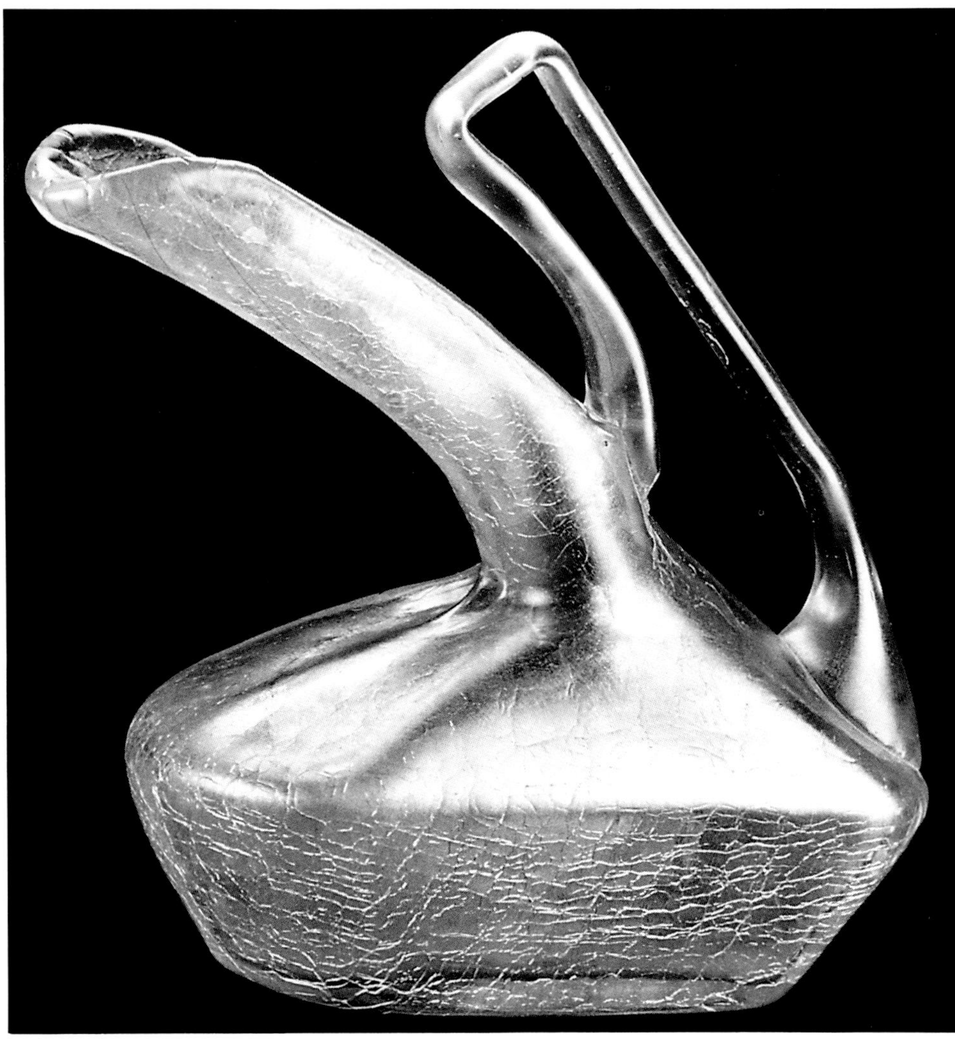

49. Vase, 1902.
Cracked iridescent glass.
Engraved signature: MK.
H. 15 cm.
Lötz Glassworks, Klášterský Mlýn.
Museum of Decorative Arts, Prague
(Inv. 21 455).

Marie Kirschner

Prague 1852-Košátky 1931.
Studied painting in private schools in Prague, Munich and Paris.
Lived in Prague, Paris and Berlin.

Marie Kirschner, a painter, throughout her career was interested in every artistic trade. She worked in glass between 1898 and 1914, and had friendly relations with Max Ritter von Spaun, proprietor of the Lötz Glassworks in Klášterský Mlýn, who executed all of her models. She created 270 vases, usually of geometric inspiration, some of them simple, some of them recherché, each of them designed for a particular kind of flower. Her colours and decorations were always sober and refined, her conception of form very personal.

Adolf Beckert

Česká Lípa, 1884-1929.
Trained at the Bor Specialised School of Glassmaking.
1905-1908: studied at the Drawing Studio of the Prague School of Decorative Arts.
1905-1906: Debschitz School in Munich.
1909-1911: Artistic Director of the Widow of Jan Lötz Glassworks in Klášterský Mlýn.
1911-1926: first professor, then, in 1918, Director of the Specialised School of Glassmaking in Kamenický Šenov.

Beckert enriched the repertoire of the Widow of Jan Lötz company with North Bohemian decoration: compositions on vegetal themes treated in a linear style, acid-etched on glass in several layers. This procedure was sometimes repeated, thus achieving a very elaborate relief. Beckert exploited both the multiple chromatic resources of the material and the possibilities of stylization offered by the acid-etching technique. His remarkable decorations from 1909-1911, and his work at the Bor school, offered a very different conception of acid engraving from that of the Lorraine manufacturers of Gallé and Daum.

50. VASE, 1910.
Acid-etched glass with enamelled details.
Acid-etched signature: AB.
H. 15 cm.
Lötz Glassworks, Klášterský Mlýn.
Museum of Decorative Arts, Prague
(Inv. 12 657).

51. Vase decorated with convolvulus flowers, 1902.
Engraved colourless glass with violet inclusions, applied colour, and cut rim. H. 18.5 cm. Harrach Glassworks, Nový Svět. Museum of Decorative Arts, Prague (Inv. 1383/60).

52. Champagne flute, 1902.
Engraved colourless glass with violet inclusions, painted in gold relief. H. 14 cm. Harrach Glassworks, Nový Svět. Museum of Decorative Arts, Prague (Inv. dep. 1383/6).

53. Vase with iris and tulip flower decoration, 1902.
Engraved colourless glass with violet inclusions and irregularly cut rim. H. 9.5 cm. Harrach Glassworks, Nový Svět. Museum of Decorative Arts, Prague (Inv. dep. 1383/4).

Harrach Glassworks, Nový Svět

The Harrach Glassworks (*cf.* page 56), whose reputation remained undiminished at the beginning of the century, was one of the first to adopt the Art Nouveau style. Its programme also included multiple techniques of heat-working as well as decorative processes like cutting, painting or engraving. Manufacturing models were created by Julius Jelínek as of 1900, but it is impossible now to measure his influence on the firm. Colourless glasses with engraved floral motifs and coloured inclusions worked into the mass remain among the firm's most interesting kinds of Art Nouveau.

54. Wine glass, 1901.
Engraved glass.
H. 15.5 cm.
Harrach Glassworks, Nový Svět, engraved by Alois Pohl.
Glass and Jewellery Museum, Jablonec nad Nisou (Inv. E 140).

Presented at the competition for the decoration of drinking glasses organized by the Liberec Museum in 1901.

Carl Lederle

Born in Friburg im Brisgau (Germany), date unknown.

Between 1890 and 1914, Lederle worked in the Museum of Industry in Liberec, where he assumed, among other responsibilities, the direction of the studio design courses. He was also himself a creator. Around 1900, he took part in various competitions organized by the museum. His floral engraved decorations, honoured in 1901 and designed to ornament drinking glasses, were adopted by the Harrach Glassworks. They were inspired by the dynamic lines of Henry Van der Velde.

Josef Riedel Glassworks, Polubný (in the Jizerské hory mountains)

The firm, founded in 1840, was bought back by the Riedel family in 1849. The Riedels—great glass industrialists who owned many other factories in the Jizerské hory Mountains—specialized in pressed glass and the manufacture of coloured glass rods used as raw material for glass bead-making and jewellery-making in the Jablonec region. Although the glassworks aimed primarily at economic profitability, a small part of its production evolved in the decorative-arts style of the period.

55. Four vases, before 1904.
Yellow and violet opalized glass, painted in black and gold.
H. 15.5 cm; 15 cm; 18.5 cm; 7.6 cm.
J. Riedel Glassworks, Polubný.
Museum of Decorative Arts, Prague (Inv. 8 776 - 779).

Right-hand page:
56. Liqueur service, after 1900.
Painted decoration in transparent enamels, contours in gold, partially frosted.
Carafe H. 31.5 cm; glasses H. 15.5 cm; plate D. 29.5 cm.
Meyr Nephew Glassworks, Adolfov.
Museum of Decorative Arts, Prague (Inv. 76 403 - 413).

Meyr Nephew Glassworks, Adolfov

Founded in 1816 by Josef Meyr, one of a large family of glass industrialists in South Bohemia. At the turn of the century, the glassworks belonged to Albert and Rudolf Kralik, relations of the Lobmeyrs of Vienna, and thus it maintained artistic and commercial contacts with the Austrian capital. Its workshops, celebrated for the brillancy and perfect transparency of their glass, as well as the richness of their cutting and engraving, produced models by Kolo Moser, O. Prutscher and Josef Hoffmann. Table glassware, decorated in a great variety of ways, represented an important part of its production.

57. Vase, 1900.
Cut and polished marbled opaque glass (called diluvium-glass).
On the label: JRS/Kosten.
H. 15.5 cm.
J. Rindskopf Glassworks, Košťany.
Regional Museum, Liberec (Inv. S. 412).

Josef Rindskopf and Son Glassworks, Košťany (Kosten)

In the second half of the nineteenth century, the Rindskopf family asserted itself in the glass-making industry of Northwest Bohemia. The family owned industrial glassworks for bottles and lighting fixtures, but the Košťany factory also manufactured a line of luxury products. Around 1900, Košťany was known for its iridescent decorations and floral-motif opaque glass (marbled in the mass and called diluvium-glass), cut and wheel-engraved or acid-etched. Some documents from the period suggest that the German architect Peter Behrens was one of the creators of the models.

The Nový Bor professional School

The school was founded in 1870 and subsidized by local industry, the city of Bor and the State. From the 1890s on, it offered training in three disciplines: glass-engraving, painting on glass and porcelain, and design. The programme of study lasted three years. From 1881 to 1907, it was directed by Daniel Hartel, and from 1907 to 1929, by Heinrich Strehblow. The establishment took part in a series of exhibitions and collaborated with regional glass-makers, who executed models designed in its studios. Under the influence of Vienna and the Wiener Werkstätte, teaching quality and creative work were considerably enriched after 1905. The school, enlivened by artists like Strehblow and Hanel, gave an original spicing to Art Nouveau.

58. Bowl, 1914.
Blue lustre glass with linear decoration painted in enamel and gold.
H. 7.1 cm.
School of Glass-making, Nový Bor.
Museum of Decorative Arts, Prague
(Inv. 13 294).

School of Glass-making, Nový Bor.
59. WINE BOTTLES AND GLASSES, 1912.
Linear decoration painted in black and enamel.
Bottle H. 39.5 cm; glasses H. 20 cm.
Museum of Decorative Arts, Prague
(Inv. 12 796).

School of Glass-making, Nový Bor.
60. Vase.
Decorated with *millefiori* painted enamels.
H. 29 cm.
Museum of Decorative Arts, Prague
(Inv. 12 764).

Anton Hanel

Kuřivody 1870 - Bor 1925.
1885-1890: trained at the School of Glass-making in Bor.
1890-1923: worked at the Bor school as head of the studio, then, from 1918, as professor.
1910: instructor at the Vienna School of Decorative Arts.

Hanel became known for his work between 1906 and 1914. He created vases with acid-etched decorations, interpreting in a highly personal manner the ornamental characteristics of the late Art Nouveau style: vegetal motifs and geometry blended with great imagination and refinement. Hanel's works were among the greatest successes of North Bohemian production, and his activity at the Bor school contributed greatly to the international reputation of the establishment.

**61. Vase in bottle form, c. 1910.
Colourless glass, cased with pink, acid-etched and cut.
H. 41.5 cm.
School of Glass-making, Nový Bor.
Glass Museum, Nový Bor
(Inv. NB 4796).**

**62. Vase, 1906.
Cased glass, acid-etched and wheel-engraved.
Engraved signature: HA.
H. 23 cm.
School of Glass-making, Nový Bor.
Glass Museum, Nový Bor
(Inv. NB 1866).**

63. Three glasses with tall stems, 1914.
Decoration painted by feather pen in black, highlighted in gold.
H. 23.5 cm; 24.5 cm; 24.3 cm.
Glass and Jewellery Museum, Jablonec nad Nisou
(Inv. S 5474 a,b,c).

Karl Massanetz

Kamenický Šenov 1890 - killed in the war in 1918.
Trained at the Specialized School of Glassmaking in Kamenický Šenov.
1908-1912: studied at the Vienna School of Decorative Arts, A. Barwig, K. Moser and M. Powolny studios.
1912: opened his own studio in Kamenický Šenov.

Massanetz, who was inspired by the decorations of Josef Hoffmann, interpreted the Viennese ornamental style in an original way. His surfaces were entirely covered with subjects executed by feather pen —tiny spirals, scales or motifs composed in lambrequins—and his forms, especially those of his stemmed glasses, were very distinctive. Glassmakers in the Kamenický Šenov area quickly adopted his decorations, and many regional glassworks executed variations on them until the beginning of the 1920's.

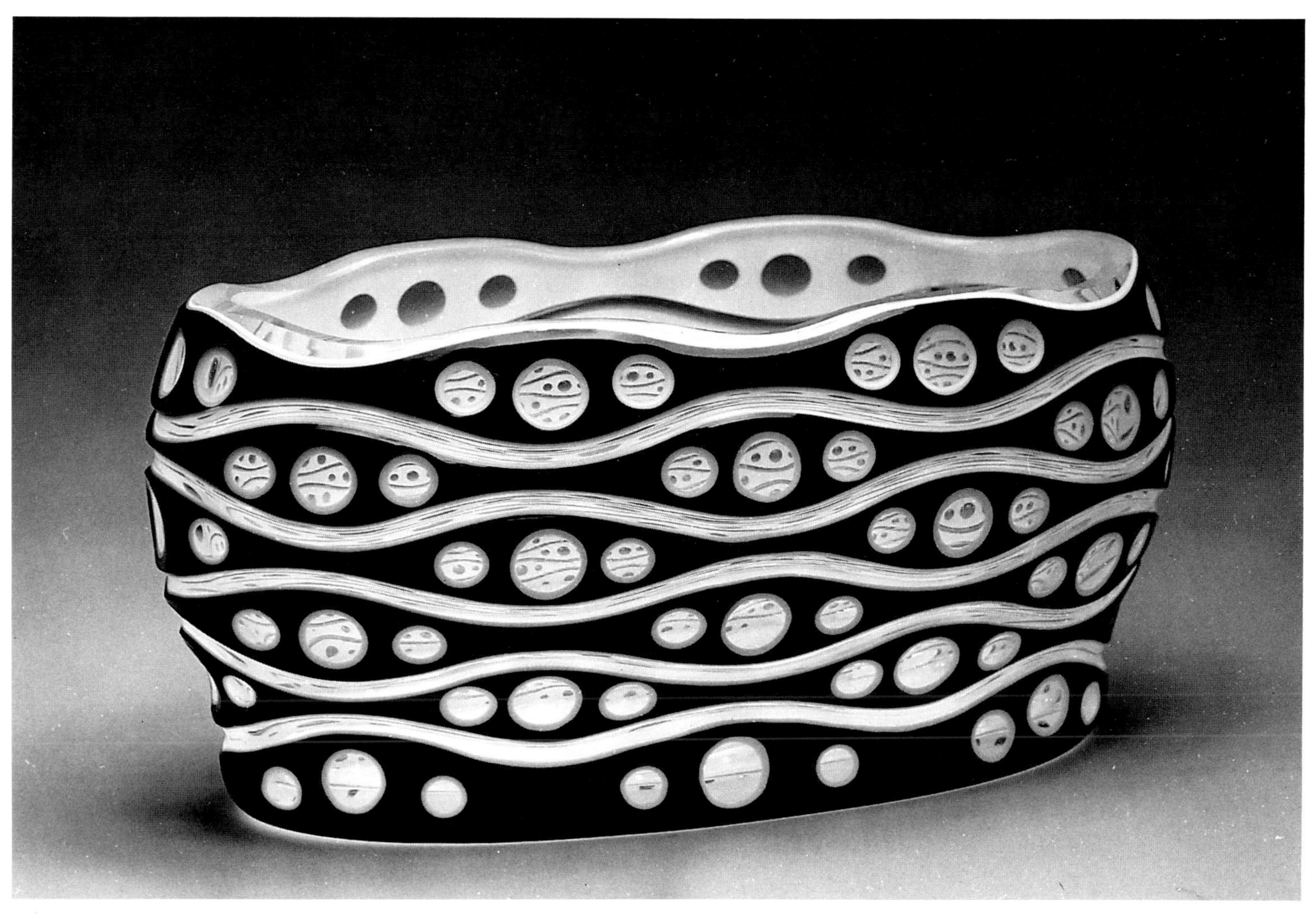

Carl Schappel Firm, Nový Bor

Founded in 1857 and dissolved in 1945; bought by J. George Stier in 1910. The firm had a cutting workshop and employed independent glass-makers, but it did not possess an oven for blowing and heat work. At the turn of the century, its decorations were among the most original of North Bohemia, and placed highly in international exhibitions. The firm created warehouses in many European countries.

64. Jardiniere, 1913.
Tripled black and white cut glass.
L. 18.4 cm.
Carl Schappel House, Nový Bor.
Museum of Decorative Arts, Prague
(Inv. 93 566).

The manufacturer received models from both the Bor School of Glassmaking and foreign artists: Otto Prutscher, Josef Hoffmann of Vienna, Emanuel Margold of Darmstadt. It was probably his design studio which produced the Borussia series of 1913, the most celebrated of Schappel's creations. Cut decoration of geometric inspiration on superimposed black and white layers of glass varied from one piece to another. A printed catalogue of this series still exists; the jardinière presented here is included therein.

65. PUNCHBOWL AND GLASSES, 1904-1910.
Facetted cut glass.
Covered bowl, H. 41.5 cm.
Glasses, H. 11.9 cm.
Harrach Glassorks, Nový Svět.
Executed for the Artěl.
Museum of Decorative Arts, Prague
(Inv. 14 170).

Jan Kotěra

Brno 1871- Prague 1923.
1894-1897: studied at the Academy of Beaux Arts in Vienna, O. Wagner's studio.
1899-1911: professor at the Prague School of Decorative Arts, Architecture and Decoration Department.
1911-1923: professor at the Academy of Beaux-Arts in Prague.

Throughout his career as architect and professor, Kotěra never lost interest in the art professions. The art of glass—table and decorative art—was inscribed in the programme of his courses. He himself created only one work in glass, a punch service presented by the School of Decorative Arts at the Universal Exposition of Saint Louis in 1904. His architect's vision and finely tuned sense of volume glitter in the simplified version of this service, executed for the Artěl after 1910. This work helped usher in the modern style of Czech glass-making.

Prague School of Decorative Arts, V.H. Brunner studio, work by Jan Bauch.
66. Prague souvenir glass, 1920.
Glass with enamelled decoration, bearing the inscription *Praga caput rei publicæ bohemicæ*.
H. 10 cm.
Museum of Decorative Arts, Prague (Inv. 89 008).

Prague School of Decorative Arts, V.H. Brunner studio.
67. Souvenir glass: Saint Cyril and Saint Methodius.
Glass with enamelled decoration.
H. 10 cm.
Museum of Decorative Arts, Prague (Inv. 89 009).

Jaromír Krejcar.
68. Souvenir glass: Charles bridge of Prague, 1922.
Glass with enamelled decoration.
H. 9.3 cm.
Museum of Decorative Arts, Prague (Inv. 93 543).

The Artěl

The Artěl, active in Prague from 1908 to 1934, grouped together creators from various branches of the decorative arts. In the beginning, there were only eight; membership increased quickly. The Artěl's programme inaugurated the struggle against the mass-production of objects and exalted the work of the artisan in daily life. The Artěl did not possess its own workshops; its members, or those who shared their convictions, operated in different factories and workshops. The Artěl then assumed the responsibility of commercial distribution. After a Cubist phase in the pre-war years, its production style usually illustrated a decorative conception of form. Around 1926, it moved towards expression devoid of functionalism.

In 1920 the Artěl decided to create souvenir glass objects of modern conception. These three works were the fruit of this initiative. The design for the first two came from the graphic art studio of the Prague School of Decorative Arts, directed by V.H. Brunner, founding member and active participant in the Artěl. The third, ornamented with a view of the Charles Bridge, was the work of Jaromír Krejcar, a young architect who collaborated on several occasions with the Artěl.

Josef Rosipal

Prague 1885 - deceased in the war in 1914.
1910-1914: collaboration with the Artěl in glass-making.

Rosipal wanted to mould his glass models to the Cubist vision, which predominated in the Artěl's ceramics and furniture. His works were geometrically stylized, but not radically so, and his decorative cutting was based on the losange, emphasized by the use of colour. Rosipal's models, mainly produced during the twenties, were presented at the 1925 International Exposition in Paris.

**69. Liqueur service, after 1910.
Colourless cut glass
cased with ruby red.
Bottle H. 33 cm; glasses H. 18 cm.
Executed for the Artěl, probably
by the Pryl Glassworks, Dobronín.
Museum of Decorative Arts, Prague
(Inv. 31 272).**

**70. Vase, after 1910.
Colourless cut glass
cased in blue.
H. 39 cm.
Executed for the Artěl,
probably by the Pryl Glassworks, Dobronín.
Museum of Decorative Arts, Prague
(Inv. 14 180).**

JAROSLAV HOREJC

Prague 1886 - Prague 1983.
Apprenticeship in metal-engraving.
Trained at the Professional School of Jewellery in Prague.
1906-1910: studied at the Prague School of Decorative Arts, E. Novák and S. Sucharda studios.
Member of the Artěl from 1909.
1918-1948: professor at the Prague School of Decorative Arts, Director of the Metal-work Studio.

Horejc, a sculptor by training who specialised in metal work, was also one of the greatest Czech glass-makers of the twentieth century. He designed his first models for the Artěl starting in 1912. It was only at the beginning of the 1920's that he fully exploited his talent as a glass-maker with the creation of four vases, executed by the engraving workshop of the J. and L. Lobmeyr House in Kamenický Šenov. Besides the three pieces shown here there was a fourth, the vase *Dance* (1923). One of the first copies belongs to the Museum of Decorative Arts in Paris. These four vases won the Grand Prize at the Paris Exposition of 1925 and secured for Horejc an important place in the evolution of modern engraved glass. In 1937 he created a monumental work, a moulded relief called *The Earth and Men* (in eight parts, 140 x 545 centimetres, originally designed for the Palace of Nations in Geneva, today conserved at the Museum of Decorative Arts in Prague). Horejc returned throughout his career to engraved glass, notably in 1957, with a vase presented at the Second Triennale of Milan.

71. VASE: « CANAAN, LAND OF ABUNDANCE AND WELL-BEING », design of 1921-1923, executed in 1926.
Engraved and cut glass, figures and fruits.
Engraved signature: JLLW AB 1926.
H. 17 cm.
Engraving workshop of the J. and L. Lobmeyr House, Kamenický Šenov, engraver August Bischof.
Museum of Decorative Arts, Prague (Inv. 1072/2).

72. « BACCHUS » VASE, design of 1921-1922, executed after 1925.
Engraved and cut glass; Bacchus, winemakers, animals.
Engraved signature: JLLW AO.
H. 17.8 cm.
Engraving workshop of the J. and L. Lobmeyr House, Kamenický Šenov, engraver Alfred Opitz.
Museum of Decorative Arts, Prague (Inv. 59 432).

73. « THREE GRACES » VASE, 1924.
Engraved glass, partly in relief, then cut; figures of Athena, Aphrodite and Hera.
Engraved signature: JLLW MR.
H. 20.8 cm.
Engraving workshop of the J. and L. Lobmeyr House, Kamenický Šenov, engraver Max Rössler.
Museum of Decorative Arts, Prague (Inv. 1072/1).

74. « ČSR » GLASS,
1928 model executed between 1945 and 1950.
Glass engraved in relief and hollowed, then cut.
Engraved signature: JLLW K. Horn.
Executed by the engraving workshop of the J. and L. Lobmeyr House, Kamenický Šenov, engraver K. Horn.
Museum of Decorative Arts, Prague (Inv. 66 537).

Later edition of a model created for the tenth anniversary of the founding of the Czechoslovakian Republic.

František Kysela

Kouřim 1881 - Prague 1941.
1900-1904 and 1905-1908: studied at the Prague School of Decorative Arts, K. Mašek's studio.
1904-1905: studied at the Academy of Beaux-Arts in Prague.
1911: instructor; then, from 1917 to 1941, professor at the Prague School of Decorative Arts, Director of the Applied Graphic Arts Studio.

Kysela, one of the first proponents of the Art Deco style in Bohemia, worked in various branches of the decorative arts. His tapestry-cycle evoking the different arts was awarded a gold medal at the 1925 Paris Exposition. His work as a glass-maker included several stained-glass windows and a glass created for the tenth anniversary of the founding of the Czechoslovakian Republic. This unique engraved glass was important to his artistic development, as it translated the values of the Baroque glass tradition of Silesia into a modern idiom.

Josef Drahoňovský

Volavec 1877 - Prague 1938.
1890-1894: student at the Turnov Professional School of Glyptics, where he learned gem-engraving.
1896-1902: studied at the Prague School of Decorative Arts, S. Sucharda and C. Klouček studios.
1904: opened his own sculpture studio.
1904: instructor at the Prague School of Decorative Arts.
1908-1938: professor at this same school; directed the Decorative Sculpture Studio, whose programme integrated training in the techniques of glyptics and engraving glass.

Drahoňovský was one of the rare artists of the twentieth century who dedicated themselves to the art of glyptics. He referred to antiquity as his authority, but also tapped into a tradition still alive in Bohemia. Although Drahoňovský himself engraved on hard stone, his glasses were engraved by his disciples and collaborators from his designs. He trained twenty or so excellent engravers, who continued his tradition until the 1950's. Drahoňovský was appreciated abroad as an artist in glyptics. Jean Babelon, former head curator of the Cabinet of Medals at the Bibliothèque Nationale in Paris, was one of his admirers in France; he wrote an introduction to a monograph on Drahoňovský, from whom he acquired several gems for the National Library. Drahoňovský's collection of gems and engraved glasses won the Grand Prize at the 1925 Exposition des Arts Décoratifs in Paris.

**75. « Clouds and stars » vase, c. 1936.
Tripled glass, acid-etched and wheel-engraved; two figures, ancient god and goddess, seated in the clouds under a starry sky.
Engraved signature: Drahoňovský.
H. 15 cm.
Executed by a collaborator of Josef Drahoňovský.
Museum of Decorative Arts, Prague
(Inv. 94 950).**

Josef Drahoňovský
76. Large covered vase: Prague, 1931.
Cut and engraved glass; panoramic view of the Castle of Prague and the Malá Strana, framed with architectural monuments and sculptures of the city. Finial on the cover in the form of the National Theatre; cover inscribed, *1896 -21 VII -1931*.
Engraved signature: J. Drahoňovský 1931.
H. 43 cm.
Executed by the A. Rückl Glassworks, Nižbor, engraved by a collaborator of J. Drahoňovský.
Museum of Decorative Arts, Prague
(Inv. 78 432).

Variant of another glass created in 1928 for the tenth anniversary of the founding of the Czechoslovakian Republic and exhibited at the time in Brno.

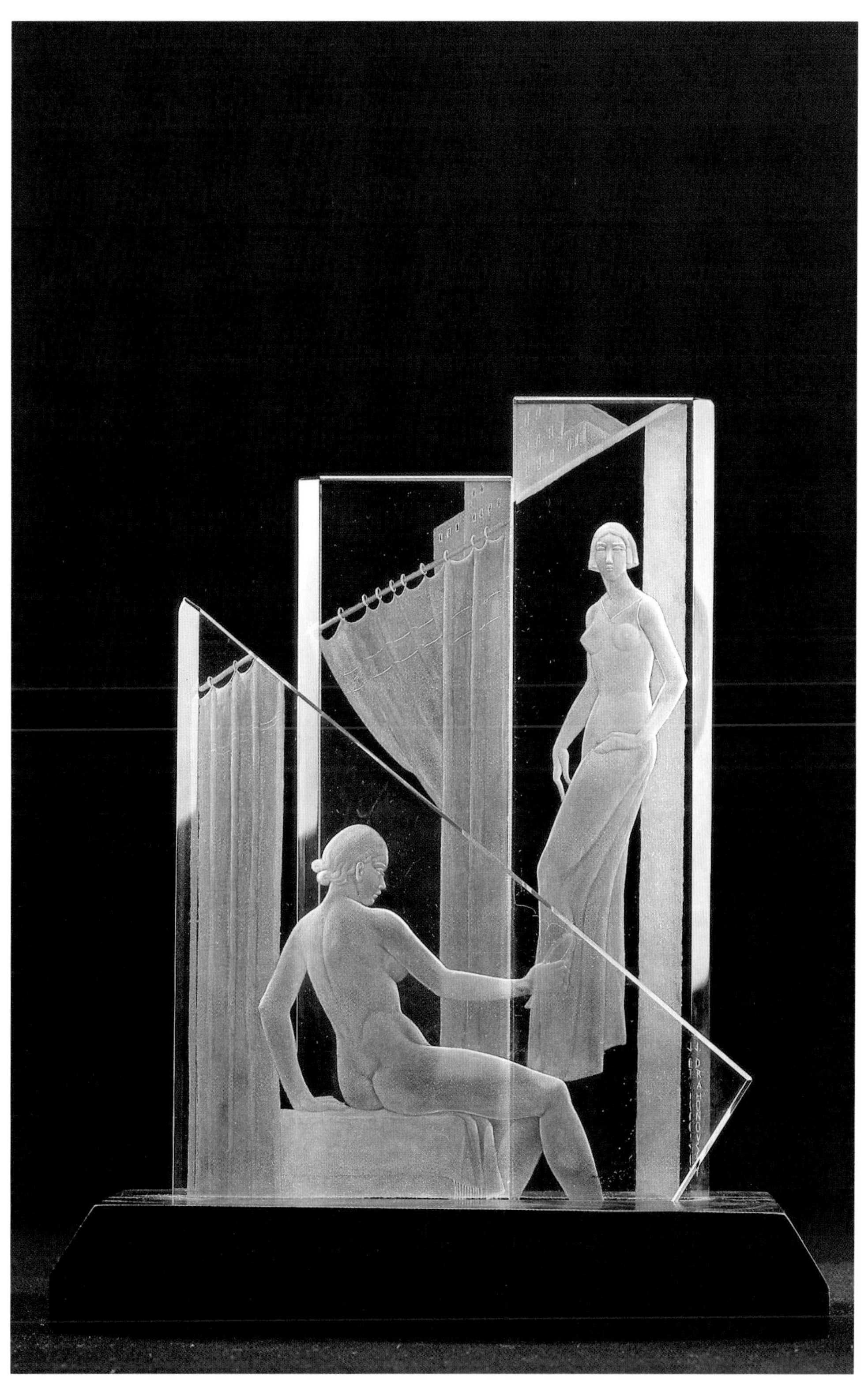

Josef Drahoňovský
77. IN FRONT OF THE WINDOW, 1932.
Three panels of glass;
engraved composition with two female
figures. Wooden stand.
Engraved signature: J. Drahoňovský.
H. 27 cm.
Engraved by Bohumil Vele.
Museum of Decorative Arts, Prague
(Inv. 1170/10).

Oswald Lippert, J. Drahoňovský's studio at the Prague School of Decorative Arts.
78. Adam and eve vase, 1931.
Glass partly coloured in black, with acid-etched linear decoration.
Acid-etched signature: O. Lippert 31.
H. 18.2 cm.
Museum of Decorative Arts, Prague (Inv. 93 557).

This vase was among the works presented by the Prague School of Decorative Arts at the Stockholm Architecture Exhibition in 1931.

Oswald Lippert

Born in 1908 in Stará Boleslav, lived in Rheinbach, Germany.
1922-1925: student at the Professional of School Glass-making in Kamenický Šenov.
1925-1933: studied at the Prague School of Decorative Arts, Josef Drahoňovský studio.
1933-1945: professor at the Specialized School of Glassmaking in Kamenický Šenov.
1949-1973: professor at the Staatliche Glasfachschule in Rheinbach.

Lippert was one of the few students of Drahoňovský who forged their own expression in glass art. A good designer of figures, he also possessed a keen sense of the expressive quality of colours. As a student, he kept abreast of the evolution in painting and contemporary graphic arts in Bohemia and France, an interest that appeared throughout his work. He experimented with and mastered various decorative techniques: painting, acid-etching, cutting by wheel, and sand-blasting.

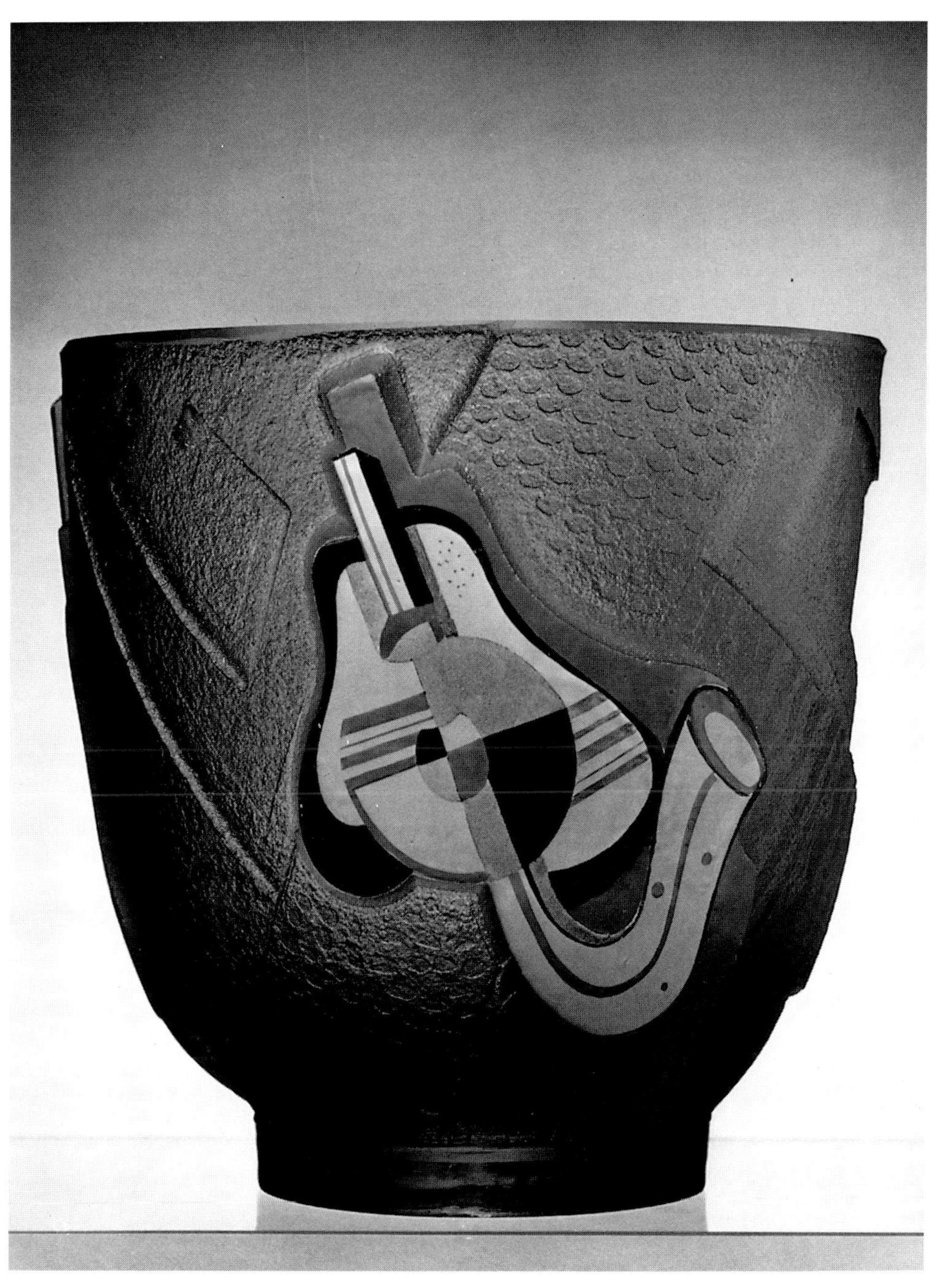

PROFESSIONAL SCHOOL,
KAMENICKÝ ŠENOV

The school was created in 1856 and trained designers for local industry. In 1880, it became a public establishment and provided education in drawing, glass-engraving, and painting on glass and porcelain. The course lasted three years. Among the directors of the school were Heinrich Zoff (1902-1914), Adolf Beckert (1918-1926) and Alfred Dorn (1933- 1945). The school collaborated with local industry, which owed it numerous technological discoveries. The school responded to the demands of the market, but also, for several decades, was influenced by the Lobmeyr House workshop in Kamenický Šenov.

79. VASE, COMPOSITION WITH MUSICAL INSTRUMENTS, 1925-1930.
Light green glass, deeply acid-etched and painted with opaque enamels.
H. 14.2 cm.
School of Glass-making, Kamenický Šenov.
Glass Museum, Kamenický Šenov (Inv. KS 2845).

Ladislav Přenosil

Příšovice 1893 - Turnov 1965.
Trained at the Specialized School of Glassmaking in Turnov.
1911-1914 and 1921-1922: studied at the Prague School of Decorative Arts, S. Sucharda and J. Drahoňovský studios.
1922-1958: professor of glass-engraving at the Specialized School of Glassmaking in Železný Brod.
1927: worked in Stuttgart, in Wilhelm von Eiff's studio.

Přenosil was one of the first artists trained in engraving gems and glass in Drahoňovský's studio; he executed a great number of his master's designs. He remained faithful to Drahoňovský's conceptions in his own work, but over the years he distanced himself more and more from neo-classical severity.

80. Intaglio: « The Woman and the Architect », 1921.
Engraved glass.
Engraved signature: LP.
H. 4.2 cm; L. 4.2 cm.
Museum of Decorative Arts, Prague (Inv. 91 848).

Gem created on the occasion of the marriage of two members of the Artěl.

Jaroslav Brychta

Pohodlí 1895 - Železný Brod 1971.
1912-1918: studied at the Prague School of Decorative Arts, J. Drahoňovský and C. Klouček studios.
1920-1960: professor at the Specialized School of Glassmaking in Železný Brod; directed the Glass Figurines Studio.

Brychta pursued the parallel careers of creator and pedagogue. In both, his most original work lay in the realization of glass figurines. He was determined to perfect their manufacturing techniques and offered new employment for glass-makers working at home in the region of Železný Brod. Brychta used glass pearls around 1921, then developed modelling and blowing by blowtorch, and, as of 1932, made certain figurines directly in the glass-maker's furnace. Brychta's characters breathe humour and good will. The subjects evoke everyday life, the occupations of country folk, sports and current events of the period; he also created fantastic characters and fairy tale heroes. He remained faithful to this kind of creation until his death, and his figurines were very successful at the Universal Expositions of Brussels (1935), Paris (1937) and Montreal (1967).

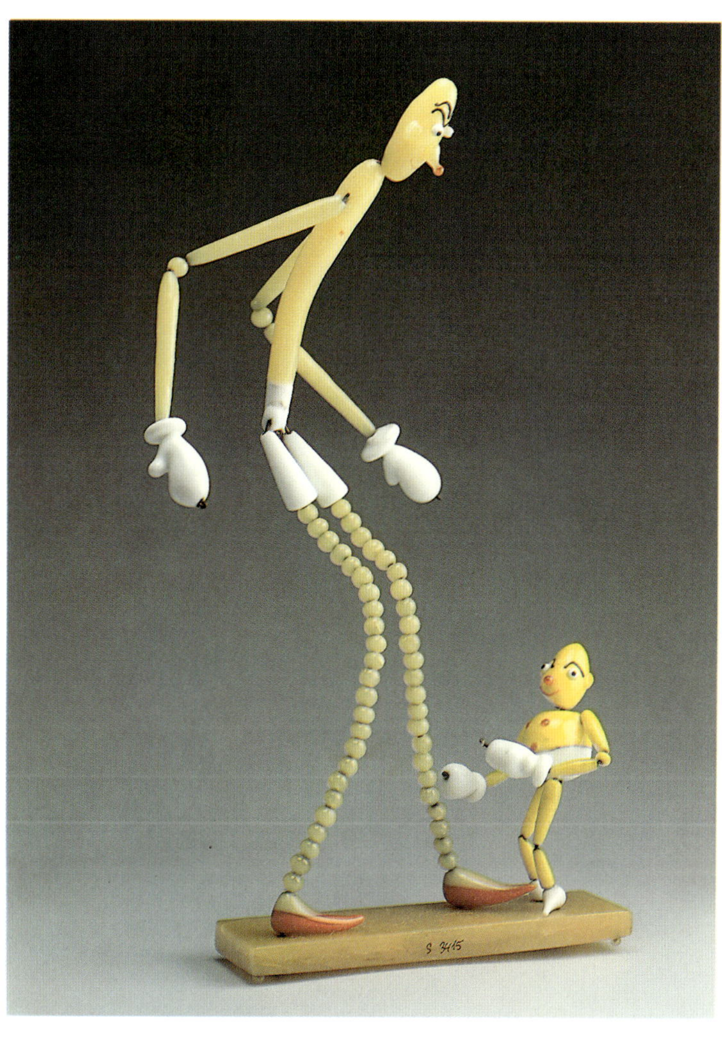

Jaroslav Brychta
81. THE BOXERS, 1921.
Group of figurines; opal glass worked with blow-torch, glass pearls.
H. 21 cm.
Železný Brod.
Museum of Glass and Jewellery, Jablonec nad Nisou
(Inv. S 3415).

JOSEF EISELT

Kamenický Šenov 1896 -
Hadamar (RFA) 1975.
1910-1914: trained at the Specialized School of Glassmaking in Kamenický Šenov.
1914-1917: worked as designer in several glassworks in Kamenický Šenov.
1917-1945: directed the Family Painting Studio in Kamenický Šenov.
1925-1945: taught painting on glass at the Nový Bor school.
1950-1956: taught at the Specialized School of Glassmaking in Hadamar.

Eisclt was one of the initiators of Art Deco in North Bohemia. His work smoothly developed its ornamental elements and chromatism.

Following double page:
82. BOX WITH COVER, 1924.
Glass painted with enamel and frosted.
H. 18.5 cm.
Josef Eiselt Studio, Kamenický Šenov.
Museum of Decorative Arts, Prague
(Inv. 16 260).

83. CUP, 1924.
Glass painted with enamel.
Signature written in gold:
Josef Eiselt, Steinschönau.
H. 14.4 cm.
Josef Eiselt Studio, Kamenický Šenov.
Museum of Decorative Arts, Prague
(Inv. 15 447).

84. Vase, around 1933.
Smoked cut glass.
H. 16 cm; D. 31 cm.
Cut by Emilian Celler, Podmoklice.
Museum of Decorative Arts, Prague
(Inv. 20 514).

Alois Metelák

Martěnice 1897 - Železný Brod 1980.
1913-1920: studied at the Prague School of Decorative Arts, J. Plečnik and F. Kysela studio.
1924-1948: director of the Specialised School of Glassmaking in Železný Brod.

Through his activity in Železný Brod, Metelák influenced not only the style of the school but even, to a certain degree, that of regional production. As professor and designer, he dedicated himself to cut glass and the study of forms; his own models and those of his studio were executed by the school and local glassworks. Metelak was sympathetic to Functionalism in the beginning, but later turned towards a more dynamic and personal expression.

LADISLAV SUTNAR

Plzeň 1897 - New York 1976.
1915-1916 and 1919-1923: studied both at the Prague School of Decorative Arts, E. Dítě, J. Benda and F. Kysela studios, and the Charles University of Prague.
1923, professor; 1932-1946, Director of the School of Graphic Arts in Prague. (He was exiled in 1939 to the United States, but still kept his title).
1929: artistic advisor for the "Krásná Jizba" firm (which may be translated as "Useful Forms").

85. TABLE GLASS SERVICE, 1930.
Blown glass.
Wine glass H. 12.7 cm;
liqueur glass H. 10.3 cm;
water glasses H. 10 cm. and 12 cm.
Museum of Decorative Arts, Prague
(Inv. 71 031).

Sutnar worked mainly in the graphic arts, particularly posters and books. As Krásná Jizba's artistic advisor, he also became interested in glass, porcelain and metal mountings. A partisan of strict functionalism, Sutnar insisted on the aesthetic and archetypal value of forms and geometric figures. He exalted them in his own work and in all of Krásná Jizba's production.

86. BREAKFAST SERVICE,
1930 design executed in 1936.
Cut and polished glass.
Engraved signature: L. Smrčková,
Cristallerie Nižbor 1936.
Tea cup H. 9 cm;
bread and butter plate D. 12 cm;
jam cup H. 4 cm;
carafe H. 11 cm.
A. Rückl Glassworks, Nižbor.
Museum of Decorative Arts, Prague
(Inv. 65 893).

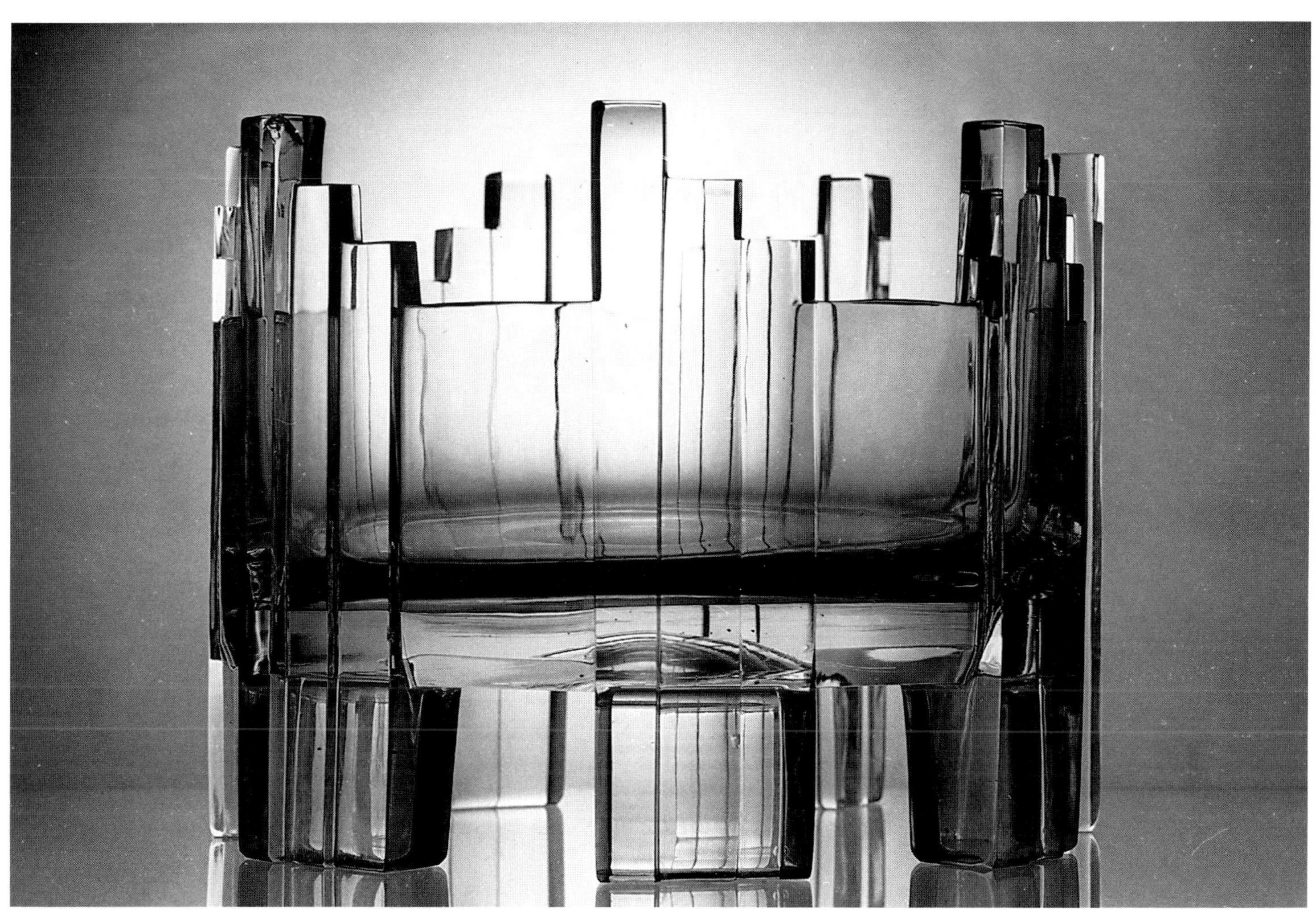

LUDVIKA SMRČKOVÁ

Kročehlavy 1903 - lives in Prague.
1921-1927: Prague School of Decorative Arts, E. Dítě, V.H. Brunner and F. Kysela workshops. Also studied drawing and mathematics at the Charles University of Prague.
1928-1948: professor at Příbor, Litomyšl, Kladno and Prague High Schools; collaboration with the Rückl glassworks of Nižbor.
1948-1958: created models for different firms: Inwald, Glassexport, Central Bureau for Research and the Glass and Ceramics Industry (see p. 198).

87. DECORATIVE PIECE, 1936.
Cut leaded glass.
Engraved signature: L. Smrčková 1936
Nižbor Crystal Manufacture.
H. 20.2 cm.
A. Rückl Glassworks, Nižbor.
Museum of Decorative Arts, Prague
(Inv. 61 697).

This piece was part of a group of works awarded the Grand Prize at the Paris Exposition of Arts and Techniques in 1937.

Smrčková is one of the founders of modern Czech glass-making. She did her best work in the 1930's, as a Functionalist, and created beautiful, robust and simple table glasses for Krásná Jizba. The same geometrical conception characterized her work in cut glass: her cutting emphasized the silhouette, which arose from an architectonic vision to monumental effect. One of Smrčková's glasses was exhibited in Paris in 1925. In the 1930's she won numerous European awards, including a Grand Prize at the Paris Exposition in 1937.

Contemporary Creators

The art of glass evolved decisively in Czechoslovakia during the forties and fifties. By the mid-fifties, glass-makers tended to the creation of unique pieces made in the studio by the artists themselves. This mode of expression constituted one of the liveliest and most interesting aspects of contemporary creation.

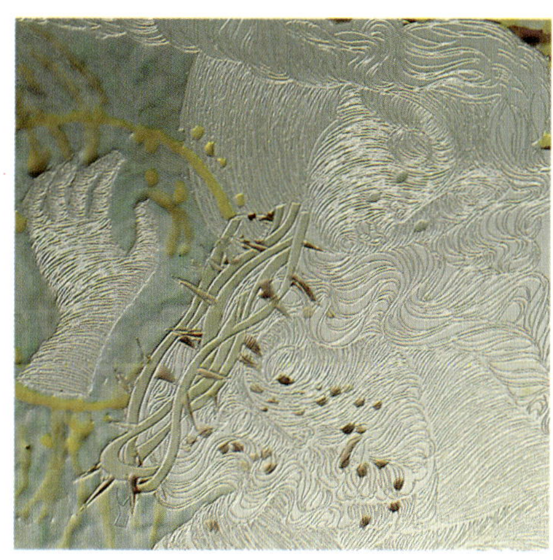

.129.

After the war, the interruption of commercial relations and the scarcity of raw materials slowed down the industrial production of glass, once highly competitive in the international market. The situation was particularly serious in North Bohemia, where it was once again a question of revitalizing the concentrated production in the areas of Bor, Kamenický Šenov and Teplice and preserving the tradition of professional training, guaranteed by the established schools in the region since the nineteenth century. The future of glass was decided in Prague, however, in the studios of the School of Applied Arts, recently upgraded to the rank of an Academy (a teaching institution training professionals and educators at the graduate level), and in Moravia, in the small Škrdlovice firm, founded during the war by Emanuel Beránek.

Czech glass-makers were obliged to prepare new production programmes that would provide them with other export possibilities, and offer high-level training to young specialists, artisans and designers. Above all, however, they had to elaborate a modern and authentically Czech conception that could serve as a sound basis in the long run. They undertook this renovation during the industrial reconstruction that lasted until 1953, but it was not until the second half of the fifties that a new blossoming in the art was observed, with successes at the large international shows (the Universal Exposition of Brussels in 1958, and the XIth and XIIth Milan Triennales of 1957 and 1960.)

The glass-making industry, and professional education in the Bor, Kamenick Šenov and Železný Brod regions, benefitted from the assistance of young graduates of the Prague Academy of Applied Arts, notably students of Josef Holeček (some of whom finished their studies in Josef Kaplický's studio), Karel Štipl and Josef Drahoňovský. These young glass-makers dug in enthusiastically to work as professors or studio heads in the schools, creators in the manufacturing firms, and organizers of exhibitions reintegrating the glass object into the contemporary aesthetic universe. Some students of the Academy of Applied Arts in Prague maintained contacts with North Bohemian industry through training programmes offered by the Prague Museum of Decorative Arts in the Lobmeyr workshop, directed by Stephan Rath until 1949. This workshop turned out remarkable models with engraved decoration, and fine-walled drinking glasses. Scholarship students, like Věra Lišková, collaborated in their production.

.203.

Their creativity was affirmed

during the fifties, when table glass manufacturing (services by Stanislav Libenský and Adolf Matura) benefitted from simple and innovative forms. Glass-cutters abandoned the traditional star motif for new designs by Miluše Roubíčková, Jiřina Žertová and Ladislav Oliva; vases by René Roubicek asserted irregular and sculptural forms in engraved and cut glass. Ladislav Oliva obtained new decorations in experiments with sand-blasting; and Adolf Matura, Pavel Hlava, Ludvika Smrčková and Jan Kotík all conducted innovative research into many-layered glass, cut into large-sided shapes. Hlava and Matura succeeded with unifloral vases in particular. At the end of the forties, glass-making reached an important stage with paintings in transparent enamels on thin-walled cups of sober line, from the drawings of Stanislav Libenský, then professor at the Nový Bor school (*Pieta, 1947; Deposition of the Cross, 1947*).

Heat-shaped glass was very important in the repertoire of utilitarian objects. The public liked it, and it was characteristic of its time; but despite certain innovations in decoration, Bohemia's contribution depended considerably upon Scandinavian creation. The Škrdlovice Glassworks, after a short period of experimentation, joined with Chřibská in this direction. Škrdlovice models were created by artists working in the internal design office of the factory (Maria Stáhlíková, Milena Velíšková, František Vízner) and by outside artists, like Jiřina Žertová, Vladimír Jelínek and Jan Kotík.

Yet undoubtedly the most important work of the period was linked to the exceptional personality of Professor Josef Kaplický. This painter, engraver, sculptor, and brilliant theoretician never created an important work of glass. Nevertheless, through the works of his disciples —today the masters of Czech glass—he animated and fulfilled his ambition: to elaborate a modern aesthetic of Czech glass responding to the national spirit.

.184.

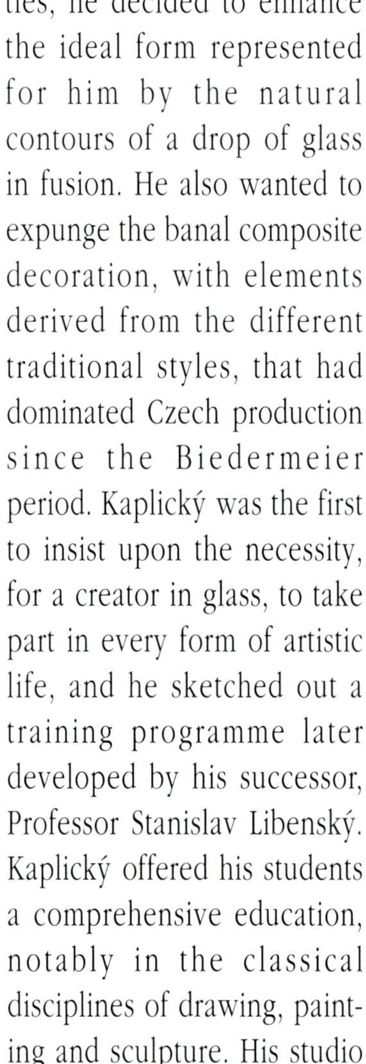

Kaplický arrived at the Academy of Applied Arts in 1945, and succeeded Professor Josef Holeček as the head of one of the establishment's two glass studios in 1947. The other studio, specialized in engraving, and later in industrial design, was directed by Professor Karel Štipl as of 1938. Kaplický devoted himself to the search for both useful and beautiful form; adapting Functionalist principles to the vision of the fifties, he decided to enhance the ideal form represented for him by the natural contours of a drop of glass in fusion. He also wanted to expunge the banal composite decoration, with elements derived from the different traditional styles, that had dominated Czech production since the Biedermeier period. Kaplický was the first to insist upon the necessity, for a creator in glass, to take part in every form of artistic life, and he sketched out a training programme later developed by his successor, Professor Stanislav Libenský. Kaplický offered his students a comprehensive education, notably in the classical disciplines of drawing, painting and sculpture. His studio executed a multitude of vases and plates with painted or engraved decoration, conceived of as utilitarian objects but works of art in and of themselves; and from these, he took the next logical step of devoting himself exclusively to the sculptural possibilites of glass. Thereby he announced the advent of unique pieces, autonomous objects invested with their own value—a conception that would take off above all in the United States during the sixties, where it was known as Studio Glass.

At a time when industry seemed saturated with

models, the effort to encourage new vocations, and to explore all resources of production, led to an attempt to liberate creative glass-making from the slavery imposed upon it by mass-production and commercial distribution. During the fifties, the evolution of the discipline in Finland, Italy and Czechoslovakia overstepped the boundary separating the decorative from art. The attention given to hot-glass processes was one of the branches of this evolution, and René Roubíček elaborated a technique inspired by the actions of the material during its passage from the liquid to the solid state.

The collaborative work of Stanislav Libenský and Jaroslava Brychtová was a fundamental influence on independent creation. Starting with their *Head-Bowl* of 1955-1956, they developed a conception of sculpture with mold-melted glass inapplicable to any other material. (See also the astonishing *Head*, 1957-1958, which renders volume visible through its transparency.) Towards the mid-fifties, they used the same technique perfected for mold-melted glass to cast elements for a monumental decoration into moulds from the Železnobroské sklo Glassworks in Železný Brod, and thus opened a new path for glass art.

.192.

But Czech glass-makers did not adhere to the classical manner of conceiving sculpture as a decorative element of architecture, as their work in Brussels in 1958 demonstrated (*Wall with Animal Reliefs* by Libenský and Brychtová or *Hommage to Glass* by Roubíček, both of which won gold medals). In their projects, monumental glass sculpture joins architecture to the surrounding space—and this tendency, by the end of the 1960s, distinguished Czech glass-making from that of other national schools. It won public commissions both for the decoration of buildings and for creations integrated into an architectural context for large exhibitions.

The 1960s were a period of stagnation for Czech glass, not only in industrial design, which no longer affected production, but also in the Studio Glass that rebounded during the following decade. But at the same time, these years marked an important stage in the evolution of sculpture in glass, which finally, accepted once and for all as artistic expression in its own right, joined in the front ranks of creation and received its due at the Universal Exposition of Montreal in 1967.

In the first half of the sixties, research at the Kaplický studio, which aimed at renewing painted decoration, bore fruit with the works of František Tejml and Vladimír Kopecký. Just as interesting were the engravings of the disciples of Štipl and Kaplicý (Pavel Hlava, Karel Wünsch, Adolf Matura, Václav Cigler, Jiří Harcuba, Vladimír Jelínek), who joined Jan Kotík and Ludvika Smrčková. Blown-glass and heat-shaped glass reached their peak with pieces by Pavel Hlava and the Roubíček couple. Pressed table glass was also developed (by František Vízner and Ladislav Oliva, who created some of the most beautiful models of the period). The competition organized as part of the preparation for Czechoslovakian participation in the Universal Exposition of Montreal in 1967 resulted in drinking glass models of a very original conception, signed by Václav Cigler, Vladimír Jelínek and Karel Holoska.

When Josef Kaplický died in 1963, Stanislav Libenský, formerly a professor at Nový Bor and Director of the Železný Brod school, was named Director of the Glass Studio of the Academy of Applied Arts in Prague. Aided by Karel Vaňura, a former disciple and then assistant,

Libenský directed the studio until 1987, and preserved a climate of tolerance favourable to inspiration.

The first objects cut by Václav Cigler spurred an immense interest in prismatic compositions with optical effects. These were among the most characteristic currents of Czech glass-making in the seventies and touched upon the work of Stanislav Libenský and his students (Marian Karel, Oldřich Plíva, Ján Zoričák, Aleš Vašíček, Pavel Trnka). Cigler also had a decided influence on contemporary Slovakian glass-makers. One of them, Askold Žáčhko, succeeded Cigler at the Bratislava Academy of Beaux-Arts.

In the 1970s, although Czechoslovakian glass triumphed in Osaka at the Universal Exposition that first year, the range of Czech glass-makers narrowed considerably. Painting on hollow glass, with a few exceptions (Karel Vaňura), was abandoned. The same was true of engraving. Even hot glass processes suffered from a certain lack of interest. The period favoured either small-format sculpture—marked by precision cutting and collage—or monumental realizations designed for architecture. Industry became automated and developed the mass-production of drinking glasses (Crystalex in Nový Bor).

.202.

During the 1980s, objects in cut optical glass have been shoved aside by new research. The most interesting is sculpture using mold-melted glass, practised essentially by Libenský, Brychtová and their students. This movement has several strains.

The first, allied somewhat with the prismatic sculptures of the preceding period, uses complex technical processes that introduce accidents, such as bubbles or lines, into the moulded object. These objects can be cut either during production or at the end. Jaromír Rybák, Gizela Šabóková, Marian Karel, and Milan Handl are the outstanding names.

The second current also reacts to prismatic compositions, but by rejecting their rational, perfect, objective forms. Its promoters also contest the value of traditional artisanal work; they insist upon the dynamic expression of structures, often linked to happenstances of the material's behaviour in fusion. This strain was announced for the first time in the thesis project of Ivan Mareš in 1982, and numerous glass-makers—Jiří Nekovář, Ivana Šolcová, Stanislav Libenský, Jaroslava Brychtová, Jaroslav Róna—have developed variations around it.

The energetic affirmation of elementary sculptural form, and the accent placed on expression, go hand in hand with a refusal of aestheticism. Although this refusal is widespread among all generations of glass-makers, it expresses itself with particular virulence in the painted pieces by the youngest ones, who abandon optical effects and properties specific to glass. The use of painting, the dynamism of sculptural form and its accidents, the opacity of the material are so many elements signifying the negation of glass in the traditional sense of the term. Instead it becomes a simple tool of the artist's thought. Its traditional beauty, grandeur and nobility are perverted by the provocative gesture and the painter's dynamics (Eliška Rožáťová, Vladimír Kopecký, Ivana Mašitová) or by a grotesque shortcut infused with humour (Ivana Šolcová, Dana Zámečníková).

On the other hand, utilitarian forms, which had lost their function, have proven a new source of inspiration for individual works. František Vízner (this was part of his

originality) for years was the lone voice in the wilderness, which has echoed anew in the young generation. Recent graduates of the Prague Academy of Applied Arts have declared their independence in glass by practising other disciplines as well: ceramics, painting, engraving, sculpture.

Besides these major tendencies stands a whole series of original, unclassifiable approaches in Czech glass-making of the eighties, along with superb work in stained glass. In this regard, Spaces I, II and II, exhibitions organized between 1982 and 1986, mark important stages in the search to integrate glass into the environment. Space I was set in a Gothic-Renaissance church; Space II in a functionalist building in Prague which had been seriously damaged by a fire; Space III in North Moravia, at the Všemina dam, in a natural setting that inspired the works on show. This series, the brainchild of theoretician Kristián Suda, has broadened the horizons of glass-making art in Czechoslovakia and added considerably to the development of this discipline in the world. In addition, three Interglassymposiums, organized in 1982, 1985 and 1988 by the Crystalex Glassworks and the glass-making artists of Nový Bor, gave international artists, curators, and theoreticians of widely divergent orientations the opportunity to meet one another.

The variety of techniques, the multiplicity of expressions, and the contribution of artists of several generations who either learned under or elaborated an original teaching method, have always been the decisive elements of Bohemian glass. In the end, Czech glass-making artists have an open spirit that puts them at the forefront of the international scene.

Sylva Petrová

.164.

88. Lock II, 1987.
Mold-melted cobalt glass, heat-shaped, engraved, and partially cut.
17 x 43 x 59 cm.
Museum of Decorative Arts, Prague
(Inv. 95 645).

Ilja Bílek

Liberec 1948 - lives in Liberec.
1965-1969: trained at the Specialized School of Glassmaking in Železný Brod.
1969-1975: studied at the Academy of Applied Arts in Prague, Stanislav Libenský's studio.
Since 1981: designer at the Železnobrodské sklo in Železný Brod.

A decade after his graduation, we know Ilja Bílek from only a few design models. He participated in the Second Interglassymposium of Nový Bor in 1985, then presented works in several group exhibits in Czechoslovakia and abroad noted for their conceptual, technological, and aesthetic originality. Bílek tried various techniques and glass compositions in his sculptures, and he collaborated with Milan Handl on two gigantic works based on a unique aesthetic (Firemen's Museum, Přisbyslav; Recreation Centre of the Ležák firm, Rabštejn nad Střelou).

Václav Cigler

Vsetín 1929 - lives in Prague.
1948-1951: trained at the School of Professional Glass-making in Nový Bor.
1951-1957: studied at the Academy of Applied Arts in Prague, Josef Kaplický's studio.
1965-1979: lecturer at the Academy of Beaux-Arts in Bratislava, Director of the Glass and Architecture Studio.
Since 1979: independent artist.

Václav Cigler is one of the most original personalities in Czech glass. His architect's vision, and a meditative philosophy, impregnate his art. He studied glass decoration under Josef Kaplický, then, at the end of his studies, created a series of engraved plates with figural compositions of monumental effect. By the beginning of the sixties, he was exploring the optical possibilities of geometric forms defined by cutting—simple lenses at first, or cylinders cut from blocks of glass. He then turned to architectural compositions, models of enormous works intended for public spaces in cities of the future.

His teaching in Bratislava has decisively influenced the evolution and character of contemporary glass in Slovakia. His projects of prismatic compositions rallied certain students of Stanislav Libenský to his side, principally during the seventies (Oldřich Plíva, Marian Karel, Ján Zoričák, Aleš Vašíček, Pavel Trnka); and he is equally distinguished in industrial design (table service, 1966), lighting, and architecture (glass walls of the Bratislava airport, 1975; chandelier-object, wall coverings and three column-sculptures in the Prague underground, 1979- 1985). He has also created both luxury and costume jewellery. Cigler has won numerous awards.

92. Object, 1979.
Leaded glass, bonded, cut, and partially metallized.
D. 26.5 cm.
Museum of Decorative Arts, Prague (Inv. 87 742).

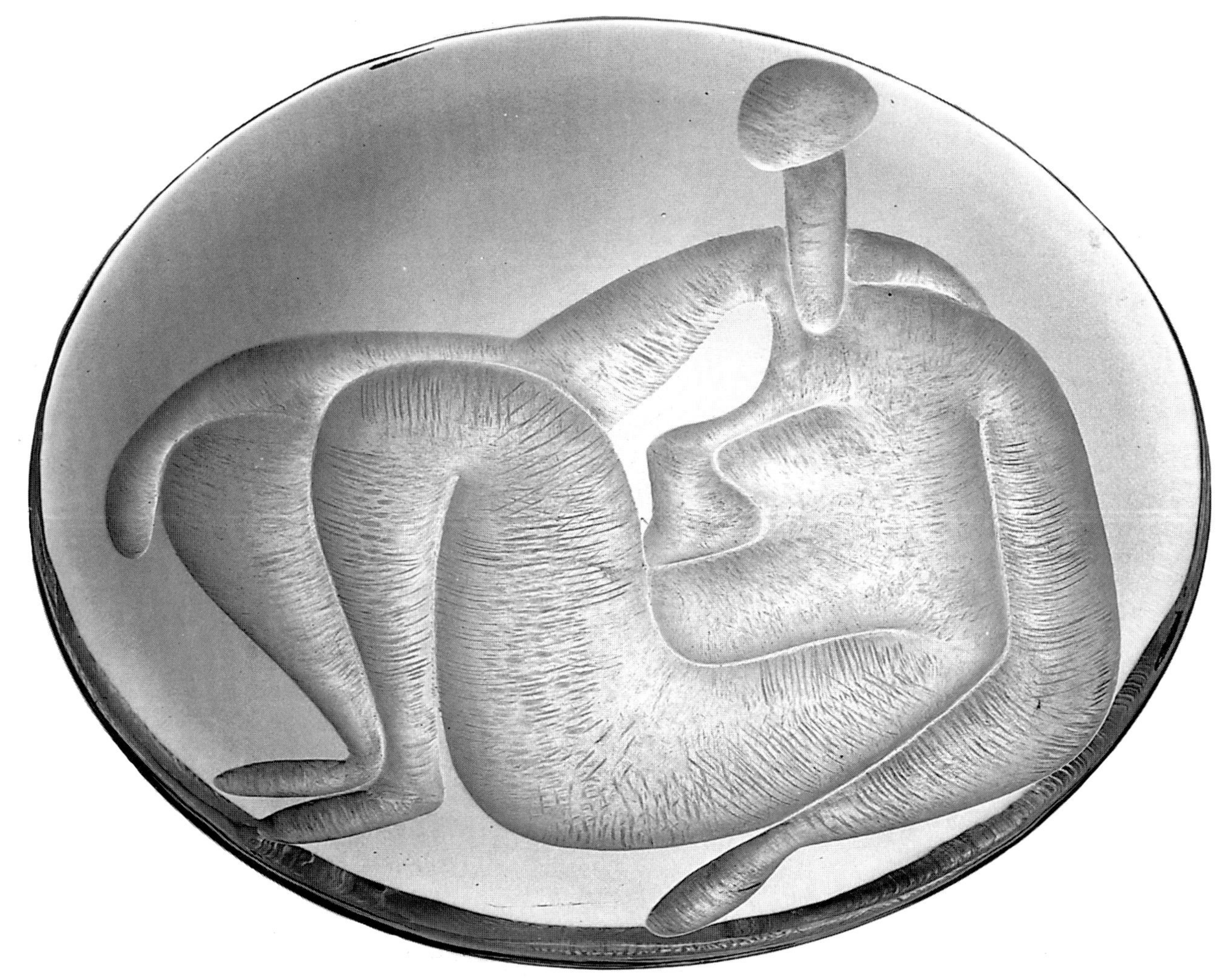

Václav Cigler
89. SCULPTURE, 1961-1967.
Model, 1961; first execution, 1964.
Cut and polished leaded glass.
H. 13.5 cm; D. 29 cm.
Executed by the Poděbradské sklo
Glassworks, Poděbrady.
Museum of Decorative Arts, Prague
(Inv. 72 552).

90. PLATE, 1964.
Engraved leaded crystal.
D. 36.5 cm.
Crystal from the Borské sklo
manufacture in Nový Bor,
engraving by the artist.
Museum of Decorative Arts, Prague
(Inv. 62 443).

91. TABLE SERVICE, 1966.
Blown glass, cut and etched surface.
H. 6.4 cm - 15.3 cm.
Moravské sklárny Glassworks, in Květná,
prototype not mass-produced.
Museum of Decorative Arts, Prague
(Inv. 72 447-454).

Václav Cigler
93. SPATIAL STUDY, 1981.
Optical glass, bonded, cut and polished, in conjunction with metallic sheet glass and black opaxite.
Base: 50 x 70 cm.
Museum of Decorative Arts, Prague (Inv. 90 265).

94. THE PRAIRIE, 1984.
Optical glass, bonded and cut, on black opaxite base.
Base: 75 x 75 cm.
Museum of Decorative Arts, Prague (Inv. 93 564).

95. PYRAMID, 1975-1987.
Metallic sheet glass, bonded and cut.
24 x 29 x 29 cm.
Artist's collection.

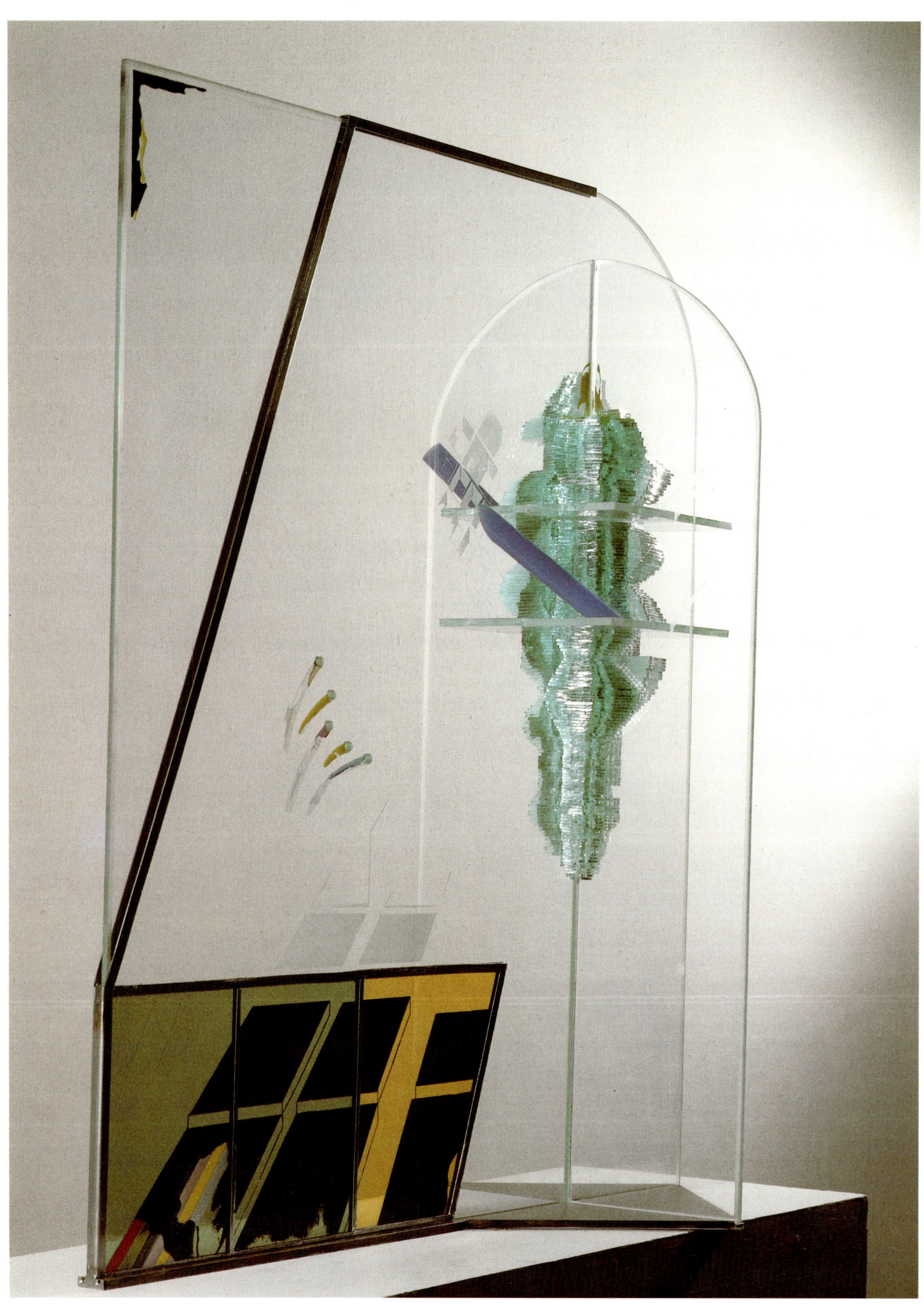

Bohumil Eliáš

Nasoburky 1937 - lives in Prague.
1954-1957: trained at the Specialized School of Glassmaking in Železný Brod.
1957-1963: studied at the Academy of Applied Arts in Prague, Professor Josef Kaplický's studio.
Since 1963: independent artist.

His training under Professor Josef Kaplický allowed Bohumil Eliáš to work simultaneously in glass-making, painting and the graphic arts. He has had well-deserved success in all three.

In 1967, he began to experiment on assemblies of sand-blasted and engraved glass sheets. His first huge works, integrating historic and modern architecture, or complementing the architectural setting of exhibits, date from this period. His grandiose *Fountain*, conceived as an object of kinetic art relying on the effects of light and presented at the Universal Exposition of Montreal in 1967, was the first of thirty or so works in the same spirit.

Eliaš worked independently in various disciplines for several years. He then blended pictorial and sculptural elements in a number of remarkable works in sheet glass, and astonished the Second Interglassymposium in Nový Bor in 1985 with his spatial paintings on hollow glass that showcased his abilities as architect, sculptor, painter, engraver, and glass-maker.

**96. Glass environment, 1985.
Assembled plates of glass, worked through sand-blasting, mixed technique and lead mounting.
H. 100 cm.
Artist's collection.**

**97. Flower of the night, 1987.
Sand-blasted blown opaline with opaque enamels and iron thread inclusions.
30 x 46.5 cm.
Museum of Decorative Arts, Prague
(1989 acquisition).**

98. **BLUE GLASS, 1989.**
Painted stained glass with cut glass panel of tin-plated lead in a metal frame.
93 x 123 cm.
Executed by the artist, Vilém Voňka, and Jiří Černohorský.
Artist's collection.

JAN EXNAR

Havlíčkuv Brod 1951 - lives in Havlíčkuv Brod.
1966-1970: trained at the Specialized School of Glassmaking in Železný Brod.
1970-1975: studied at the Academy of Applied Arts in Prague, Professor Stanislav Libenský's studio.
Since 1975: independent artist.

Jan Exnar's double orientation as glass-maker and painter brought him logically enough to stained-glass windows, assembled with lead. He invaded this area towards the end of his studies, and has executed works large and small. He forged his science of design and of painting under Stanislav Libenský and Karel Vaňura.

Exnar has also worked with hot glass processes, and presented at the Seventh, Eighth, and Ninth Škrdlovice Symposiums and at the First Interglassymposium of Nový Bor in 1982 (small-sized objects, the *Cushions* and *Arms* cycles). Since 1975, he has realized twenty or so works designed for building decoration, first in collaboration with Milan Handl, later with his wife, ceramist Hana Exnerová. With her he has experimented in new techniques blending ceramics and heat-shaped glass. In 1981 he won a Special Mention in the Jugend Gestaltet competition, organized under the auspices of the International Handwerkmesse of Munich. He has also designed drinking glasses.

99. **INTERIOR SPACE, 1968.**
Moulded and cut glass with metal support.
19.5 x 30 cm.
Executed by the Železnobrodské sklo Glassworks, Železný Brod.
Artist's collection.

JAN FIŠAR

Hořovice 1933 - lives in Nový Bor.
1948-1952: School of Decorative Arts, Prague.
1953-1959: Academy of Applied Arts in Prague, Professor Josef Wagner's studio.
1960-1966: independent sculptor in stone and wood.
1966-1971: designer at the Železnobrodské sklo Glassworks in Železný Brod.
Since 1971: independent artist.

In 1966 the Železnobrodské sklo Glassworks, in Železný Brod, invited Jan Fišar, an experienced sculptor, to collaborate on the execution of models by Stanislav Libenský and Jaroslava Brychtová, who represented Czechoslovakia at the 1967

Universal Exposition in Montreal. Ever since then, Jan Fišar has devoted himself entirely to glass. His years in this firm, as a creator of moulded or heat-shaped glass models, allowed him to acquire vast technological knowledge.

He was interested briefly in moulded sculpture, then found his real voice in heat-shaped glass used in conjunction with metal (*Birth of a Serpent, Anomaly*). Between 1966 and 1980 he collaborated with Eliška Rožátová on several monumental works. Since 1980, he has created pieces in arched form for the cycle *Twins*, and complex compositions in heat-shaped, expanded and cut glass.

Jan Fišar
100. Stone marked with red, 1985.
Smoked glass on metal base
with cut red sticks.
13 x 27 x 27 cm.
Museum of Decorative Arts, Prague
(Inv. 92 148).

Jan Fišar
101. Brawl, 1987.
Smoked glass, mould-blown and heat-shaped,
expanded, cut and polished.
35 x 50 x 100 cm.
Executed at the Crystalex Glassworks,
Nový Bor, and in the artist's studio.
Museum of Decorative Arts, Prague
(Inv. 95 644).

Milan Handl

Příbram 1952 - lives in Prague.
1968-1972: trained at the Specialized School of Glassmaking in Železný Brod.
1972-1978: studied at the Academy of Applied Arts in Prague, Professor Stanislav Libenský's studio.
Since 1978: independent artist.

During his student days, Handl specialized in painting on glass, then turned to table glass design and lighting, cut glass, mould-blown glass and enormous works meant to be integrated into natural settings.

At the beginning of his career, although prismatic and optical compositions dominated Czech glass, Handl chose to work with opaque blown tubes, joined by bonding. Towards the middle of the eighties, he substituted the hollow cylinder with the moulded and cut trihedron. This elementary figure generated a cycle of cobalt glasses of architectonic conception much appreciated at the Ebeltoft Young Glass 87 competition in Denmark. Handl is now developing these forms in a new series of mysterious pieces in black opaxite and coloured cut glass (*Bird*, 1988-1989).

Although he remains attached to three-dimensional sculptured glass, Handl also embraces sheet glass in mirror form; he has executed window panes, partially opacified by colour, and spatial compositions in sheet glass (*Storm*, 1988, Museum of Finnish Glass, Riihimäki). He created several gigantic works with Ilja Bílek (The Firemens' Museum, Přibyslav; Recreation Center of the Ležák firm, Rabštejn nad Střelou).

103. Bird, 1988-1989.
Bonded black opaxite with elements of coloured and cut glass.
30 x 80 x 37 cm.
Artist's collection.

Right:
102. Table n° 401, 1986.
Cut and polished moulded cobalt glass.
24.5 x 25.5 x 25.5 cm.
Museum of Decorative Arts, Prague
(Inv. 94 945).

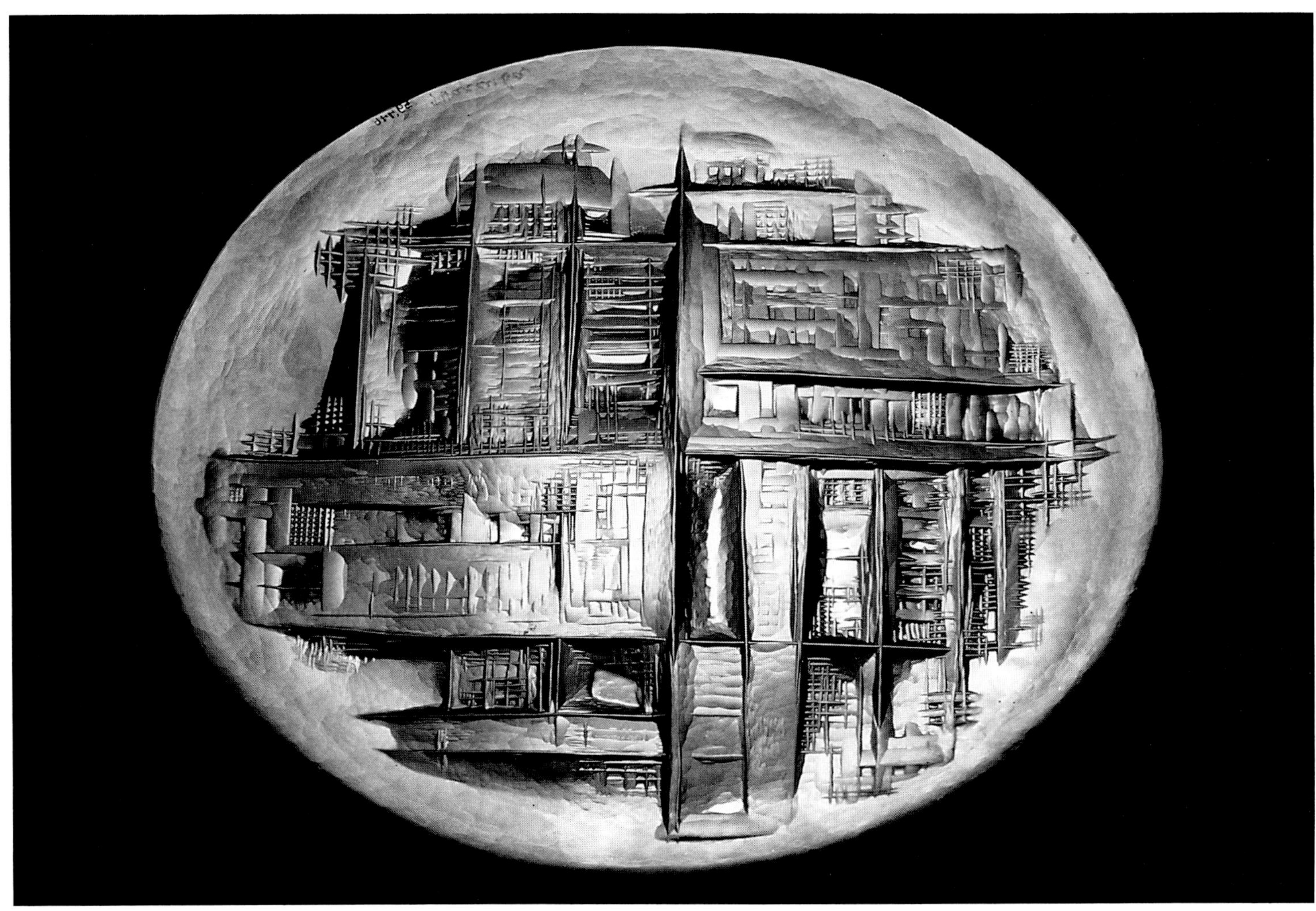

104. **La Ville, 1962.**
Cristal au plomb gravé.
D. 34 cm.
Gravure de l'artiste sur forme de la verrerie Borské sklo, Nový Bor.
Musée des Arts décoratifs, Prague (Inv. 59.446).

Jiří Harcuba

Harrachov 1928 - lives in Prague.
1942-1945: learned glass engraving in the Harrach Glassworks.
1945-1948: trained at the Specialized School of Glassmaking in Nový Bor.
1948: Department of Pedagogy at Palacký's University in Olomouc.
1948-1949: glass engraver in the Umêlecké sklo firm in Nový Bor, Karel Hrodek's studio.
1949-1957: studied at the Academy of Applied Arts in Prague, Professor Karel Štipl's studio.
1958-1961: training session at the Academy of Applied Arts, Prague.
1961-1971: Assistant Professor at the Academy of Applied Arts in Prague, Professor Karel Štipl's studio, then Professor Stanislav Libenský's studio.
1969-1970: training period at the Royal College of Art in London.
Since 1983: has taught medal engraving and engraved glass at the California College of Arts and Crafts in Oakland; the Rochester Institute of Technology; Penn State University; and the Pilchuck Glass Summer School, all in the United States, as well as at the Baden Glass Art Academy of West Germany.

Jiří Harcuba has devoted himself completely to engraved glass. At the beginning of his career, he engraved almost exclusively on crystal; during the sixties, he began to experiment with crystal cutting as well. His initially decorative pieces became increasingly more sculptural (*The Cities*), and at the beginning of the seventies he created the first of his portaits in intaglio (D. Biemann), a technique to which he dedicates all of his time He has created effigies in both glass and bronze, and he pursues the double career of glass-maker and medallion maker—in the latter of which capacities he has created several coins. He has also done portraits of personalities from Czech and international culture, as well as medals representing the great glass-making artists of different countries: K. Fujita, S. Valkema, F. Lynggaard, H. Littleton, D. Chihuly, Stanislav Libenský.

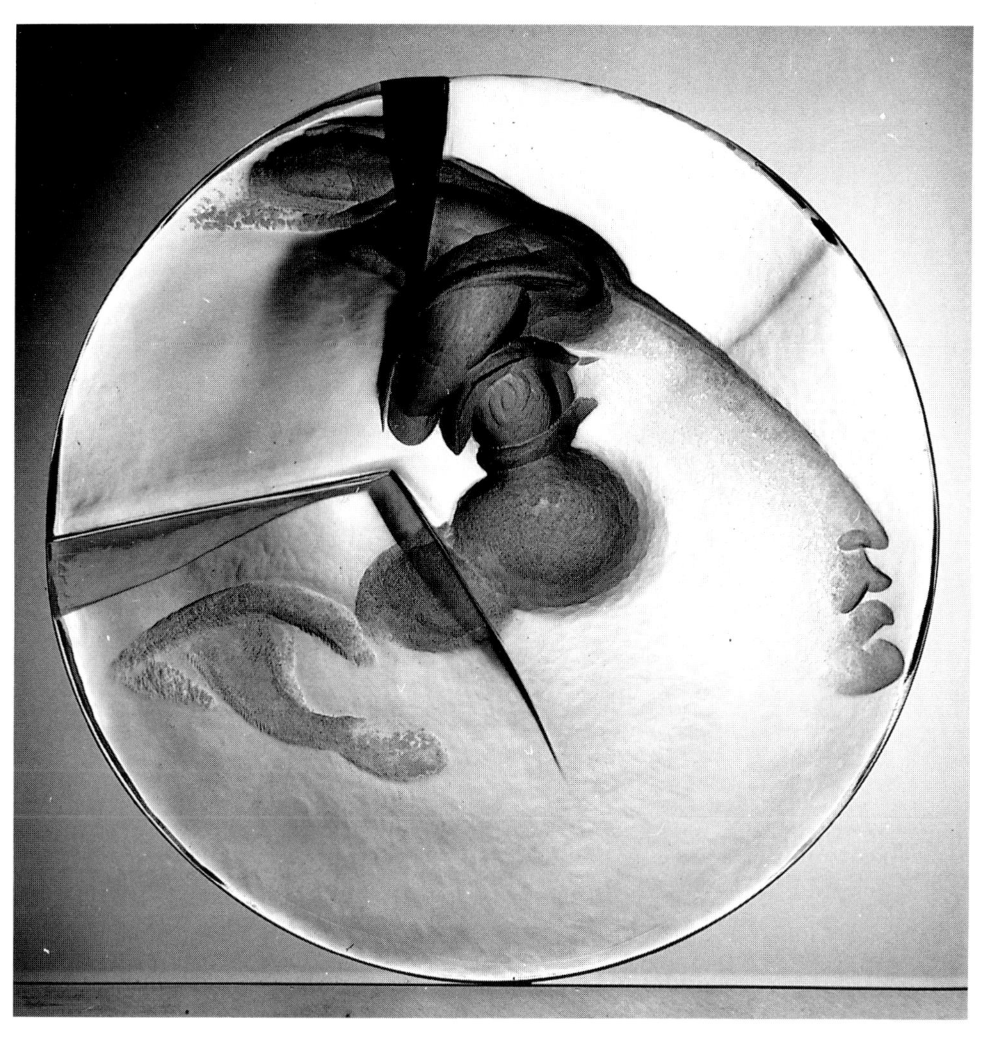

105. IMAGINARY PORTRAIT
OF FRANZ KAFKA, 1984.
Engraved and cut glass.
D. 17.3 cm.
Engraved by the artist.
Museum of Decorative Arts, Prague
(Inv. 92 149).

106. Liqueur service, 1959.
Colourless blown glass.
Carafe H. 30.5 cm; glass H. 9.5 cm.
Borské sklo Glassworks,
Hantych firm, Nový Bor.
Museum of Decorative Arts, Prague
(Inv. 54 790-54 791).

107. Unifloral vase, 1959.
108. Unifloral vase, 1960.
Cased cut crystal.
H. 19 cm; H. 33.5 cm.
Borské sklo Glassworks, Hantych firm,
Nový Bor, Josef Rozinek's studio.
Museum of Decorative Arts, Prague
(Inv. 54 880 and 54 882).

Shown at the XIIth Milan Triennale, 1960.

Pavel Hlava

Semily 1924 - lives in Prague.
1939- 1942: trained at the Specialized School of Glassmaking in Železný Brod.
1942-1948: studied at the Academy of Applied Arts in Prague, Professor Karel Štipl's studio.
1952-1958: designer at the Central Bureau of Design for the Glass and Ceramics Industry, Prague.
1948-1985: designer in the Glass Department at the Institute of Furnishings and Clothing Culture, Prague.
1967: taught at the Royal College of Art in London.
Since 1985: independent artist.

Pavel Hlava has assimilated every technique and even innovated in some. He has pursued his own work while exercising his profession as a designer, and he is also one of the organizers of the Nový Bor Interglasssymposiums. In the forties and fifties, he devoted himself above all to engraved glass; in the sixties and seventies, he made bottle-vases blown in reinforced moulds, as well as vases and objects with sunken decorations (see p. 145). During the eighties he has moved to cut objects similar in spirit to his first unifloral vases, and today he works in Studio Glass, a summary of all his technical and formal experiments (the *Biology, Civilization*, and *Energy cycles*). As a designer, he has created several models, including the drinking glasses *Gina*, *Elisabeth*, *Ideal* and *Isabella*, manufactured by automatic and semi-automatic processes in the workshops of the Crystalex firm, whose artistic council he has directed since 1972.

Since 1967 and the Montreal Universal Exposition, Hlava has realized a variety of monumental works, like the luminous sculpture of the new stage's staircase at the National Theatre of Prague, in collaboration with J. Štursa. He has also won, among other awards, the Second Prize of the First Coburger Glaspreis, 1977, and the Prize of Honor of the Second Coburger Glaspreis, 1985, in Coburg, West Germany.

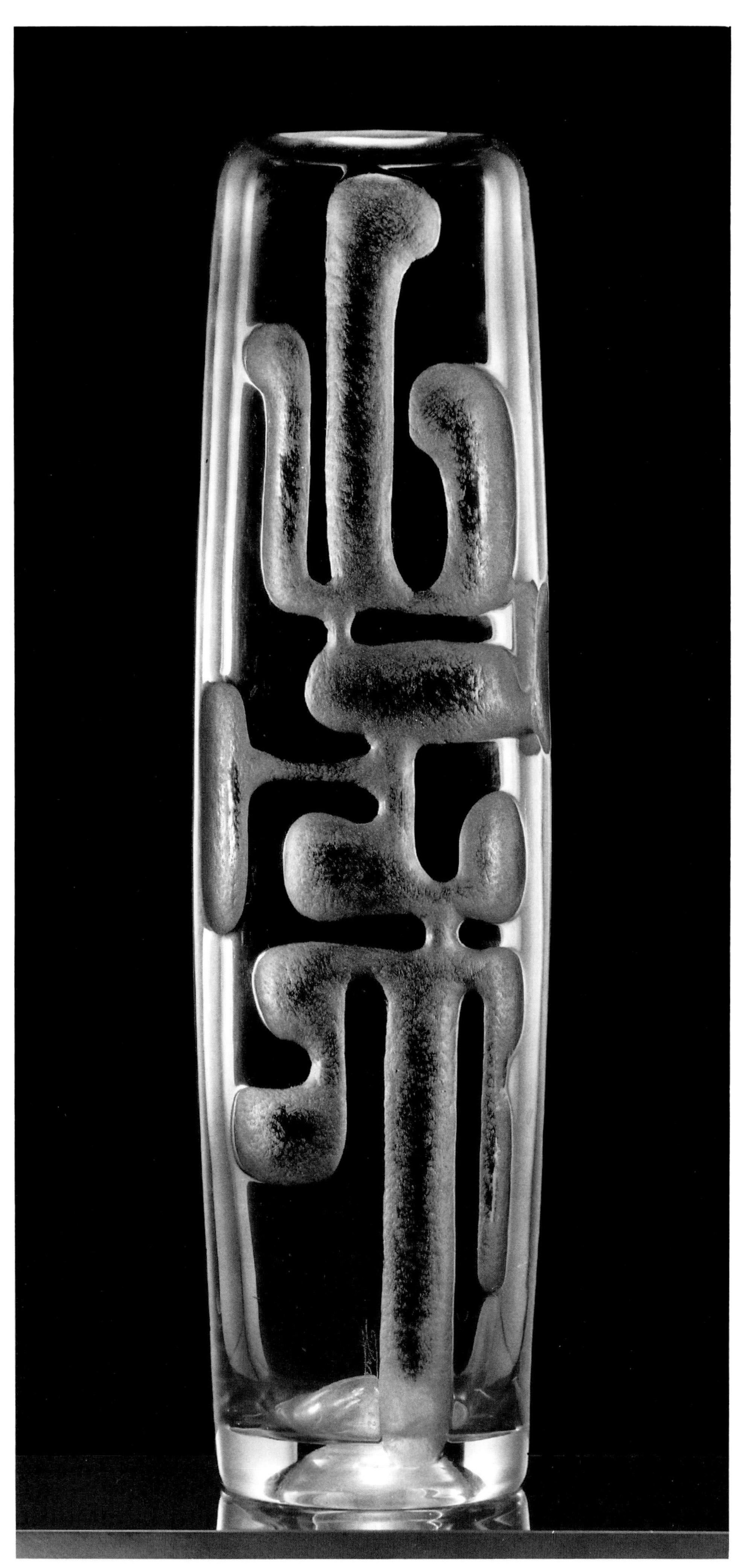

Pavel Hlava
109. Vase with Greek Decoration, 1962.
Engraved lead crystal.
Engraved signature: P. Hlava 62.
H. 32 cm; D. of the base 7.5 cm.
Glass from Borské sklo, Nový Bor,
engraved decoration by the artist.
Museum of Decorative Arts, Prague
(Inv. 59 448).

Pavel Hlava
110. Vase with sunken decorations, 1964.
Blown glass with elements sunk in
by panel pin while hot.
Engraved signature on the bottom: P. Hlava 64.
H. 56 cm; D. 9 cm.
Executed by the Český Křišťál Glassworks,
Chlum u Třeboně, Včelnička firm.
Museum of Decorative Arts, Prague
(Inv. 63 517).

Pavel Hlava
112. CIVILIZATION, 1985.
Mould-blown glass with heat-sunk elements
and applications of cut and
bonded pieces.
Engraved signature:
P. Hlava, Czechoslovakia 1985.
51 x 7.5 x 97 cm.
Museum of Decorative Arts, Prague
(Inv. 92 150).

Pavel Hlava
111. TWO HEMISPHERES, 1975.
Mould-blown glass with heat-sunk elements
and cut pedestal.
37 x 46 cm.
Executed by the Český Křišťál Glassworks,
Chlum u Třeboně, Včelnička firm.
Museum of Decorative Arts, Prague
(Inv. 81 181).

113. Glass service, 1980.
Blown and cut crystal.
H. 9 cm. to 11.8 cm.
Elements of a graduation portfolio for the Academy of Applied Arts, Prague, Professor Stanislav Libenský's studio.
Conceived for the Moser Glassworks, Karlovy Vary.
Museum of Decorative Arts, Prague (Inv. 89 032-89 037).

Ivana Houserová

Jablonec nad Nisou 1957
- lives in Krásná-Bratříkov and Prague.
1972-1976: trained at the Specialized School of Glassmaking in Železný Brod.
1976-1982: studied at the Academy of Applied Arts in Prague, Professor Stanislav Libenský's studio.

Ivana Houserová's industrial designs and remarkable sculptured glasses, of supple plasticity and artisanal savoir-faire, breathe with her inventive spirit, first recognized in Stanislav Libenský's studio. She is a purist in composition, and stresses the optical effects of the interpenetration of the object's geometrical forms. She cuts her glasses herself.

As a designer-mainly of table glass with multiple functions, she has created blown pieces with a simple line and either smooth surfaces or soberly-cut embellishments. These have aroused public interest but have not been widely distributed. In 1984 the Jugend Gestaltet competition, organized as part of the International Handwerkmesse of Munich, awarded her its Diploma, and in 1985, the Bayerischer Stadtpreis.

František Janák

Havlíčkuv Brod 1951 - lives in Prague.
1966-1967: glass-cutting apprenticeship in Josefodol, training centre of the Bohemia glassworks of Světlá nad Sázavou.
1967-1971: Specialized School of Glassmaking in Kamenický Šenov.
1972-1975: worked as a glass engraver in the Art Trades' Studios, Prague.
1976-1981: studied at the Academy of Applied Arts in Prague, Professor Stanislav Libenský's studio.
1986-1988: designer in the Glass Department of the Institute of Furnishings and Clothing Culture, Prague.
Since 1989: independent artist.

František Janák combines an artisan's experience with an artist's imagination. He makes cut objects in optical glass that evoke the architecture and sculpture of antiquity or of primitive civilizations (*Stonehenge*, 1985; *Dolmen I*, 1982), and his works often emphasize irony, humour and the grotesque (the *Small Ghost, Bald Man* cycles of 1983; *My Subject* or *Small Venus*, 1984). Besides his Studio Glass works, Janák has also been successful with several mass-produced cut glass models (Europäisches Kunsthandwerk prize in 1988).

He has widened his repertoire recently through experiments with mould-melted glass, which have led to objects of great expressiveness, whose surfaces often preserve a certain primitive roughness (the cycle *Head*). In 1982 he received the Jugend Gestaltet competition certificate, organized as part of the International Handwerkmesse of Munich; in 1985, he won the Special Prize in the Second Coburger Glaspreis, and in 1986, the First and Fourth Prizes in the Quadriennale for Art Crafts of Socialist Countries, held in Erfurt.

**114. Desire, 1982.
Cut block of optical glass.
26 x 27 cm.
Cut by the artist.
Museum of Decorative Arts, Prague
(Inv. 90 271 ab).**

**115. Idol IV, 1988.
Cut lead crystal.
31.5 x 23 cm.
Cut by the artist.
Artist's collection.**

Vladimír Jelínek

Žižice near Slaný 1934 - lives in Prague.
1949-1952: trained at the Specialized School of Glassmaking in Kamenický Šenov.
1952-1958: studied at the Academy of Applied Arts in Prague, Professor Josef Kaplický's studio.
1961-1968: designer at the Moravské sklárny Glassworks, Karolinka firm.
1966-1977: designer in the Glass Department at the Institute of Furnishings and Clothing Culture, Prague.
1978-1982: independent artist.
Since 1982: designer in the Glass Department of the Institute of Furnishings and Clothing Culture, Prague.

Vladimír Jelínek belongs to the fifties generation of designers. While still at school, he distinguished himself with models for glass services using hot work processes designed for the Škrdlovice Glassworks. The extremely fragile appearance of his engraved glasses is equally remarkable. As a designer, Jelínek exploits the full potential of industrial glass, both as an artisan, through one-of-a-kind pieces, and in automated manufacturing. His luxurious and decorative drinking glass services, produced by the Moser Glassworks, are characteristic of his art.

Both in his unique pieces and in the designs of models intended for small-scale production, Jelínek studies the relationships between the colour of glass and its structure; he also plays on the contrasts of optical effects in the thickness of the material. He uses simple volumes: spheres, or pebble-like pieces with large bubbles, sometimes associated with cut lenses. He has recently returned to engraving, where he specializes in highly stylized figures integrated into three-dimensional pieces.

His work is appreciated abroad: he obtained the First Prize for drinking glasses in a competition organized by the Institut für neue technische Formen in West Germany in 1969, and the Bayerischer Stadtpreis, and Gold Medal at the Munich International Handwerkmesse in 1970.

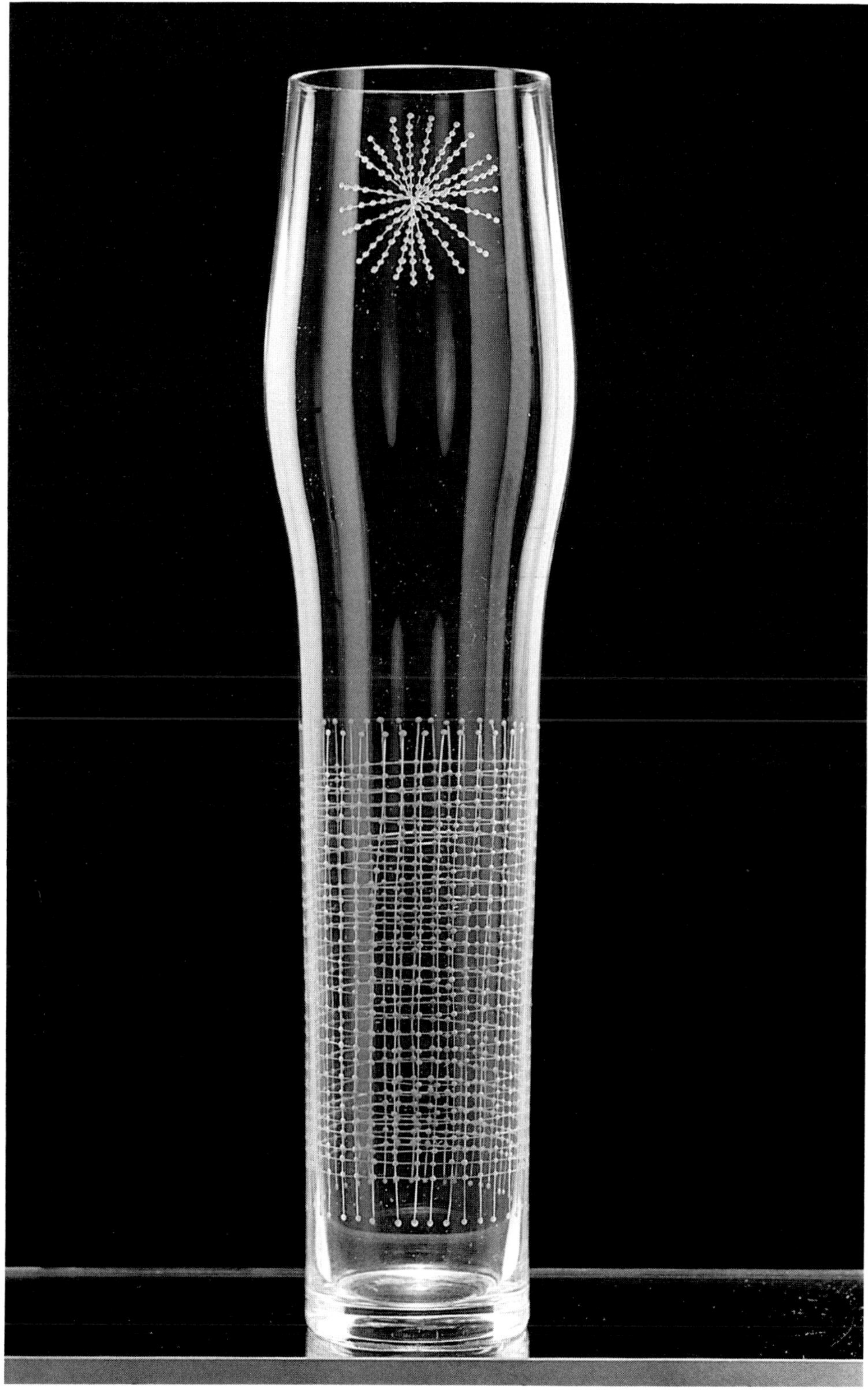

117. Vase, 1969.
Thick-walled glass, heat-worked and partially cut.
Signature: V. Jelínek 69.
H. 31 cm.
Executed by the Karlovarské sklo Glassworks, Karlovy Vary.
Museum of Decorative Arts, Prague (Inv. 73 474).
Gold Medal at the International Handwerkmesse of Munich, 1970.

116. Vase, 1960.
Engraved crystal.
Engraved signature: V. Jelínek 1960.
H. 31 cm.
Borské sklo Glassworks, Nový Bor.
Museum of Decorative Arts, Prague (Inv. 54 865).
Exhibited at the XIIth Milan Triennale, 1960.

Marian Karel

Pardubice 1944 - lives in Prague.
1959-1963: trained at the Specialized School of Jewellery-making in Jablonec nad Nisou.
1965-1972: studied at the Academy of Applied Arts in Prague, Professor Stanislav Libenský's studio.
Since 1972: independent artist.

At the end of the 1960s, Marian Karel took up sculpting objects cut from blocks of glass. He was soon recognized as a leader in prismatic sculpture, a mode of expression he has never entirely abandoned. In the eighties he has worked in mould-melted glass, to which he brings a concrete vision of space. Karel's talent is fully revealed in his vast architectonic compositions made of sheet-glass panels, usually bonded, and assembled with the support of a metallic frame. The decoration consists of cutting, painting, and bands of bonded colour; sometimes, in purist spirit, the surfaces remain entirely unadorned (the wall at the entrance of the Museum of Finnish Glass, Riihimäki, 1988; the cubic object shown in front of the Czechoslovakian Pavilion at the Biennale of Venice, 1988.) Since 1976, Karel has frequently turned to monumental decoration, sometimes in collaboration with Karel Vaňura and Vladimír Kopecký. His installations in the Prague-Motol Hotel (1987) and the Teplice bank (1988) are his most important works in this area.

119. Ruby red towers, 1981.
Golden ruby red cut and polished glass.
H. 29 cm.
Museum of Decorative Arts
(Inv. 90 270).

118. Agglomerate, 1980.
Moulded, partially cut and polished glass.
20.5 x 18 x 18 cm. and 13.5 x 20 x 20 cm.
Moravian Gallery, Brno
(Inv. 27 166).

MARTA KERHARTOVÁ-PEŘINOVÁ

Prague 1935 - lives in Prague.
1953-1959: studied at the Academy of Applied Arts in Prague, Professor Kaplický's studio.
1959-1969: independent artist.
Since 1970: secondary school professor.

In Josef Kaplický's studio, Marta Kerhartová-Peřinová successfully practised painting and acid-etching on hollow glass. During the sixties, she enlarged her production with acid-etched window panes (the Sokolov Theatre, the Cultural Centre of Nové Sedlo, near Sokolov). She has taught art history, drawing and painting in a secondary school since 1970, and only returns to creative work on rare occasions. At the XIth Milan Triennale, in 1957, she received a Gold Medal for her acid-etched vases.

120. VASE, 1962.
Blown glass with acid-etched decoration.
H. 21.3 cm.
Decoration executed by the artist.
Museum of Decorative Arts, Prague
(Inv. 61 693).

121. VASE, 1962.
Blown glass with acid-etched decoration.
H. 21.3 cm.
Decoration executed by the artist.
Museum of Decorative Arts, Prague
(Inv. 61 692).

Vladimír Kopecký

Svojanov 1931 - lives in Prague.
1946-1948: trained at the Specialized School of Glassmaking in Kamenický Šenov.
1948-1949: trained at the Specialized School of Glassmaking in Nový Bor.
1949-1956: studied at the Academy of Applied Arts in Prague, Professor Josef Kaplický's studio.
1958-1961: training session at the Academy of Applied Arts, Prague, Professor Josef Kaplický's studio.
Since 1961: independent artist.

At the beginning of the 1960s, Vladimír Kopecký's interest turned towards acid-etched and painted decoration, especially during his training at the Prague Academy of Applied Arts. His innovative works, products of a vast cultural background, rapidly became original works of art. His glassmaking is intimately linked to his activity as painter and engraver.

From the mid-sixties on, as his vision became more geometrical, he banished Expressionist tendencies from his work, and created objects imbued with an impression of space from panels of superimposed glass, with geometric motifs engraved by sand-blasting and later painted. Kopecký elaborated these compositions in his monumental decorative works (six realizations for the Bank of the City of Nieuwegein in the Netherlands, 1975). He has also collaborated with architects since 1950 (painted leaded glass window, XIth Milan Triennale, 1957; mosaic of the Czechoslovakian Pavilion, Universal Exposition of Brussels in 1958), and has worked on several occasions with Marian Karel and Karel Vaňura. By the beginning of the eighties, an Expressionist current with a strong emotional charge re-emerged in his works (the glass window-objects or three-dimensional compositions using painted glass in conjunction with other materials, like wood or metal).

123. Vase, 1962.
Colourless blown glass
with acid-etched decoration.
H. 34 cm.
Decoration executed by the artist on a form from the Borské sklo Glassworks, Nový Bor.
Museum of Decorative Arts, Prague
(Inv. 58 827).

122. Vase, 1958.
Blown glass
with smooth surface and smoked frosting.
Decoration painted in black.
H. 29 cm.
Painting by the artist.
Museum of Decorative Arts, Prague
(Inv. 53 719).

Vladimír Kopecký
124. Corridor, 1972.
Flat glass with sand-blasted decoration, metal frame and reinforcement.
69 x 77 cm.
Executed in the Kepka Brothers studio, Kostelec nad Labem.
Museum of Decorative Arts, Prague (Inv. 76 451).

125. The rooms, 1987.
Metal, glass, mirror, paint.
100 x 50 x 56 cm.
Executed by the artist.
Artist's collection.

Vladimír Kopecký
126. PAINTING WITH LANDSCAPE, 1988.
Metal, glass, paint.
Material from the Crystalex glassworks of
Nový Bor, executed by the artist.
Artist's collection.

Jan Kotík

Turnov 1916 - lives in West Berlin.
1935-1941: studied at the Academy of Applied Arts, Jaroslav Benda's studio.
1947-1968: member of the editorial board and paste-up artist for the review *Tvar*, Director of the Design Studio of the Centre for Folk Art Production, Prague.
1949-1967: collaborated with the glass industry in the design field.

Painter, engraver and designer, Jan Kotík is also a highly esteemed critic and theoretician of applied arts and industrial design. He devoted himself to glass-making for fifteen years, from 1950 on. The Škrdlovice glassworks executed his heat-worked vase and cup models with appliqués and string inclusions. Some of Kotík's models marked a new stage in this manufacture technology: use of inserted mica powders, pieces with bubbled glass in asymetrical forms and raised gadroons, partially cut tubular vases of great plastic quality. Kotík also contributed to the revival of the cut glass style found at the Borské sklo Glassworks in Nový Bor, as well as the engraved glass of the engraving workshop in Kamenický Šenov and the Karlovarské sklo factory in Karlovy Vary. He also collaborated with the Železnobrodské sklo Glassworks in Železný Brod. His painted leaded glass window, designed as an autonomous piece, received a award at the 1958 Brussels Universal Exposition.

Although considered one of the major figures in glass-making, Kotík abandoned this area relatively early. The wall realized in collaboration with René Roubíček, and exhibited in 1967 at the Universal Exposition of Montreal, was his last work in glass.

127. Vase with red center, 1956.
Cut multi-layered blown glass.
H. 13 cm.
Borské sklo Glassworks, Nový Bor.
Museum of Decorative Arts, Prague
(Inv. 48 136).

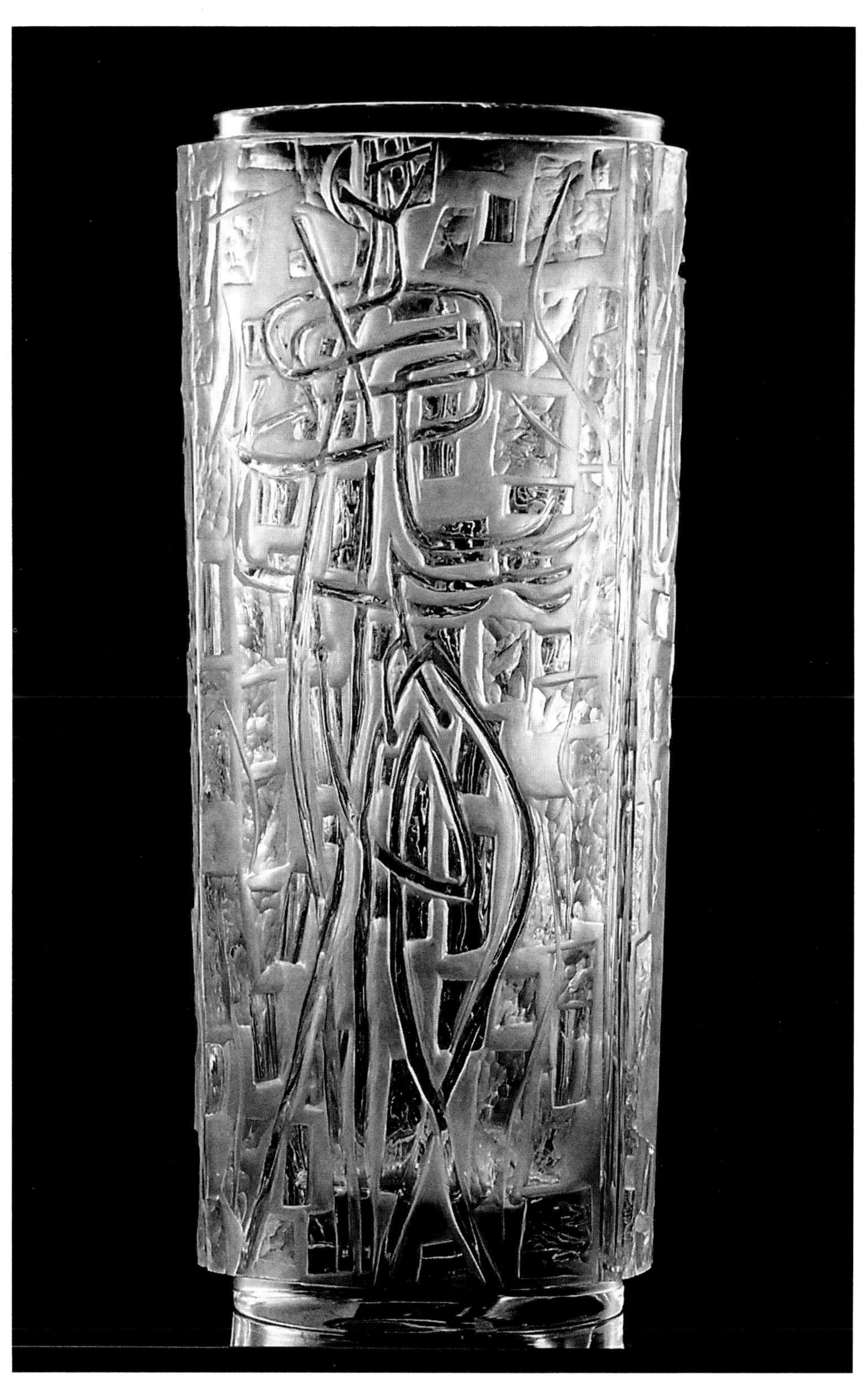

128. Vase, 1957.
Engraved crystal.
H. 29 cm.
Executed by Čestmír Cejnar,
Borské sklo Glassworks, Lobmeyr firm,
Kamenický Šenov.
Museum of Decorative Arts, Prague
(Inv. 58 714).

STANISLAV LIBENSKÝ
JAROSLAVA BRYCHTOVÁ

STANISLAV LIBENSKÝ
Sezemice 1921 - lives in Šelezný Brod and Prague.
1937-1939: trained at the Specialized Schools of Glassmaking in Nový Bor and Železný Brod.
1939-1944: studied at the Academy of Applied Arts in Prague, Professor Josef Holeček's studio.
1949-1950: studied at the Academy of Applied Arts, Prague, Professor Josef Kaplický's studio.
1945-1954: instructor at the Specialized School of Glassmaking in Nový Bor and designer in local glassworks.
1954-1963: Director of the Specialized School of Glassmaking in Železný Brod.
1963-1987: professor at the Academy of Applied Arts, Prague, Director of the Glass Studio.
Since 1987: independent artist.

Stanislav Libenský
129. PIETA VASE, 1947.
Colourless blown glass with transparent enamels and acid-etching.
Engraved signature: S. Libenský 1947.
H. 16 cm; D. 22 cm.
Executed by Věra Gottwaldová, Specialized School of Glassmaking, Nový Bor.
Museum of Decorative Arts, Prague
(Inv. 93 563).

JAROSLAVA BRYCHTOVÁ
Železný Brod 1924 - lives in Železný Brod and Prague.
1945-1951: studied at the Academy of Applied Arts in Prague, Karel Štipl's studio.
1947-1950: studied at the Beaux-Arts Academy in Prague, Professor Jan Lauda's studio.
1950-1984: directed the Glass in Architecture Department of the Design Studio of the Železnobrodské sklo Glassworks in Železný Brod.
Since 1984: independent artist.

Stanislav Libenský has occupied the world of glass since the thirties. He excelled in several disciplines: table and utilitarian glass, with acid-etched or painted decoration, blown or mould-melted. He used this last technique for both isolated small objects and for large scale works. In 1963, Libenský succeeded Professor Josef Kaplický as the head of the Glass Studio at the Prague Academy of Applied Arts, where he has since trained several generations of students with a key role in Czech glass-making today, notably in glass sculpture.

Jaroslava Brychtová, as of the mid-forties, devoted herself to small-sized sculptures and jewellery. With the help of her father Jaroslav Brychta, she experimented in different approaches to mould-melted glass. In the mid-fifties she met Stanislav Libenský, who had already created numerous industrial models and, more important still, admirable painted decorations with transparent enamels. Their collaboration began with the famous *Head-Bowl* (1955-1956). They then adapted the technique of mould-melted glass to the creation of monumental works. By the end of 1957, they used mould-melted glass exclusively, and thereafter moved to the architectural domain, studying the relationships between glass objects and their surrounding space, and creating a series of works situated in contemporary and historic buildings all over the world. These multiple creations give the two artists a pre-eminent position in the history of modern glass: 1962–twelve panels of relief-decorated windows, crystal wall, luminous objects, for a UIC building in Paris; 1971-1972–hall of the Czechoslovakian Embassy in Stockholm; *Flower, Meteor, Bird*; 1978-1980–new building of The Corning Museum of Glass. They are responsible for numerous installations in Teheran, Prague, New Delhi, Geneva, etc., as well as important creations for the Czechoslovakian Pavilions at the Universal Expositions of Brussels (1958), Montreal (1967) and Osaka (1970).

The collaboration between Libenský and Brychtová has been splendidly rich, and this book has space to evoke only a few stages in their evolution. First, during the *Heads* cycle they elaborated an approach specific to glass. In the mid-sixties, a new phase began that privileged colour relief, but was rapidly surpassed by very pure cut compositions in colourless glass.

Stanislav Libenský
130. Vase, 1959.
Painted blown colourless glass.
H. 24.2 cm; D. 10.5 cm.
Executed by the students of the Specialised School of Glassmaking, Železný Brod.
Museum of Decorative Arts, Prague
(Inv. 58 927).

Stanislav Libenský
Jaroslava Brychtová
131. HEAD-BOWL, 1955-1956.
Mould-melted green cut glass.
11.5 x 30 cm.
Železnobrodské sklo Glassworks, Železný Brod.
Museum of Decorative Arts, Prague
(Inv. 47 755).

132. HEAD, 1957-1958.
Mould-melted smoked glass, partially cut and polished, with sculpted interior cavity.
H. 36 cm.
Železnobrodské sklo glassworks,
Železný Brod.
Museum of Decorative Arts, Prague
(Inv. 76 894).

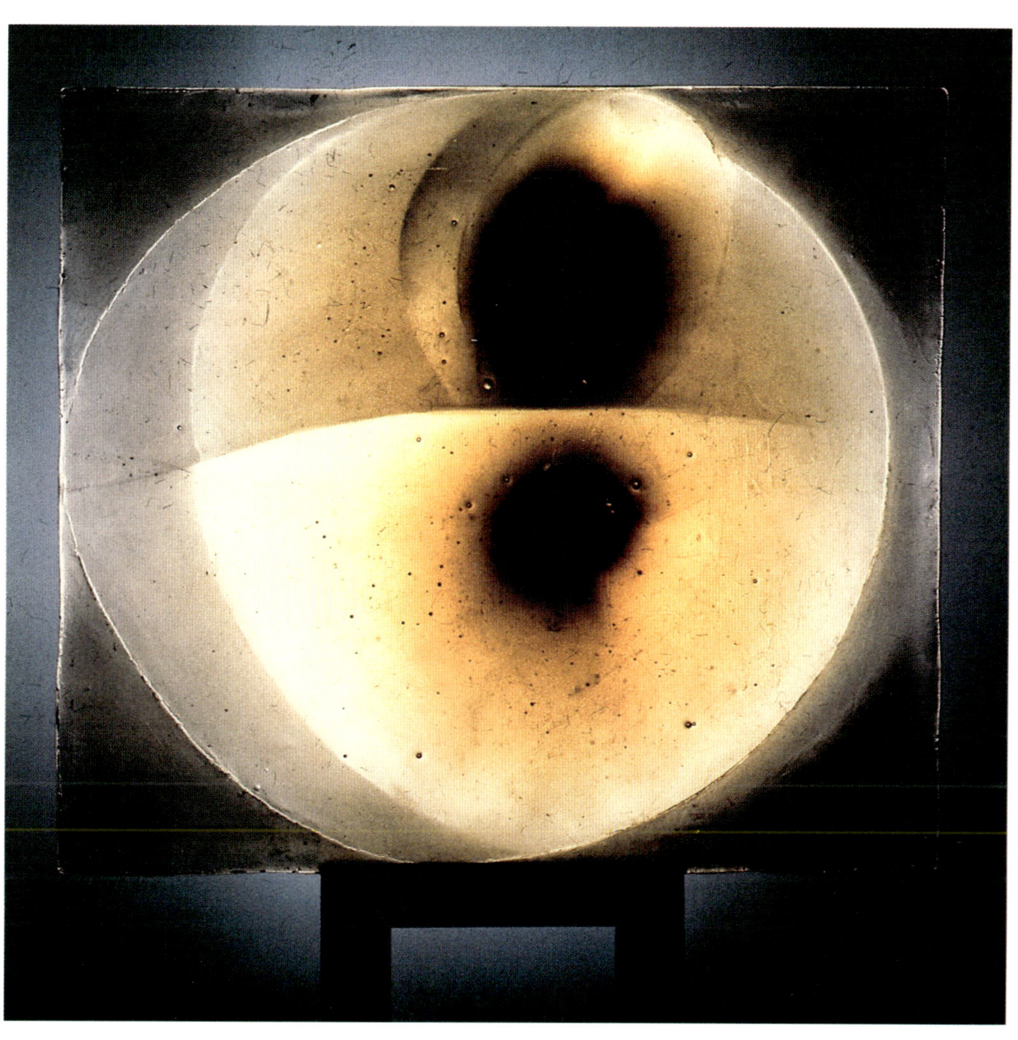

Colour has reappeared in the eighties (*Metamorphoses*), announcing a new direction that led the two artists from perfect finishing touches towards strong, expressive sculptural form. The work of Stanislav Libenský and Jaroslava Brychtová has received numerous prizes: 1958, Grand Prize from the Brussels Exposition; 1966, Special Medal in the Eighth Sao Paulo Biennale; 1967, Gold Medal in the Munich International Handwerkmesse; 1969, Gold Medal of the International Art Professions Fair in Stuttgart; 1975, the Herder Prize given by the University of Vienna; 1977 and 1985, Special Prize of the First and Second Coburger Glaspreis, Coburg; 1981, the Glaskunst Special Prize, 1981, Kassel; 1984, the Rakow Award, The Corning Museum of Glass, Corning. They also teach at the Pilchuck Summer School and in other establishments in the United States.

Stanislav Libenský
Jaroslava Brychtová
133. Heart, 1968.
Mould-melted smoked yellow cut and polished glass.
Overall H. 170 cm; 73.5 x 55 cm.
Executed by the Železnobrodské sklo Glassworks, Železný Brod.
Pedestal designed by Bohuslav Rychlink, in 1983.
Museum of Decorative Arts, Prague (Inv. 75 059).

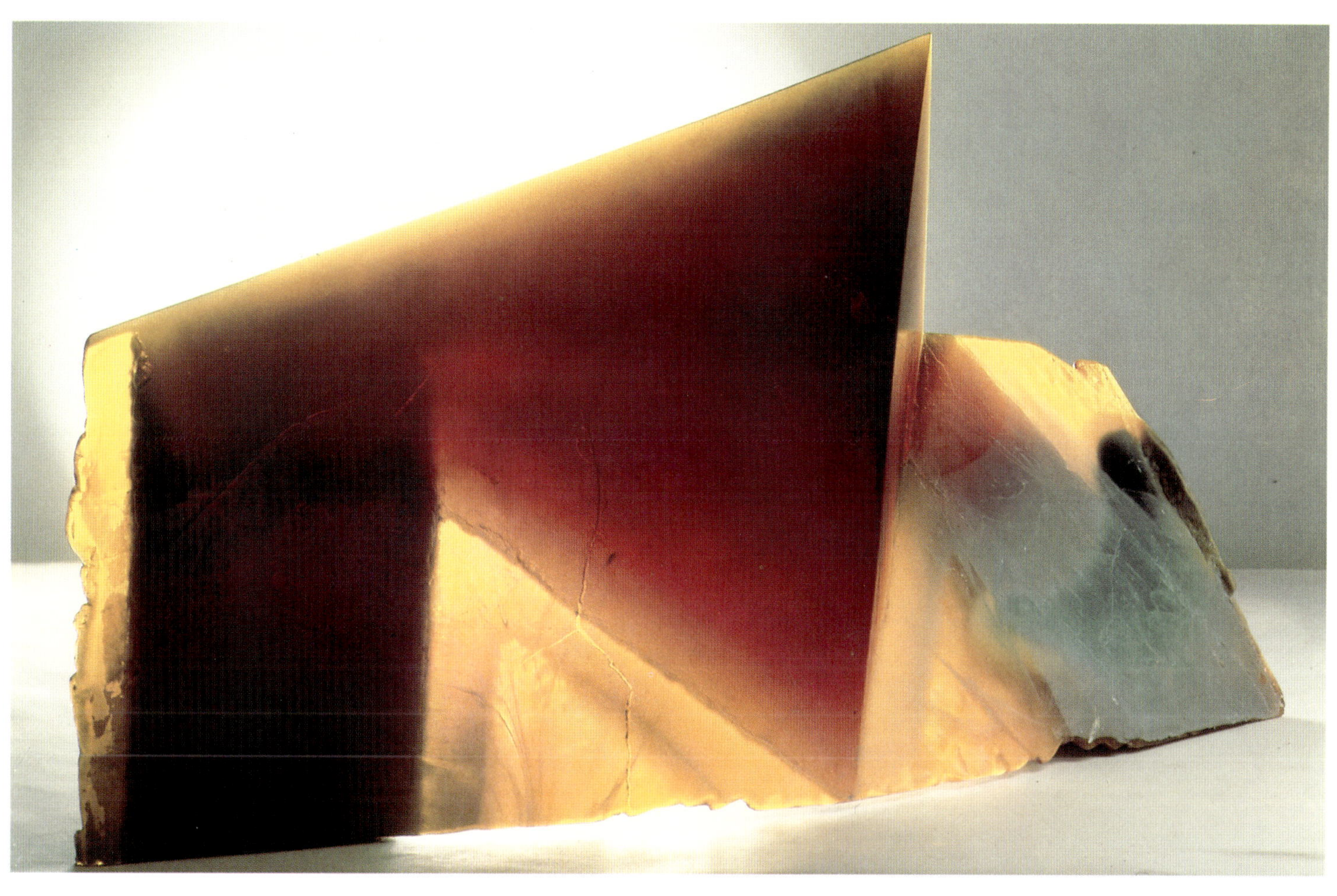

Stanislav Libenský
Jaroslava Brychtová
134. RED FLOWER, 1975-1984.
Mould-melted cut ruby red glass.
H. 85 cm; pedestal H. 30 cm.
National Gallery Prague
(Inv. P 7445).

Stanislav Libenský
Jaroslava Brychtová
135. RED TABLE SETTING SUN, 1988.
Mould-melted ruby red glass.
40 x 90 cm.
Executed in the artists' studio,
with the collaboration of Jaroslav Zahradník.
Museum of Decorative Arts, Prague
(acquired in 1989).

VĚRA LIŠKOVÁ

Prague 1924 - Prague 1985.
1939-1941: studied at the School of Graphic Arts in Prague.
1941-1943: studied at the Academy of Applied Arts in Prague, Professor Josef Holeček's studio.
1945-1949: studied at the Academy of Applied Arts in Prague, Professors Karel Štipl's and Josef Kaplický's studios.
1946-1985: independent artist.

Between 1946 and 1951, Věra Lišková worked as a trainee in the Lobmeyr workshop in Kamenický Šenov, where she created, with her director Stephan Rath, several excellent models adopted for production. (She excelled in thin-walled table glasses, sometimes ornamented with engraved motifs of great precision.) Liškova herself executed several pieces in the Lobmeyr workshop, mainly vases and engraved glass decorated with the signs of the zodiac, animals and flowers.

Her collaboration with the Karlovarské sklo Glassworks in Karlovy Vary, where her luxury cut glass models were produced for many years, began in 1950. In 1952 she also worked for the Central Bureau of Design for the Glass and Ceramics Industry. At the beginning of the sixties, she abandoned design and turned to the creation of individual pieces, working in flame-worked glass. She first created utilitarian and decorative pieces, then devoted herself to sculpture, inspired by animals and vegetables. Věra Lišková also collaborated occasionally with architects (lighting for the hall of the Federal Assembly of Prague, 1972). In 1973, she received the Bayerischer Stadtpreis as part of the Munich International Handwerkmesse, and in 1977, the Special Prize from the First Coburger Glaspreis.

**136. GLASS SERVICE, 1947.
Blown chiffon glass;
one glass monogrammed.
H. 3.5 to 7.3 cm.
Umelecké sklo Glassworks, Lobmeyr firm,
Kamenický Šenov, 1947-1950.
Museum of Decorative Arts, Prague
(Inv. 31 613 / 1,3,5,6).**

**137. BIRD OF PARADISE, 1950.
Egraved colourless glass.
H. 15.5 cm.
Karlovarské sklo Glassworks, Karlovy Vary.
Museum of Decorative Arts, Prague
(Inv. 32 177).**

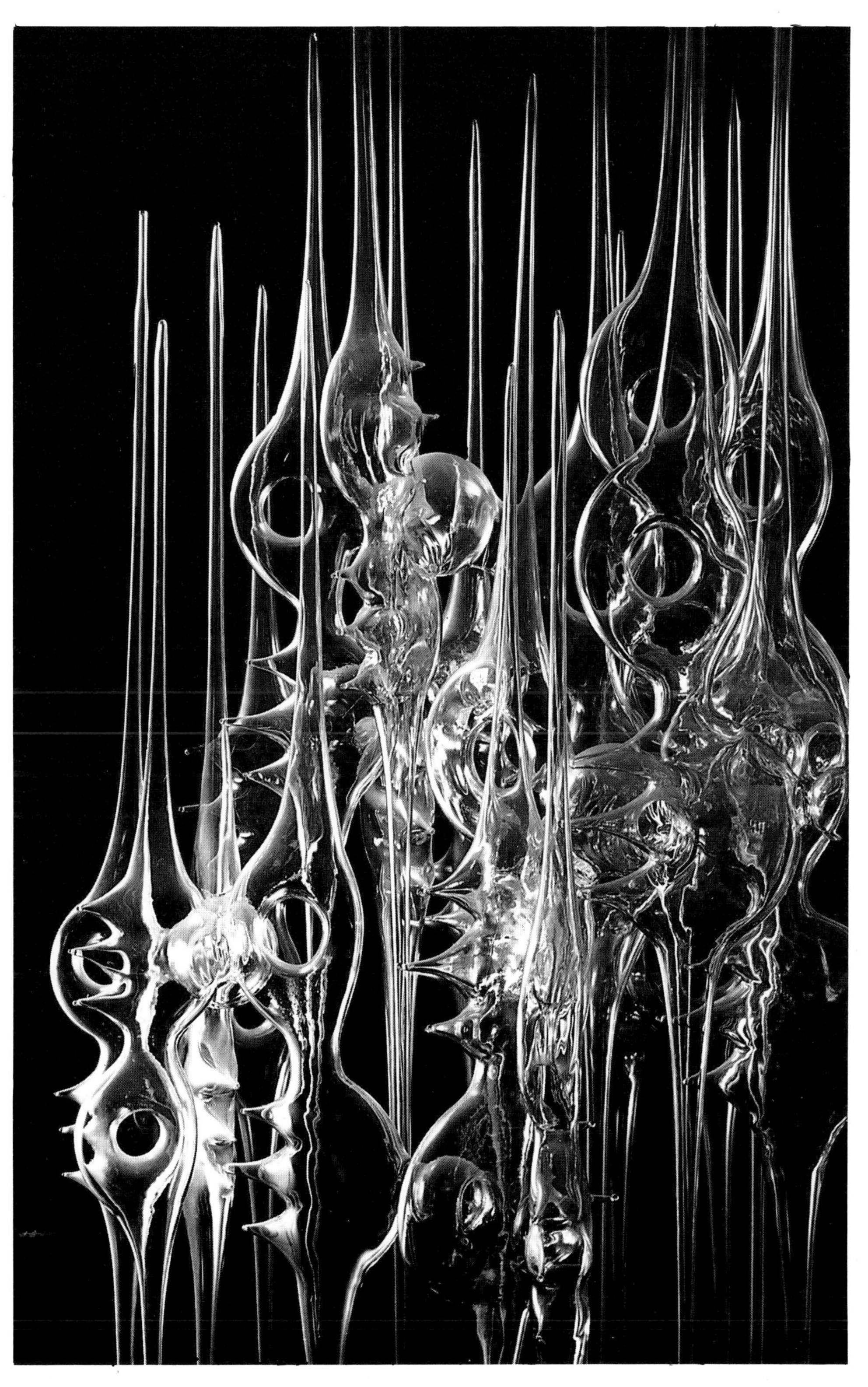

138. Moving forms, 1976-1982.
Tubes of flame-worked glass.
H. 128 cm.
Executed in the artist's studio.
Museum of Decorative Arts, Prague
(Inv. 89 683).

VÁCLAV MACHAČ

Kamenice nad Lipou 1945 -
lives in Nový Bor.
1959-1963: trained at the Specialized School of Glassmaking in Nový Bor.
1965-1971: studied at the Academy of Applied Arts in Prague, Professors Stanislav Libenský's and Jozef Soukup's studios.
Since 1978: instructor at the Specialized School of Glassmaking in Nový Bor, Department of Hot-worked Glass Processes.

In his glass sculptures, Václav Machač combines the classical processes of three disciplines: sculpture, glass-making (mould-blown glass) and painting (cold techniques and polychromatics). His works stand half-way between realist representation and expressive abstraction; evoking body fragments (animals or human heads), they exploit the tension between these two types of vision.

Machač has also practised portraiture, often choosing his models from different sports (*Cyclist, Mountain Climber, Jockey*, 1984). Since 1980, when he visited the Mediterranean seashore, his work has drawn on ancient Etruscan themes (*Head of an Etruscan*, 1982; *Fragments of an Ancient Wreckage*, 1980-1981; *The Foot*, 1982). His suggestive horse and zebra heads, marked by the same influence, betray great psychological sensitivity. In 1985, Václav Machač received a Diploma from the Second Coburger Glaspreis in Coburg.

139. FRAGMENTS OF AN ANCIENT WRECKAGE, 1980-1981.
Green mould-blown glass with inserted layers of cut crystal and elements in metal.
48.5 x 35.3 x 46.5 cm.
Museum of Glass and Jewellery, Jablonec nad Nisou
(Inv. S 6162).

Ivan Mareš

Děčín 1956 - lives in Prague and Děčín.
1971-1975: trained at the Specialized School of Glassmaking in Kamenický Šenov.
1977-1983: studied at the Academy of Applied Arts in Prague, Professor Stanislav Libenský's studio.
Since 1983: independent artist.

In 1983, Ivan Mareš finished his studies in Staislav Libenský's studio by presenting an admirable group of mould-melted sculptures (executed in the Železnobrodské sklo Glassworks of Železný Brod) and a deluxe drinking glass service. The surfaces of his sculptures maintain all their primitive roughness, as the artist has chosen not to touch up his forms from the moulds. This process, which he was the first to use, spread quickly throughout Czech glass-making. Mareš's work, although small in numbers, is imposing.

Recently he has moved towards monumental objects in mould-melted glass, where he alternately introduces opacity and transparency, organic structures, forms evoking the texture of crystal, and the geometry of a beehive's structure. *Egg* (1987) represented Czechoslovakia in the 43rd International Biennale of Venice.

**140. Egg, 1987.
Mould-melted glass,
partially cut and polished.
70 x 38 cm.
Executed by the Železnobrodské sklo
Glassworks, Železný Brod.
Museum of Decorative Arts, Prague
(Inv. 95 642).**

Ivana Mašitová

Česká Lípa 1961 - lives in Prague.
1976-1980: trained at the Specialized School of Glassmaking in Kamenický Šenov.
1980-1988: studied at the Academy of Applied Arts in Prague, Professors Stanislav Libenský's and Jaroslav Svoboda's studios (1987-1988).
Since 1988: independent artist.

Ivana Mašitová began her training at the age of fifteen. Three distinctly defined groups are clear in her production: blown and painted glass, mould-melted glass, and stained-glass windows. Her expression is determined by her engraving experience and a refusal of the aestheticism common to her generation.

For Mašitova, the form of the traditional container serves as material for plastic research. She assimilates her containers and blown objects to stained-glass windows, and highlights them with enamel painting, hot-applied sheet metal with repoussé work, coloured fabrics, or red, black and yellow lustre paint. These works do not entirely lose their utilitarian function, but they are striking first and foremost because of their plastic quality. In cast sculpture, Mašitová has also borrowed from architecture. She uses several techniques like sand blasting, painting, and engraving to realize her stained-glass windows.

142. Cone II, 1987.
Mould-blown painted glass.
50 x 40 cm.
Painting executed by the artist.
Artist's collection.

141. Cone I, 1987.
Mould-blown painted glass.
50 x 40 cm.
Painting executed by the artist.
Artist's collection.

Adolf Matura

Bystřice 1921 - Prague 1979.
1938-1940: trained at the Specialized School of Glassmaking in Železný Brod.
1940-1946: studied at the Academy of Applied Arts in Prague, Professor Karel Štipl's studio.
1947-1954: independent artist.
1954-1958: designer at the Central Bureau of Design for the Glass and Ceramics Industry, Prague.
1958-1979: designer in the Glass Department of the Institute of Furnishings and Clothing Culture, Prague.

Adolf Matura was actively involved in several glassmaking disciplines, particularly those of pressed, cut, and engraved glass. He was also adept at organization, and from 1954 presided over the Artistic Advisory Council for the design of pressed and packaging glass of the Sklo-Union firm in Teplice.

Matura maintained great sobriety in his forms and decorations, but enriched them with optical and tactile effects (the *Prague* series, 1971). He collaborated with Ludvika Smrčkova in engraved glass, and was himself an excellent engraver. In the second half of the fifties, he concentrated on multi-layered coloured glass, and from 1964 onwards focussed on pressed glass design. Matura took the best from the Czech tradition and adapted past values to modern conceptions. His glass models, intended for both artisanal and industrial manufacturing, represented a real triumph for Czech glasswork production. In 1960, he received the Gold Medal at the XIIth Triennale of Milan.

143. Lemonade service, 1959-1960.
Mould-blown glass.
Bottle H. 27 cm.; glasses H. 7 cm.
Borské sklo Glassworks;
Hantych firm, Nový Bor.
Museum of Decorative Arts, Prague
(Inv. 54 776 - 54 780).

Gold Medal
at the XIIth Milan Triennale in 1960.

Jiří Nekovář

Pardubice 1956 - lives in Pardubice.
1971-1975: trained at the Specialized School of Glassmaking in Železný Brod.
1977-1983: studied at the Academy of Applied Arts in Prague, Professor Stanislav Libenský's studio.
Since 1983: independent artist.

Jiří Nekovář completed his training under Stanislav Libenský by presenting an elegant drinking glass service and a remarkable group of mould-blown fish made in opaque marbled glass, which caught the eye of specialists. He then turned to mould-melted sculpture and studied the opposition between the precision of an abstract form and the spontaneity of an organic structure. In 1988, at the Third Nový Bor Interglasssymposium, he exhibited astonishing objects linked to his early works: cobalt mould-blown glass woven with metallic fibres which become an integral part of the sculptured work themselves.

144. Conflict in a triangle, 1986.
Mould-melted smoked glass with metallic frame.
25 x 73 x 51 cm.
Executed by the Železnobrodské sklo Glassworks, Železný Brod.
Museum of Decorative Arts, Prague (Inv. 94 944).

145. PLATE, 1957.
Lead crystal, engraved by sandblasting.
D. 35.5 cm.
Borské sklo Glassworks, Nový Bor.
Museum of Decorative Arts, Prague
(Inv. 62 476).

LADISLAV OLIVA

Chuderice near Bílina 1933
- lives in Železný Brod.
1948-1951: trained at the Specialized School of Glassmaking in Kamenický Šenov.
1951-1957: studied at the Academy of Applied Arts in Prague, Professor Kaplický's studio.
1957-1964: designer at the Nový Bor Glassworks.
1964-1969: designer at the Bohemia Glassworks of Podebrady, instructor at the Specialized School of Glassmaking in Kamenický Šenov.
Since 1969: professor at the Specialized School of Glassmaking in Železný Brod.

As a student, Ladislav Oliva was interested in cut lead crystal and sandblasting. His rustic-looking plates, deeply engraved by sandblasting, are among the most beautiful realizations of Czech glass in the second half of the 1950s, and he was awarded the Gold Medal at the XIIth Milan Triennale in 1960. During the 1960's Oliva created several pieces in lead-pressed glass (jardinières, plates) which were not mass-produced in spite of their quality.

Among his numerous models in cut glass is a series, created for Crystalex of Nový Bor, that includes ashtrays, vases and dishes whose decoration combines exquisite cutting and transparent, smoked or frosted surfaces (Frankfurt Fair in 1988). His personal work is marked by its cultural depth and achieved form. The same qualities characterize his monumental works. He has won numerous prizes, including the Bronze Medal at the International Fair of Stuttgart in 1963 and the Special Medal at the Consumer Goods Fair of Leipzig in 1965.

Oldřich Plíva
146. CUBE, 1971.
Cut optical glass.
14 x 14 cm.
Cut by the artist.
Regional Museum of Liberec
(Inv. S 3845).

OLDŘICH PLÍVA

Mšeno nad Nisou 1946
- lives in Jablonec nad Nisou.
1961-1965: Specialized School of Glassmaking in Železný Brod.
1965-1971: studied at the Academy of Applied Arts in Prague, Professor Stanislav Libenský's studio.
Since 1971: independent artist.

Oldřich Plíva has ingeniously developed the principle of prismatic compositions with optical effects. His early designs (1968-1969 but executed much later) treated the relationship between cube and sphere, and the register of forms has allowed him to study both the interior and the surrounding space of a sculpture, which he then deepens with columns, cylinders, stelae and pyramids. He executed especially accomplished works in the second half of the 1970s (*Three Sides, Triangular Prism*, 1978-1980), and since 1982-1983 has created enormous sculptures planned for public and outdoor spaces (*Promenade*, 1986), using metal or wooden frames in conjunction with sheet glass panels and a metallic surface. This work was spurred on by the exhibitions Space I and Space II.

In 1983, Plíva became interested in small-scale projects, especially many-sided objects, some of which were rendered opaque by means of metal leaves, while others opened up surprising views into their interior structure. Plíva has also created monumental works in materials traditionally used by sculptors, like stone. In 1985, he received a Diploma from the Second Coburger Glaspreis in Coburg.

147. OBJECT, 1974.
Cut optical glass.
10.5 x 20 cm.
Material from the Corning Glass firm, France.
Cut by the artist.
Museum of Decorative Arts, Prague
(Inv. 80 555).

Oldřich Plíva
148. ONE IS NUDE, 1986.
Cut optical glass and lead leaf.
12.5 x 12.5 x 5 cm; base 1.5 x 14.5 x 5.6 cm.
Artist's collection.

Oldřich Plíva
149. Untitled, 1988.
Partially squared, partially cut glass block, metallized by vacuum.
Executed by the artist.
Artist's collection.

151. The tower, 1986-1987.
Partially cut and polished brown-red mould-melted glass.
33 x 13 x 26 cm.
Museum of Decorative Arts, Prague
(Inv. 95 202).

Jaroslav Róna

Prague 1957 - lives in Prague.
1975-1978: trained at the Prague Art School.
1978-1984: trained at the Academy of Applied Arts in Prague, Professor Stanislav Libenský's studio.
Since 1984: independent artist.

Paroslav Róna is a typical representative of the youngest generation of Stanislav Libenský's students. A glass-maker by profession, he has also delved into painting, engraving, ceramics and scenogaphy. His glass sculptures have attracted attention, but they represent a relatively limited portion of his activity. At the origin of his work lie blown bottle-vases, deformed and cased with opaline; then mould-blown dogs, inspired by Pop-Art; and finally monster-dogs harking back to Constructivism (glass placed in lead, iron, blown elements). After a transitional period with mould-melted sculpture, Róna returned to mould-blown objects, exhibited at the Third Interglassymposim of Nový Bor in 1988. These works assert both the symbolism of archetypal forms and the ironic and healthy provocative spirit of the artist. Róna has also executed three-dimensional objects and leaded glass windows.

150. THE SERPENT, 1986-1987.
Partially cut and polished mould-melted green glass.
33 x 23 x 29 cm.
Museum of Decorative Arts, Prague
(Inv. 95 201).

152. THE FORTRESS, 1986-1987.
Partially cut and polished mould-melted green glass.
23.5 x 29 x 29 cm.
Museum of Decorative Arts, Prague
(Inv. 95 200).

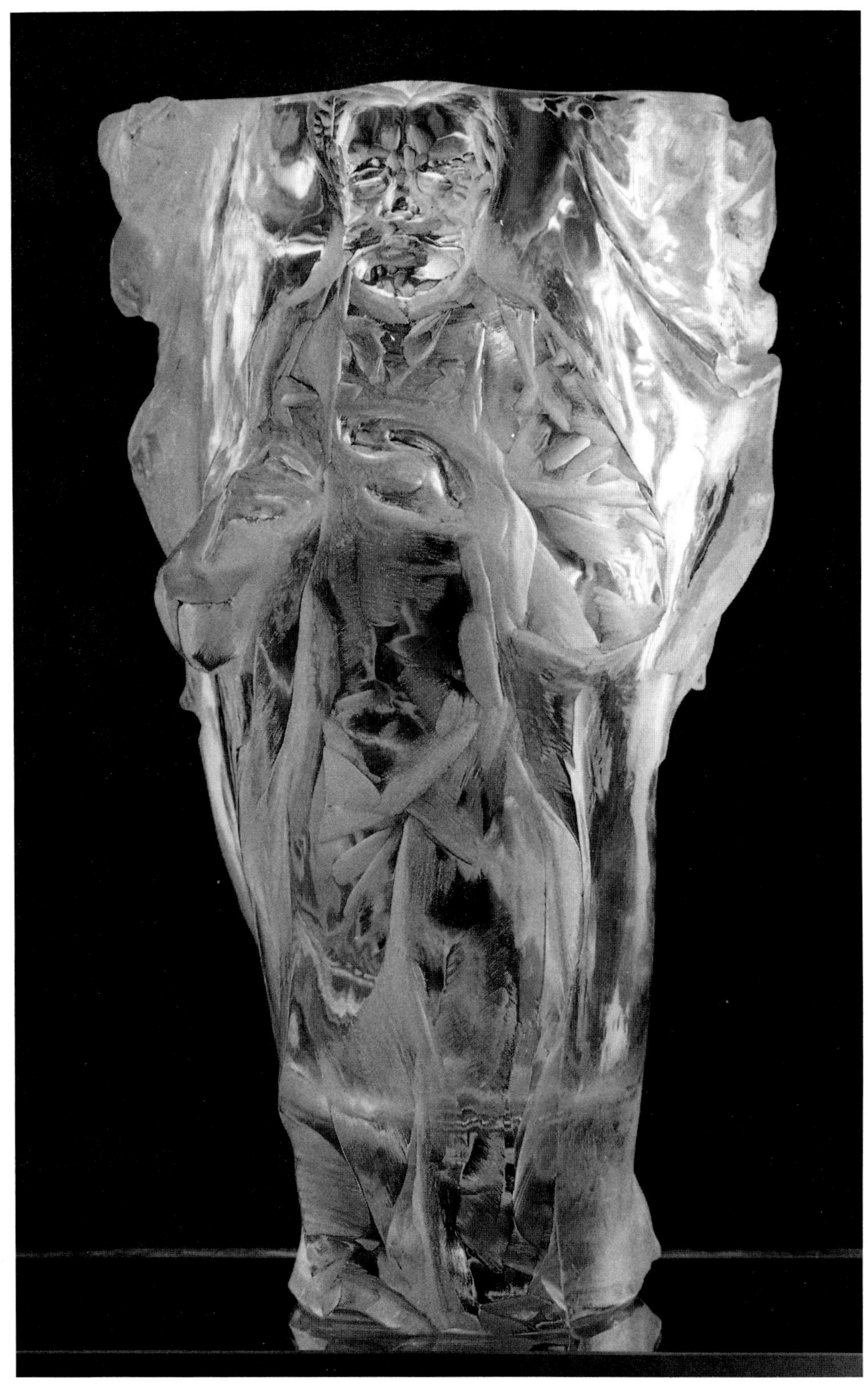

**153. ANTONÍN DVOŘAK VASE, 1946.
Deeply engraved colourless glass.
H. 23.5 cm.
Executed by the artist at the Specialized School of Glassmaking, Kamenický Šenov.
Museum of Decorative Arts, Prague
(Inv. 84 566).**

RENÉ ROUBÍČEK

Prague 1922 - lives in Kamenický Šenov and Prague.
1940-1944: studied at the Academy of Applied Arts in Prague, Josef Holeček's studio.
1945-1952: professor at the Specialised School of Glassmaking in Kamenický Šenov.
1951-1952: Academy of Applied Arts in Prague, Professor Josef Kaplický's studio.
1952-1965: Director of the Design Office of the Borské sklo Glassworks, Nový Bor.
1966-1968: course at the Academy of Beaux-Arts in Prague.
Since 1969: independent artist.

René Roubíček is one of the first Czechoslovakian artists to develop all of glass's potential as a specific support for plastic thought. In the second half of the 1950s, he enriched Czech sculpture with heat-worked or blown pieces that put him squarely in the trend of hot glass process work that thrived during the 1960s. Today he remains one of the rare Czech glass-makers who systematically perfect these techniques.

Roubíček's first pieces—vases with engraved decoration of dynamic lines and sculptural conception—date back to his teaching days at the Kamenický Šenov School of Glassmaking, immediately after the war, but it is his monumental works, integrated into the architectural spaces of large exhibitions, that lastingly mark the history of Czech glass (*Hommage to Glass*, Grand Prize at the 1958 Brussels Universal Exposition; the Czechoslovkian Pavillon's decorative wall at the Universal Exposition of Montreal in 1967, realized in collaboration with Jan Kotík; *Glass Cloud*, a dynamic composition presented at the 1970 Osaka Exposition.) Roubiček's long collaboration with master glass-maker Josef Rozinek has been very fruitful.

In the 1960s Roubiček, who knew how to exploit all the physical and optical resources of the material, worked on themes taken from nature, in cycles like *Water* or *Trees*. He also created his first works of monumental decoration, which are essentially light-objects of a very original design (stairway at the Czech Children's House at the Castle of Prague, 1963; Intercontinental Hotel in Prague, 1973; the Most Theatre, 1986). In the seventies and eighties, he created one of his most beautiful works, the admirable *Heads* cycle.

In addition to the prizes mentioned above, Roubiček has garnered a fistful of distinctions, notably the Bayerischer Stadtpreis, awarded during the Munich International Handwerkmesse (1969); the Special Prize at the First Coburger Glaspreis of Coburg (1977); the First Prize from the sculpture division of the Zentralschweizerisches Glaspreis of Lucerne (1980); and the Special Prize at the Second Coburger Glaspreis of Coburg (1985).

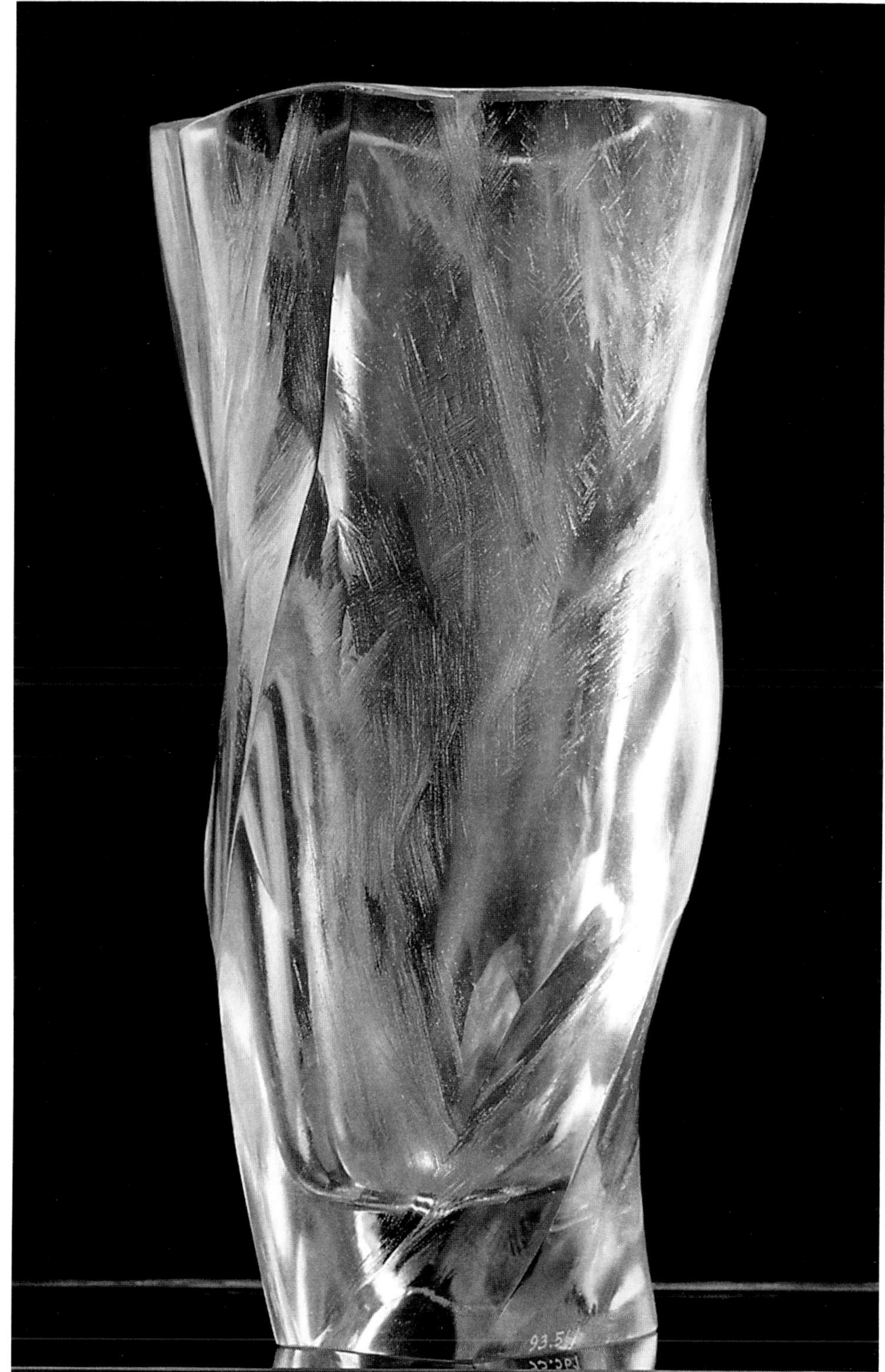

154. Vase, 1947.
Cut and engraved colourless glass with unpolished surface.
Engraved signature: R. Roubiček 1947.
H. 23.5 cm.
Executed by the artist in the Specialized School of Glassmaking, Kamenický Šenov.
Museum of Decorative Arts, Prague (Inv. 93 561).

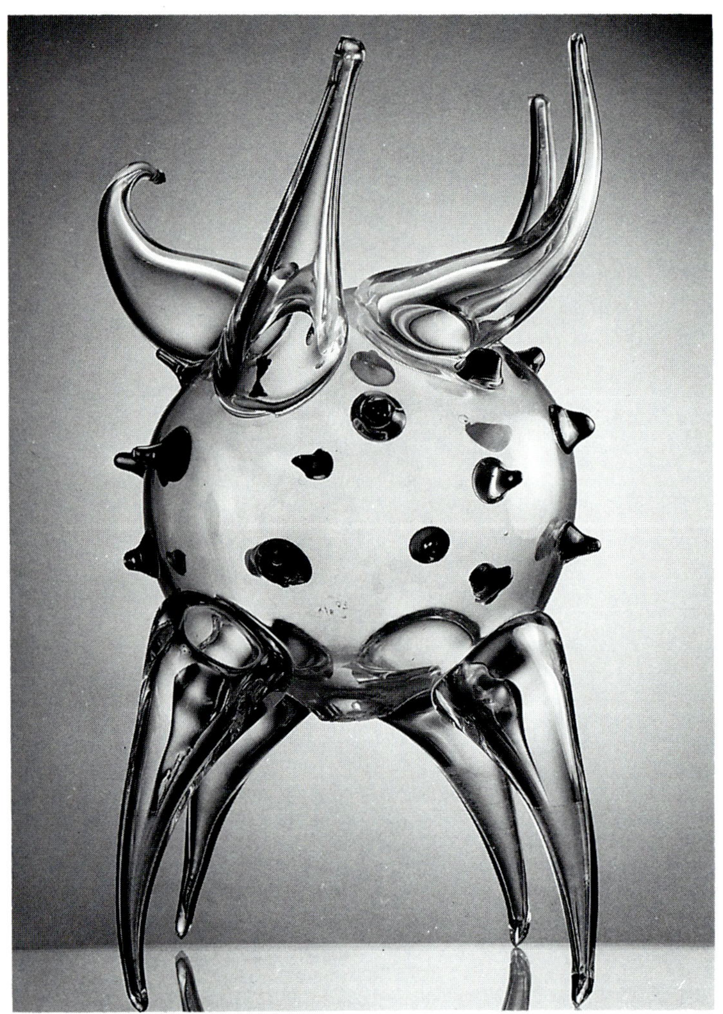

René Roubiček
155. DECORATIVE SCULPTURE, 1960.
Heat-shaped blown crystal and brown glass.
H. 29 cm.
Executed by the Borské sklo Glassworks,
Nový Bor.
Museum of Decorative Arts, Prague
(Inv. 54 875).

René Roubiček
156. BOTTLE, 1965.
Heat-shaped mould-blown green
and blue glass.
H. 43.5 cm.
Executed by Josef Rozinek,
Borské sklo Glassworks, Nový Bor.
Museum of Decorative Arts, Prague
(Inv. 66 583).

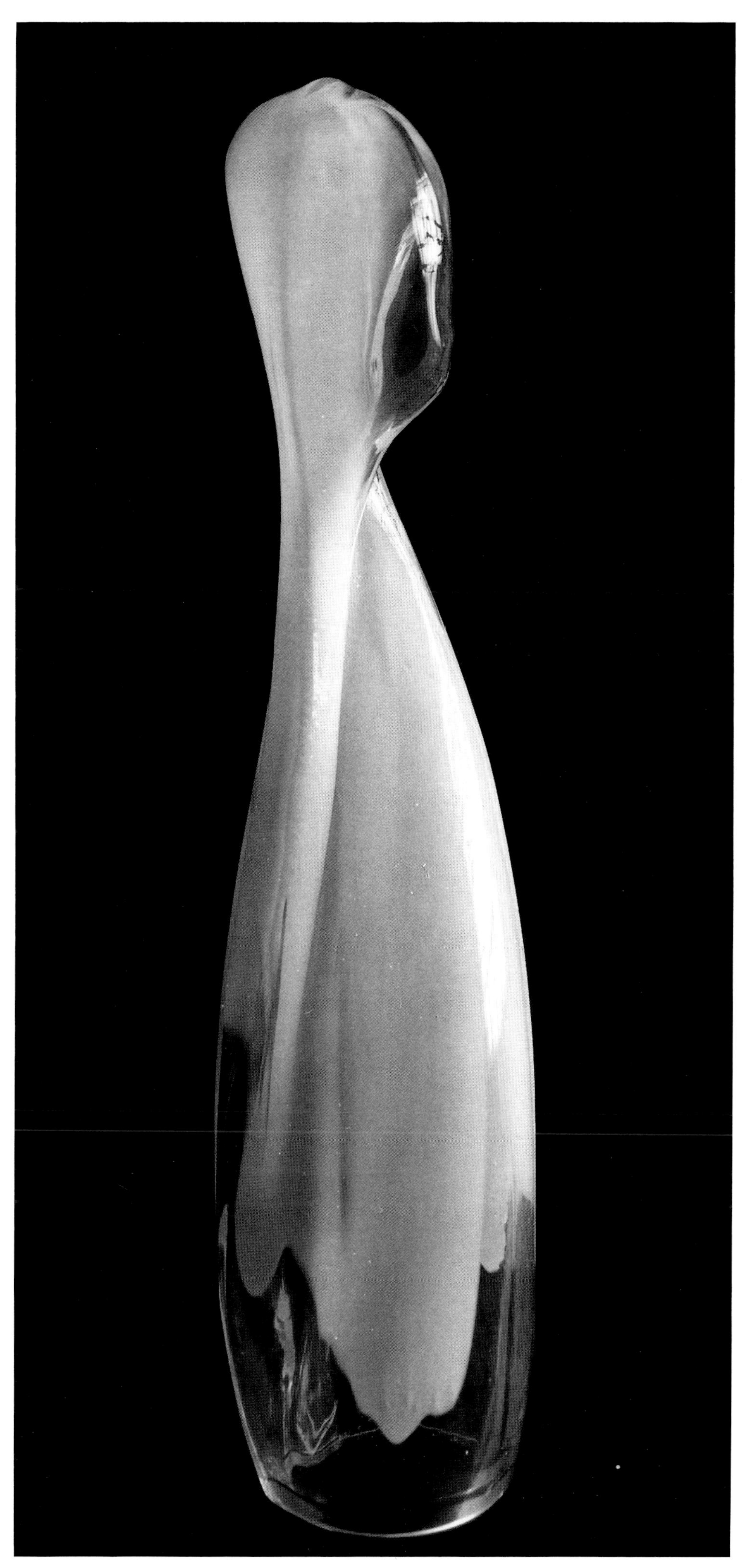

René Roubiček
157. Head, 1981.
Blown heat-worked glass
with white inserted layer.
H. 86 cm.
Executed by Josef Rozinek, Crystalex
Glassworks, Nový Bor.
Museum of Decorative Arts, Prague
(Inv. 89 042).

159. Bowl, 1957.
Cut lead crystal.
D. 45 cm.
Borské sklo Glassworks, Nový Bor.
Museum of Decorative Arts, Prague
(Inv. 54 905).
Presented at the XIIth Milan Triennale in 1960.

Miluše Roubičková-Kytková

Prague 1922 - lives in Kamenický Šenov and Prague.
1941-1943: studied at the Academy of Applied Arts in Prague.
1944-1949: studied at the Academy of Applied Arts, Prague, Josef Holeček's and Josef Kaplický's studios (1945-1949).
Since 1950: independent artist.

Miluše Roubíčková took part in the evolution of Czech glass after the war through her industrial models and glass sculptures. She is a true non-conformist who constantly proposes new forms and decorations, and has created numerous drinking glass models, heat-worked glasses decorated in cut lead crystal, and pieces in coloured glass for the Nový Bor and Škrdlovice glassworks. The 1957 Milan Triennale awarded her a Silver Medal in the design division.

Her personal work lies on a completely different plane—glass inspired by the popular tradition and Baroque techniques, wafting a charm reminiscent of naive art. Her works (kuglofs, bouquets of flowers in vases, cabbages and marmelade pots), inject poetry and humour into everyday life. In 1977 she received the Special Prize at the First Coburger Glaspreis, and in 1984 a prize from the exhibition of the World Crafts Council in Bratislava.

158. Bottle, 1956.
Blown glass.
H. 33 cm.
Borské sklo Glassworks, Nový Bor.
Museum of Decorative Arts, Prague
(Inv. 48 263).
Silver Medal at the 1957 Milan Triennale.

Miluše Roubíčková
160-161. Vases with optical decoration, 1960.
Multi-layered mould-blown glass.
H. 32 cm.; H. 28 cm.
Nový Bor.
Museum of Decorative Arts, Prague
(Inv. 54 459 and 51 352).

Miluše Roubíčková
162. Bouquet in a vase, 1972.
Blown heat-worked glass.
H. 70 cm.
Museum of Decorative Arts, Prague
(Inv. 76 456).

163. Danger II, 1987.
Heat-deformed glass with reflecting surfaces and paint in metal frame.
44 x 60 cm.
Executed by the artist.
Museum of Decorative Arts, Prague
(Inv. 95 192).

Eliška Rožátová

Prague 1940 - lives in Prague.
1954-1958: trained at the Specialized School of Glassmaking in Železný Brod.
1960-1966: studied at the Academy of Applied Arts in Prague,
Professors Josef Kaplický's and Stanislav Libenský's studios (1963-1966).
1966-1970: designer at the Železnobrodské sklo Glassworks in Železný Brod.
Since 1970: independent artist.

From the beginning of her career, Eliška Rožátová has been active in three fields: design, monumental decoration, and sculpture. Before 1970 (her first personal work dates from that year), she created a series of blown glass models, sometimes finished by cutting, that were mass-produced with some success. In monumental decoration, she has created numerous leaded windows, mosaics and glass walls. Her transparent mosaics, applied by heat to flat glass panels (window-mosaic of the Cultural Centre of Levoča, 1975) aroused a decided interest in her work. She has also practised acid-etching (official convention in the Smíchov station, Prague, 1975). In the 1970s she collaborated with Jan Fisar, and during this period she used blown cylinders in conjunction with metal elements and graphics (*Cylinders* cycle, 1973; *Fingers*, 1981). Next came the *Hats* period, which achieved notoriety at the First Interglassymposium of Nový Bor in 1982. In 1985, she began a series of windows and expressively painted objects.

164. **Danger I, 1987.**
Heat-deformed glass with reflecting surfaces and paint in metal frame.
44 x 60 cm.
Executed by the artist.
Museum of Decorative Arts, Prague
(Inv. 95 191).

Ivo Rozsypal

Brno 1941 - lives in Nový Bor.
1959-1961: trained at the Specialized School of Glassmaking in Kamenický Šenov.
1963-1966: worked in the Borské sklo Glassworks in Nový Bor.
1966-1973: studied at the Academy of Applied Arts in Prague, Professor Stanislav Libenský's studio.
1973-1984: designer at the Crystalex Glassworks of Nový Bor.
Since 1984: independent artist.

As a designer at the Crystalex Glassworks, Ivo Rozsypal created a series of models with painted decoration in pressed, blown or heat-worked glass. These were mass-produced and found considerable favour in industrial design competitions in Czechoslovakia and abroad. His individual pieces with engraved or painted decoration have also remained close to design: Rozsypal takes functional form into account but is always sensitive to the graphic quality of decoration (*Cyclist*, 1978-1980).

Since 1985, he has dedicated himself entirely to glass sculpture. His complex spatial compositions symbolize imaginary civilizations but also the three elements: earth, water and air; and he likes to explore the possibilities of new technological procedures, especially collage, engraving and cutting of coloured opaxites. Occasionally he creates works intended for building decoration (light fixtures for the Nový Bor Theatre, in collaboration with Milan Handl).

165. Energy, 1987.
Engraved and cut bonded opaxite, partially painted glass.
45 x 35.5 cm.; 10 x 10 x 25 cm.
Museum of Decorative Arts, Prague (Inv. 95 639).

Jaromír Rybák

Plzen 1952 - lives in Prague.
1967-1971: trained at the Specialized School of Glassmaking in Železný Brod.
1973-1979: studied at the Academy of Applied Arts in Prague,
Professor Stanislav Libenský's studio.
Since 1979: independent artist.

Jaromír Rybák presented a highly-appreciated functional table service as his final graduation portfolio, but now devotes himself exclusively to individual works, especially sculpture; and although he has experimented with various techniques, he generally mould-melts his sculptures and finishes them by cutting. He also creates heat-worked objects, paints on hollow glass and executes stained-glass windows using the classical lead process. Rybák has met the problems posed by the multiple areas of his activity in a variety of original ways. He has also accepted commissions for important works to be integrated into an architectural setting (lighting elements, light-objects, and windows), and has worked with Gizela Šaboková on both the design and the execution of these works (lighting elements at the Odeon Bookstore in Prague, 1987-1988; light-objects and windows of the Nebozízek Restaurant in Prague, 1985). In 1981 he received the Diploma from the Jugend Gestaltet competition, organized as part of the Munich International Handwerkmesse, and in 1985, the Third Prize of the Second Coburger Glaspreis of Coburg.

**166. Night over the lake, 1984-1985.
Leaded glass window with tin-plated lead sheets, purple opaxite, frosted glass, cut crystal, and metal frame.
120 x 120 cm.
Executed by Vilém Voňka and Jiří Černohorský.
Museum of Decorative Arts, Prague (Inv. 95 199).**

Jaromír Rybák
167. GOLDEN ARCH, 1985.
Mould-melted cut and polished glass with
engraving and gold leaf inclusions.
11 x 33 x 33 cm.
Executed by the artist and Jan Štohanzl.
Artist's collection.

Jaromír Rybák
168. THE APOCALYPSE, 1988.
Mould-melted gold-coloured lead crystal,
engraved and irradiated with
cobalt gamma rays.
49 x 49 x 20 cm.
Artist's collection.

169. LOOK BACK, 1988.
Painting (various techniques) on glass panel with metallic frame.
95 x 70 cm.
Executed by the artist in the Crystalex Glassworks, Nový Bor.
Artist's collection.

Gizela Šabóková

Nové Zámky 1952 - lives in Prague.
1967-1969: trained at the apprenticeship centre of the Český Křišťál Glassworks in Chlum near Třebon.
1969-1973: Specialized School of Glassmaking in Železný Brod.
1973-1979: studied at the Academy of Applied Arts in Prague, Professor Stanislav Libenský's studio.
Since 1979: independent artist.

Gizela Šabóková entered Professor Libenský's studio even though she already possessed solid experience in glass cutting, which has permanently influenced her work. In her mould-melted sculptures, executed in 1980, cutting represents an important stage in the creation. By 1981, however, she began to concentrate on painted windows, usually figural, that emphasize her gifts as painter and her lively wit and humour.

Gizela Šabóková has spent a great deal of time collaborating with architects. She created lighting elements, light-objects and windows (lighting at the ČKD House in Prague) with fellow student Jaromír Rybák. In 1982 she received the Diploma from the Jugend Gestalt competition, organized as part of the Munich International Handwerkmesse of Munich. That same year, her works were honoured by the Third Quadriennale for Art Crafts of Socialist Countries, held in Erfurt.

170. FIGURE IN A LANDSCAPE, 1988.
Painting (various techniques)
on glass panel with metallic frame.
95 x 70 cm.
Executed by the artist
in the Crystalex Glassworks, Nový Bor.
Artist's collection.

LUDVIKA SMRČKOVÁ
(see also p. 117)

Kročehlavy 1903 - lives in Prague.
1948-1952: designer at the Inwald Glassworks.
1952: designer at the Umělecké sklo Glassworks of Nový Bor.
1952-1958: directed the Central Bureau of Design for the Glass and Ceramics Industry in Prague.
Since 1958: independent artist.

Ludvika Smrčková taught in secondary schools in Prague and the provinces before 1948. Since then, and her entry into the Inwald Glassworks, she has been completely absorbed with glass-making, from heat-work to engraved and cut glass. She designed a series of drinking glass models, fruit bowls and dessert plates, tackled flame-worked glass during the war, and since the 1950s has collaborated with the Škrdlovice glassworks in this area.

Her work on cut glass brought her back to the pre-war models whose decorative values she had helped develop (cut plates, Inwald Glassworks, 1948; cut vase, Crystalex Glassworks, Nový Bor, 1970). From 1941 onwards, she collaborated with Adolf Matura, who executed her decorations. Smrčkova has been partial to floral themes and views of Prague, and, in her conception of engraving and her choice of subjects, she is the artist closest to the Biedermeier style among Czech glass-makers. She has created numerous engraved and cut glasses and objects, intended as official gifts (*Coventry Cathedral*, 1974). During the eighties, she has also done many highly original cut sculptures.

171. VASE, 1956.
Cut and polished purple glass.
Engraved signature: L. Smrčková.
H. 17 cm; D. 12 cm.
Moser Glassworks, Karlovy Vary.
Museum of Decorative Arts, Prague
(Inv. 86 910).
Created for the XIth Milan Triennale, 1957.

172. VASE, 1957.
Cut and polished topaze glass.
H. 16 cm; D. 10 cm.
Karlovarské sklo Glassworks; Karlovy Vary.
Museum of Decorative Arts, Prague
(Inv. 48 162).

Ivana Šrámková-Šolcová

Liberec 1960 - lives in Prague.
1976-1980: Specialized School of Glassmaking in Železný Brod.
1980-1981: worked in the Železnobrodské sklo Glassworks in Železný Brod.
1981-1987: studied at the Academy of Applied Arts in Prague, Professor Stanislav Libenský's studio.
Since 1987: independent artist.

Like many other artists of her generation, Ivana Šrámková-Šolcová has not limited herself to only one discipline. She was known as a painter, engraver and sculptor in Stanislav Libenský's studio, which always offered a great deal of freedom to its students, and created her first glass sculptures at school: the blown and painted crazy-autos, which she followed up with many variants that introduced a note of freshness and gaiety into Czech glass creation through their refusal of aestheticism.

Her graduation portfolio comprised painting on hollow glass (vase), mould-melted sculpture, models of pressed glass designed for mass-production, and stained-glass windows. Today, Ivana Šrámková-Šolcová has abandoned design, but continues all other glass-making disciplines in a characteristically innovative spirit.

175. Yellow vase, 1987.
Mould-blown and painted colourless glass.
H. 52 cm; D. at the base 27.3 cm.
Painted by the artist.
Museum of Decorative Arts, Prague
(Inv. 95 196).

Ivana Šrámková-Šolcová
173. AUTO I, 1985.
Mould-blown and painted glass.
25 x 16 x 47 cm.
Painted by the artist.
Regional Museum, Liberec
(Inv. S 3821).

Ivana Šrámková-Šolcová
174. AUTO II, 1985.
Mould-blown and painted glass.
24 x 24 x 65 cm.
Painted by the artist.
Regional Museum, Liberec
(Inv. S 3820).

176. Vase, 1960.
Opal mould-blown heat-shaped glass.
H. 24 cm.
Borské sklo Glassworks, Nový Bor.
Museum of Decorative Arts, Prague
(Inv. 54 813).

Vratislav Šotola

Hermanuv Městec 1931
- lives in Prague.
1946-1948: Specialized School of Glassmaking in Kamenický Šenov.
1948-1949: Specialized School of Glassmaking in Nový Bor.
1949-1954: studied at the Academy of Applied Arts in Prague,
Professor Josef Kaplický's studio.
1958-1962: designer in the glassworks of Nový Bor.
1962-1978: designer and art theoretician at the Institute of Furnishings and Clothing Culture in Prague.
Since 1979: designer at the Sklo-Union OBAS Glassworks, Teplice.

Vratislav Šotola allies his artistic preoccupations with the necessities of production. In the second half of the 1950s, at the beginning of his career, he devoted himself to many-layered coloured glass, fashioned by cutting, and to thin-walled blown glass. By the end of the sixties he had moved towards utilitarian pressed glass, to be manufactured by automatic processes and artisanal means. In the mid-seventies, he adapted the technique of many-layered coloured glass, shaped by the cut, to modern conceptions. He thus created a collection of particularly successful table glasses for the Karlovarské sklo Glassworks of Karlovy Vary.

At the Institute of Furnishings and Clothing Culture, he triumphed in the multiple roles of organizer, theoretician and art critic, and in the multiple fields of glass, design, and ceramics. He has also created several monumental works: a lighting-sculpture in the hunting pavilion at Hluboká nad Vltavou, 1980, and a glass figure in the ballroom at the Prague III Town Hall, 1979-1981.

Jiří Šuhájek

Pardubice 1943 - lives in Prague.
1957-1961: Specialized School of Glassmaking in Kamenický Šenov.
1962-1964: designer at the Moser Karlovarské sklo Glassworks - Karlovy Vary.
1964-1971: studied at the Academy of Applied Arts in Prague, Professor Stanislav Libenský's studio.
1968-1971: training period at the Royal College of Art in London, Professor Queensbury's studio.
1972-1978: designer at the Moser Karlovarské sklo Glassworks - Karlovy Vary.
Since 1979: designer in the Glass Department of the Institute of Furnishings and Clothing Culture in Prague.

Jiří Šuhájek is one of the rare Czech glass-artists who blow and shape their pieces by heat in the oven themselves; and he is as gifted a designer as he is an artist.

Šuhájek's models, designed for both small- and large-scale manufacturing, have achieved distinction in Czechoslovakia and abroad: cut drinking glass service (Moser), drinking glass service of post-modernist inspiration using mixed techniques (Crystalex), and the series of table glasses moulded by centrifugation (Crystalex). In his personal work, Šuhájek uses blowing and hot glass processes. He has created a universe of animals, birds and vegetables, populated over the last few years by female figures. At the Third Interglassymposium of Nový Bor in 1988, he experimented with different mould-melted glass techniques for his compositions with characters. He has received numerous foreign prizes, among them the Bayerischer Stadtpreis awarded by the Munich International Handwerkmesse in 1976; the International Prize of Valencia, in 1980; and the Exhibition Prize of the World Crafts Council of Bratislava in 1984.

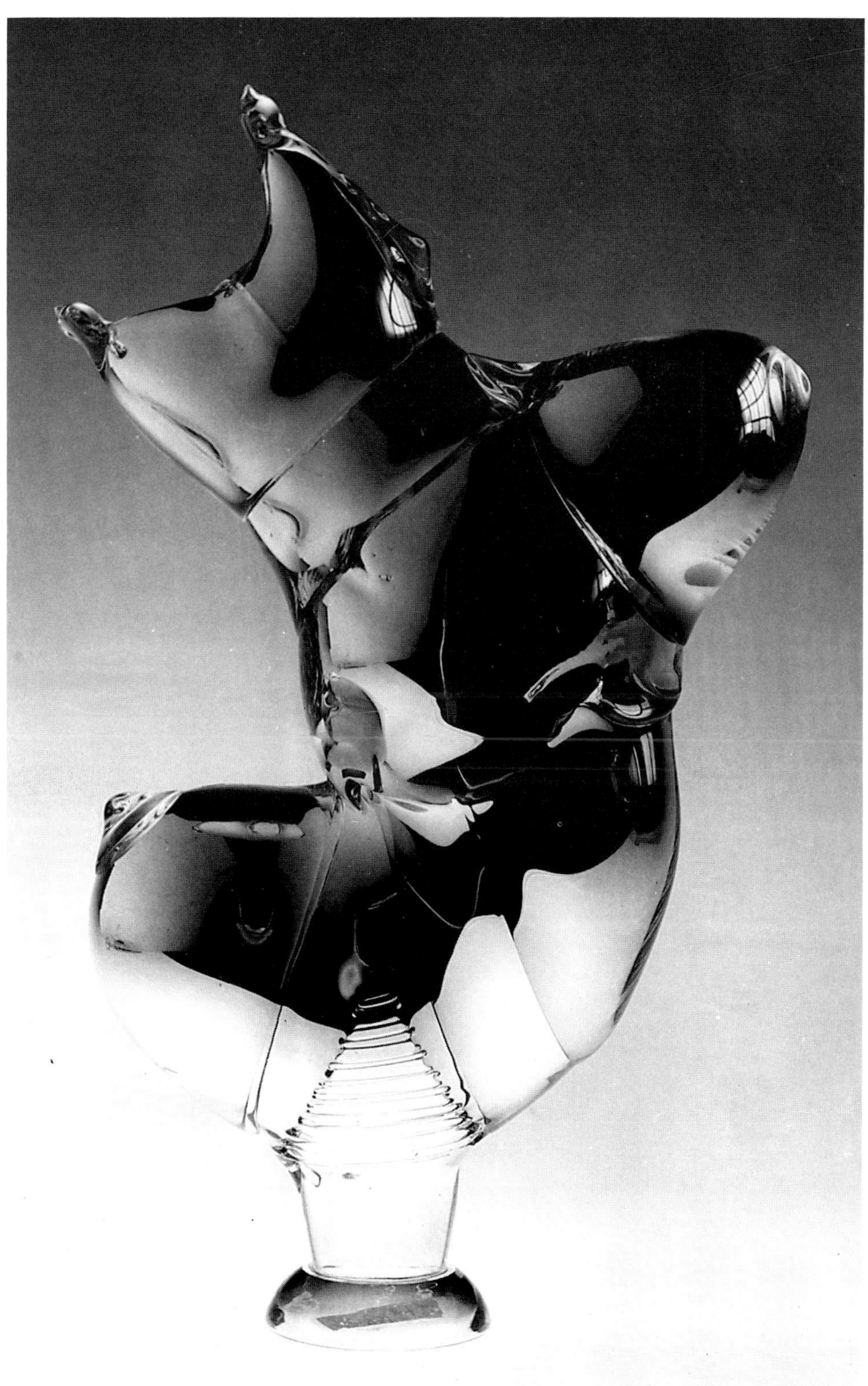

177. Zoomorphic object, 1974.
Silver-plated blown and heat-shaped glass.
H. 39.5 cm.
Executed by the artist at the Moser-Karlovarské sklo Glassworks, Karlovy Vary.
Museum of Decorative Arts, Prague
(Inv. 80 557).

Jiři Šuhajek
178. Bird, 1974.
Heat-shaped gilded glass.
Executed by the artist at the Moser-Karlovské
sklo Glassworks, Karlovy Vary.
Museum of Decorative Arts, Prague
(Inv. 80 556).

Jaroslav Svoboda

Sokoleč near Poděbrady 1938
- lives in Škrdlovice and Prague
1953-1957: Specialized School of Glassmaking in Železný Brod.
1959-1960: glass cutter in the art trade workshops in Prague.
1960-1968: glass cutter for the Arts and Crafts Center in Prague.
1963-1969: studied in the Department of History and Philosophy at the Charles University of Prague.
1969-1987: director and designer of the Škrdlovice factory.
Since 1987: professor and director of the Glass Studio at the Academy of Applied Arts in Prague. Designer at the Škrdlovice glassworks.

Jaroslav Svoboda was born into a family of glass-makers. After starting out as an artisan, he rapidly became an independent creator. His first models date from 1964, and he has devoted himself both to utilitarian glass design produced on a small-scale in Škrdlovice and to monumental decoration and glass sculpture. His Škrdlovice models conformed to the technical possibilities of this glassworks and usually combined heat-work glass processes with cutting. Svoboda has also adapted his monumental works to concrete architecture (glass objects at the Ždar nad Sázavou Museum, 1983).

In his personal work, he insists upon a precise, simple and highly aesthetic form highlighting his abilities as a cutter. From the beginning of the 1980s, he has explored more complex compositions in mould-melted glass, which he finishes by cutting or frosting. This work puts into play his earlier research on the relationships between the opaque and transparent surfaces of a sculpture and between the sculpture and its environment. In 1987, Jaroslav Svoboda succeeded Professor Stanislav Libenský as the Head of the Glass Studio at the Academy of Applied Arts in Prague.

179. The contact, 1988.
Cast and cut smoked glass with marble.
47 x 43 cm; pedestal 10 x 24 x 25 cm.
Executed in the Škrdlovice factory,
cut by the artist.
Artist's collection.

František Tejml

Born in 1933 - lives in Prague.
1948-1951: Specialized School of Glassmaking in Kamenický Šenov.
1951-1957: Academy of Applied Arts in Prague,
Professor Josef Kaplický's studio.
1957-1970: collaboration with different glassworks.

Frantisek Tejml was one of Josef Kaplický's most talented students, especially in the art of painted decoration on hollow glass. His works, models designed for production, perfectly adapt ornament to form. In spite of this, they have no real commercial use and are, because of their rarity and expressiveness, original works of art. During the sixties, František Tejml realized many monumental works and participated in various glass competitions and exhibitions. In 1970, he abandoned glass-making.

184. Vase, 1964.
Blown glass with glazed and enamelled decoration.
Signature on the bottom: TEJML. H. 34.5 cm.
Painted by the artist.
Museum of Decorative Arts, Prague (Inv. 63 533).

183. Vase with fish, 1960.
Blown glass with glazed and enamelled decoration.
H. 19 cm.
Painted by the artist.
Museum of Decorative Arts, Prague (Inv. 53 620).

180. VASE WITH SERPENT, 1958.
Blown glass with glazed
and enamelled decoration.
H. 42 cm.
Museum of Decorative Arts, Prague
(Inv. 52 690).

181. VASE DECORATED WITH BLACK DROPS, 1958.
Blown glass with glazed
and enamelled decoration. H. 28 cm.
Painted by the artist.
Museum of Decorative Arts, Prague
(Inv. 52 667)

182. BIRD VASE, c. 1965.
Blown glass with glazed
and enamelled decoration. H. 34.5 cm.
Painted by the artist.
Museum of Decorative Arts, Prague
(Inv. 73 827).

Pavel Trnka

Poděbrady 1948 - lives in Prague.
1963-1967: Specialized School of Glassmaking in Železný Brod.
1967-1973: Academy of Applied Arts in Prague,
Professor Stanislav Libenský's studio.
1973-1974: taught drawing in a primary school in Prague.
Since 1973: independent artist.

Pavel Trnka is an artist with well-defined theories. His work lies in prismatic compositions precision-cut in lead glass, and he has studied colour mixtures and the optical qualities of glass since his graduation. He has also explored the fracturing of glass and the substance's inner tension, themes that appear in his *Non-Vessel* cycle and elsewhere. To the elementary geometric form, he opposes debris and cracked glass, which he mixes with fragments of colour.

Trnka is interested as well in the relationships among space, the glass object and the play of light. In his large scale spatial creations, he uses a computer to harmonize the effects of large glass panels with light-streams (the fountain in the Národní underground station in Prague). In addition to the fountains, he has also created light fixtures and leaded-glass windows.

**186. Untitled, 1980.
Optical leaded cut glass.
10 x 7.5 x 7.5 cm. (3 parts).
Moravian Gallery, Brno
(Inv. 28 804).**

Pavel Trnka
187. NON-VESSEL, 1982.
Blown and cut-out glass.
H. 23.5 cm.
Museum of Decorative Arts, Prague
(Inv. 89 651).

185. Object, 1981.
Heat-shaped mould-melted glass.
Engraved signature: Tichý.
H. 19 cm.
Museum of Decorative Arts, Prague
(Inv. 89 038).

Dalibor Tichý

Kolín 1950 - Prague 1985.
1965-1970: Specialized School of Glassmaking in Kamenický Šenov.
1970-1976: Academy of Applied Arts in Prague,
Professor Stanislav Libenský's studio.
1976-1980: designer at the Crystalex Glassworks, Nový Bor.
1980-1985: independent artist.

During his brief career, Dalibor Tichý devoted himself to industrial design and individual works. In Stanislav Libenský's studio, he realized a number of original ashtrays and vases, and from the beginning of the seventies he concentrated on heat-work glass processes. His sculptures took shape in the contrast between the massive mould-melted base and the fragile composition of spirals and vegetal forms above it, which he drew out with a special technique. Another group of his works consisted of objects in engraved and assembled sheets (*Castle of Spain*, 1981).

Tichý designed several models for small-scale manufacturing that emphasized the artisanal fluency he acquired at the Kamenický Šenov school. In 1985, the Diploma from the Second Coburger Glaspreis of Coburg was awarded to one of his sculptures.

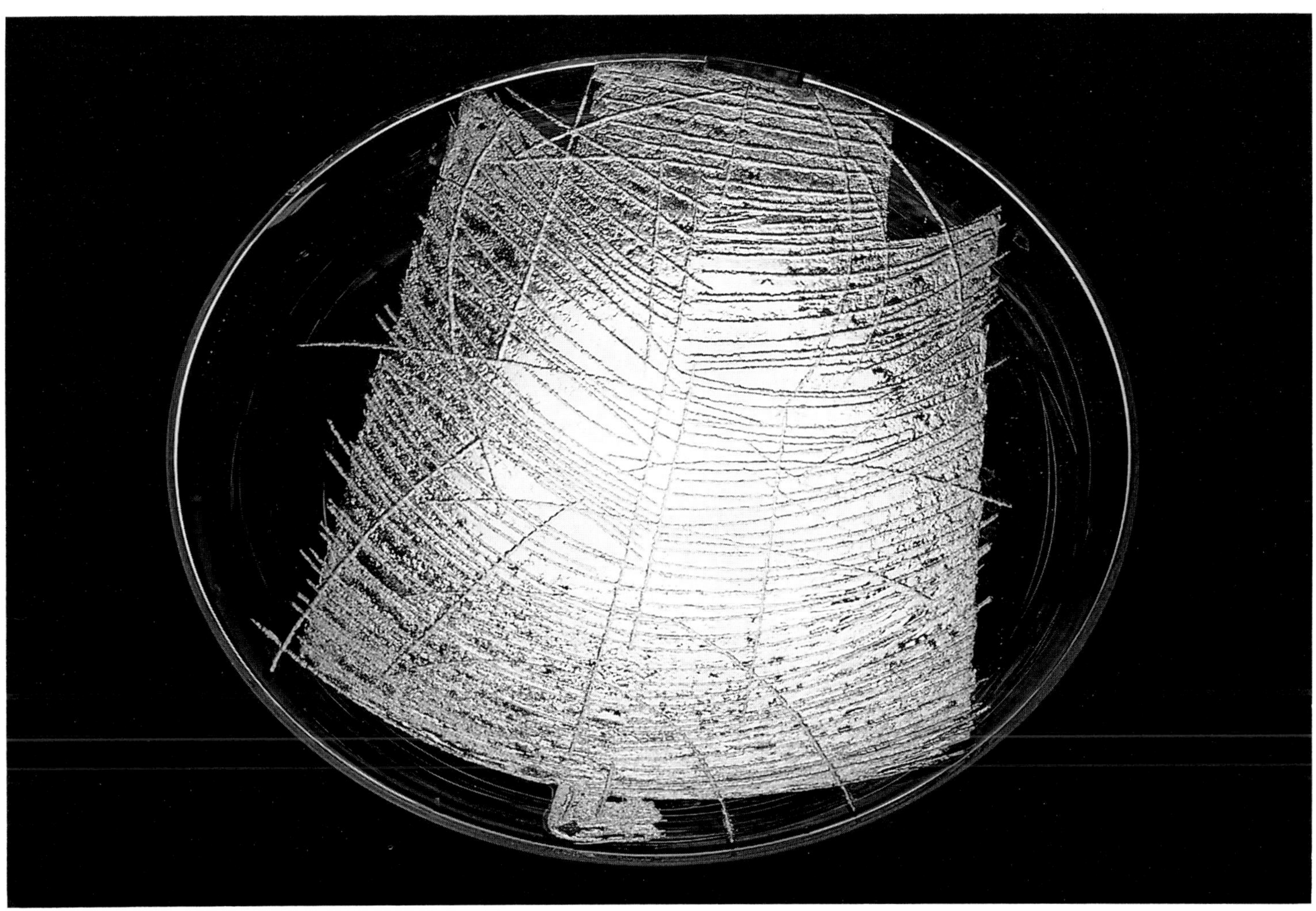

188. PLATE, 1964.
Acid-etched blown glass.
D. 34 cm.
From from the Borské sklo Glassworks, Nový Bor.
Decoration executed by the artist.
Museum of Decorative Arts, Prague
(Inv. 66 575).

DANA VACHTOVÁ

Prague 1937 - lives in Prague.
1952-1956: Prague Art School.
1956-1963: Academy of Applied Arts in Prague,
Professor Kaplický's studio.
Since 1963: independent artist.

Dana Vachtová is a glass-making artist with a sculptor's ability. She works not only in glass but in metal and wood, traditional materials of the latter art.

In the 1960s, she also worked in design. The drinking glass service she created at the end of her studies was produced by the Květná Glassworks and presented at the Universal Exposition of Montreal in 1967. Although she occasionally practised industrial design, Dana Vachtová deliberately moved towards glass sculpture, where she has used mould-melted and blown techniques. She refuses to touch up the surfaces of the cooled object, which she sometimes combines with metal elements. Her style is characterized by dynamism, the interpenetration of forms, and a clear delimitation of the spatial relationships among the various components of the work qualities typical of modern sculpture; and she was acclaimed at the exhibitions Space I, Space II, and Space III, between 1982 and 1986. She has also, on occasion, produced monumental works (glass relief in the ballroom at the Dačice Town Hall, 1973; sculptures at the Gomel Hotel in České Budějovice, 1983).

Dana Vachtová
189. DIALOGUE, 1982.
Mould-blown smoked glass
with copper sheets.
84 x 44 cm; 83 x 50 cm.
Museum of Decorative Arts, Prague
(Inv. 91 816).

190. Bowl, 1971.
Painted and engraved blown glass.
Signature on the bottom: K. Vaňura 1971.
H. 20 cm; D. 26 cm.
Decoration executed by the artist.
Museum of Decorative Arts, Prague
(Inv. 75 376).

Karel Vaňura

Hořovice v Podkrkonoší 1937
- lives in Prague.
1952-1956: Specialized School of Glassmaking in Železný Brod.
1957-1963: Academy of Applied Arts in Prague, Professors Josef Kaplický's and Stanislav Libenský's studios.
1965-1988: assistant at the Academy of Applied Arts, Prague, Professor Libenský's studio.
Since 1988: lecturer at the Academy of Applied Arts, Prague.

Since 1965, Karel Vaňura has designed and realized more than thirty works of monumental decoration, sometimes with Marian Karel, Vladimír Kopecký or Dana Zámečníková. He has also created individual works, restored historic stained-glass windows, and executed copies of them. He was Libenský's assistant for painted and acid-etched decoration, and contributed to the evolution of glass-making through his pedagogical activity.

Vaňura's glass creations are reflected in his painting and engraving. At the beginning of the seventies, he was the sole Czech glass-maker to practise painting (or, more precisely, mixed techniques) on hollow glass. He then took up blown-glass sculpture, in metallic structures, and opaxite objects, also in metallic frames. In 1974, he returned to the classical technique of leaded stained-glass windows, a process marking both his monumental and his small-scale works (stained-glass windows of great quality, painted with inserted cut elements). His acid-etched plates with painted decorations, created for the First Nový Bor Interglassymposium in 1982, are equally remarkable.

191. Shell ashtray, 1950.
Colourless heat-shaped glass with bubbles and inserted threads.
D. 16 cm.
Škrdlovice Glassworks;
Artist's Collection.

Milena Velíšková

Buenos Aires 1917
- lives in Prague.
1936-1938: Graduate School of Architecture in Prague.
1942-1945: designer at the Českomoravské sklárny Glassworks, Krásno nad Bečvou.
1945-1946: Pedagogical Faculty of the Charles University of Prague.
1950-1960: directed the design office of the Škrdlovice factory.
1960-1962: designer at the Lustry Glassworks, Kamenický Šenov.

Milena Velíšková is a specialist in heat-worked glass processes; in the 1950s she was one of the most influential figures in this discipline. She first took up the technique with Emanuel Beránek, founder of the Škrdlovice factory. Her pieces are characterized by their inserted decorations: bubbles, coloured mica, grains of sand, colour threads; but she also worked in acid-etched and sand-blasted cut glass, and has created decorative walls and lighting fixtures integrated into architecture.

Her work has been frequently honoured: Grand Prize at the 1958 Brussels Universal Exposition, Gold Medal from the Munich International Handwerkmesse in 1959. Milena Velíšková now creates furniture fabrics and tapestries.

Martin Velíšek

Teplice 1963
- lives in Prague.
1979-1983: trained at the Specialized School of Glassmaking in Kamenický Šenov.
1983-1989: studied at the Academy of Applied Arts in Prague, first under Stanislav Libenský, then under Jaroslav Svoboda.

Martin Velíšek is typical of the recent generation of Czech glass-makers trained at the Academy of Applied Arts in Prague. His inspiration lies in drawing, painting and engraving, which he freely applies to glass work. Man and animal are the main themes of his work, which at once recalls Art Nouveau, primitive art and Expressionist influences in painting, popular engraving, and the work of Jean Dubuffet, as Velíšek himself affirms.

He was one of the most gifted pupils of the Academy's Glass Studio and received seven prizes in academic and state competitions while still a student. Velíšek has participated in several exhibitions in Czechoslovakia.

192. Tzigane bottles and tumblers, 1989.
Painted blown crystal glass.
Class project, Academy of Applied Arts, Prague,
Professor J. Svoboda's studio.
Bottle, H. 40 cm, D. 24 cm;
bottle H. 44.5 cm, D. 11 cm.
Cups, H. 10 cm., D. 10 cm.
Academy of Applied Arts, Prague.

František Vizner

Prague 1936
- lives in Žďár nad Sázavou.
1951-1953: Specialized School of Glassmaking in Nový Bor.
1953-1956: Specialized School of Glassmaking in Železný Brod.
1956-1962: Academy of Applied Arts in Prague,
Professor Karel Štipl's studio.
1961-1967: designer at the Sklo-Union Glassworks of Teplice.
1967-1975: designer at the Glass Studio of the Škrdlovice Art Professions' Centre.
Since 1975: independent artist.

František Vízner has marked the history of Czechoslovakian art as artisan, industrial designer, and sculptor in glass. In the 1960s, he created a series of pressed glass models manufactured in various colours, and helped to improve the style of this method of production. His pressed glasses were inexpensive and highly competitive products, and his activity was essential to the Škrdlovice factory. He created numerous models there specifically adapted to the factory's technology, which was geared towards manual work and heat techniques. This period produced pieces with robust and simple forms, as well as optical decorations.

Vízner is particularly well-known for a special technique that blends cutting and the boring of holes with various procedures, like polishing, used in the final phase. His vases, plates and dishes, with delicate forms and colours possessing a perfectly finished velour or silk surface, forego their utilitarian function to become aesthetic objects in themselves.

Vízner has also created enormous decorations in glass, like the wall covering in the Karlovo náměstí underground station in Prague, 1984. In 1974 he won the Grand Prize at the Quadriennale for Art Crafts of Socialist Countries held in Erfurt; in 1978, he recieved the Bayerischer Stadtpreis, accorded as part of the Munich International Handwerkmesse.

**196. Jardinière, 1962.
Colourless pressed glass.
10.4 x 15.5 x 7 cm.
Executed by the glass container manufacturer, Rudolfova hut factory, Dubí near Teplice.
Museum of Decorative Arts, Prague (Inv. 59 437).**

František Vízner
193, 194 and 195. VASES, 1962.
Brown and colourless bored glass, cut and acid-etched, with mat surface.
I. 7.2 x 7.2 x 8.5 cm.
II. 10.5 x 10.5 x 10.5 cm.
III. 19 x 8 x 5.5 cm.
Works forming part of a graduation portfolio for the Academy of Applied Arts in Prague executed by the artist under the direction of Václav Plátek, instructor.
Museum of Decorative Arts, Prague
(Inv. 58 823 and 58 824).

197. VASE, 1983.
Smoked and colourless bored glass, cut and acid-etched, with mat surface.
H. 47 cm.
Block of glass from the Škrdlovice Glassworks, worked on by the artist.
Museum of Decorative Arts, Prague
(Inv. 91 813).

František Vízner
198. Vase, 1983.
Bored smoked glass, cut and acid-etched,
with mat surface.
D. 19.5 cm.
Block of glass from the Škrdlovice
Glassworks, worked by the artist.
Museum of Decorative Arts, Prague
(Inv. 91 814).

František Vízner
199. Bowl, 1972-1986.
Cut and polished opal glass.
H. 9 cm; D. 26 cm.
Glass block from the Škrdlovice Glassworks,
worked on by the artist.
Artist's collection.

Karel Wünsch

Bor 1932 - lives in Nový Bor.
1946-1950: Specialized School of Glassmaking in Nový Bor.
1953-1959: Academy of Applied Arts in Prague,
Professor Josef Kaplický's studio.
1959-1969: designer at the Borské sklo Glassworks, Nový Bor.
Since 1969: independent artist.

Until 1969, Karel Wünsch practised three disciplines: design, monumental decoration, and Studio Glass. In his models for the Borské sklo Glassworks, he insisted upon the value of artisanal work. For the XIIth Milan Triennale of 1960, he designed a group of elegant pieces with painted and engraved decorations. The Nový Bor Glassworks manufactured different variations of his vases and dishes ornamented with cut lenses that were popular in foreign markets. In 1965, Wünsch created his first stained-glass window, which marked the beginning of his interior decoration period: ornamented indoor and outdoor walls, glass reliefs and lighting fixtures. His work also includes decorative objects, linked together in cycles (*Solar Disk* in the seventies, and *Stability* in the eighties).

**200. Jardinière, 1960.
Engraved crystal.
H. 19 cm.
Borské sklo Glassworks, Nový Bor.
Museum of Decorative Arts, Prague
(Inv. 54 862).
Executed for the XIIth Milan Triennale, 1960.**

Karel Wünsch
201. Vase, 1960.
Smoked mould-blown glass,
painted in black with scratched motifs.
H. 26.5 cm.
Borské sklo Glassworks, Nový Bor.
Museum of Decorative Arts, Prague
(Inv. 54 855).

202. Spaces VII, 1986.
Cut and polished bonded optical glass on an opaxite base.
24 x 25 x 27 cm.
Museum of Decorative Arts, Prague
(Inv. 94 942).

Askold Žáčko

Bratislava 1946 - lives in Bratislava.
1960-1964: trained at the Specialized School of Glassmaking in Železný Brod.
1965-1971: studied at the Bratislava Academy of Beaux-Arts,
Václav Cigler's studio.
1971-1978: independent artist.
Since 1978: lecturer, then professor at the Bratislava Academy of Beaux-Arts. Directs the Glass Studio.

Askold Žáčko's work is remarkably rich, including models designed for large and small-scale production, monumental works, objects and jewellery. Žáčko elaborated his earliest industrial designs, already elegant and refined, during his studies in Václav Cigler's studio, and indeed he has never entirely abandoned this form of activity. He now collaborates with the Lednické Rovně Glassworks (the table service *Winter*, 1986; liqueur service decanter, 1986).

Žáčko has devoted himself for more than ten years to precision-cut objects of geometrical and optical inspiration, resting on opaxite or mirror bases. These technically innovative and brilliantly aesthetic pieces today represent a finished chapter in his work. Since 1988, he has adopted a new language of Expressionist bent (*Clown Head*). Among his monumental works are the show-room of the Tatrasklo firm in Trnava (1983).

Askold Žáčko continues to exert a strong influence on glass-making in Slovakia, both through his work and through the quality of his teaching. He was successively awarded prizes at the First and Second Quadriennale of Art Professions of Socialist Countries, in 1974 and 1978, and then, in 1984, from the Bratislava International Exhibition of Art Professions.

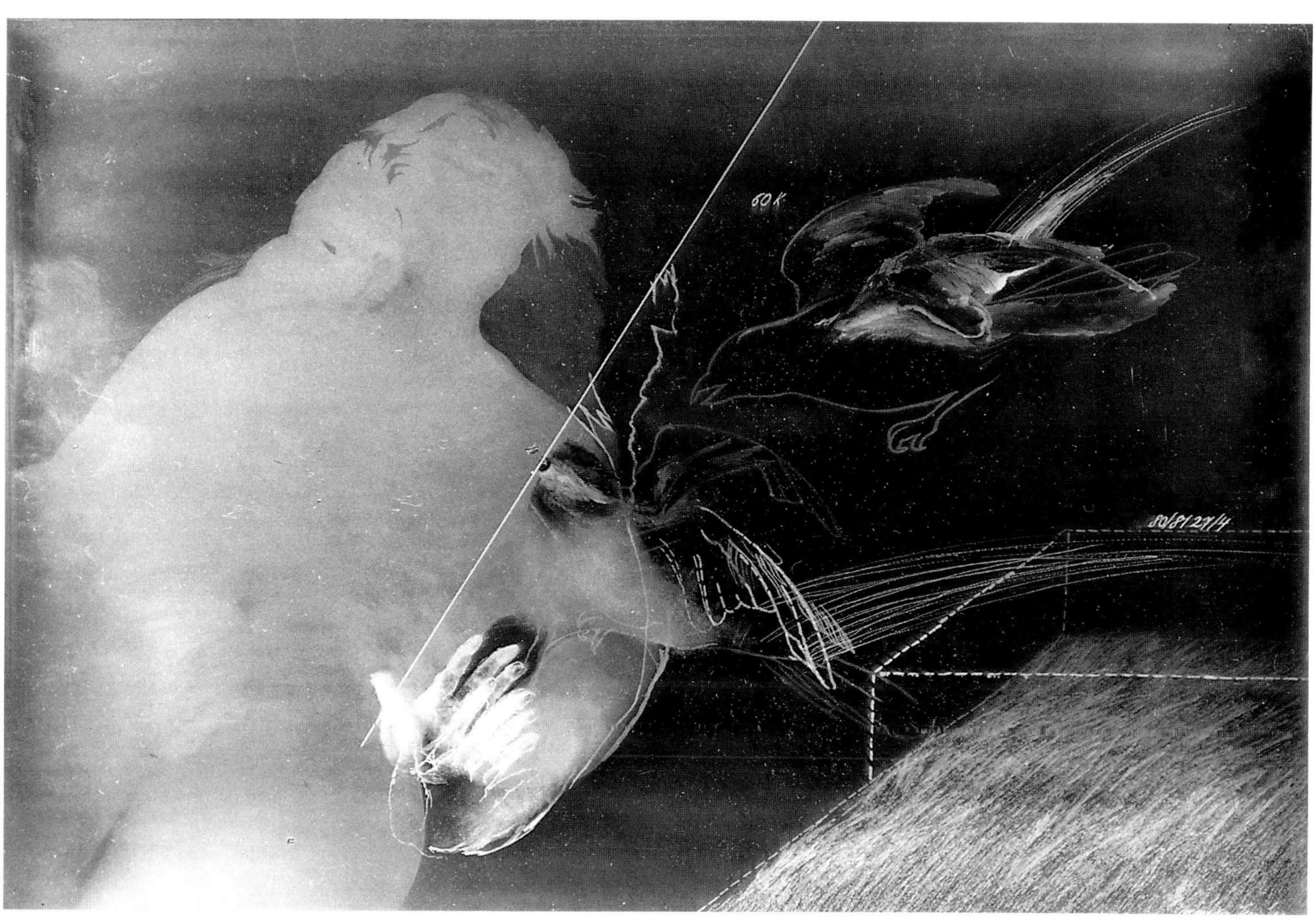

204. HOW TO CATCH A BIRD, 1981.
Engraved and painted sheet glass in metal frame.
27 x 28 cm.
Executed by the artist.
Museum of Decorative Arts, Prague
(Inv. 88 374).

DANA ZÁMEČNÍKOVÁ

Prague 1945 - lives in Prague.
1962-1968: architecture studies at the Graduate Technical Institute in Prague.
1969-1972: Academy of Applied Arts in Prague,
Professor Josef Svoboda's studio (architecture and scenography).
Since 1980: independent artist specializing in industrial design.
1985: lecturer at the Pilchuck Summer School, U.S.A.

At the beginning of her career, Dana Zámečníková worked in several fields: painted furniture, toys (The Child's Universe, Montreal, 1979), cartoons, scenography, and design. In 1978 she began to concentrate on glass-making, and proved especially adept at glass panels embellished with paint, acid-etching and scratched decoration, or with different collages composing very original objects. These large-scale works are meant to be integrated into a specific space; her small-scale ones are used to animate living interiors. The objects, enclosed in metal or glass frames, are grouped into cycles and thus allow glimpses of the artist's thought processes. Zámečníková first looks for the illusion of space and the scenic effect. Then her interest is displaced towards the expressive quality of the painting, emphasized by the presence of figurines and animals in pressed glass, evolving among the debris of the material. Today she creates aquarium-objects where space is once again unified.

Her large leaded-glass windows (*Breaking In*, 1984) are remarkable, and they sometimes decorate building interiors (window executed with Marian Karel for the Czech Restaurant in Budapest, 1988). Her sculptures (*Dogs* cycle) from 1985 on are fresh and exciting and attest to a sharp sense of expressive detail. In 1981, Dana Zámečníková received the Special Prize from the Kassel Glaskunst 1981.

Dana Zámečníková
203. THEATRE, 1980.
Engraved and painted sheet glass
in metal frame.
20.5 x 27 cm.
Executed by the artist.
Museum of Decorative Arts, Prague
(Inv. 88 375).

Dana Zámečníková
205. THE DOG, 1987-1988.
Sheet glass, wood, feathers,
mixed techniques.
155 x 180 cm.
Executed in collaboration
with Antonín Vojáček.
Artist's collection.

207. Undertow, 1988.
Colourless mould-blown and hot-shaped glass with chrome ring.
H. 27 cm; base 62 x 80 cm.
Artist's collection.

***Page right*:**
206. Tension, 1984.
Mould-blown glass with steel wire.
60 x 42 x 26 cm.
Museum of Decorative Arts, Prague (Inv. 93 542).

Jiřina Žertová

Prague 1932 - lives in Prague.
1947-1950: trained at the School of Graphic Arts in Prague.
1950-1955: studied at the Academy of Applied Arts in Prague,
Professor Josef Kaplický's studio.
Since 1956: independent artist.

Jiřina Žertová contributed to the reputation of Czech glass-making as early as 1957, when the XIth Milan Triennale awarded her a Silver Medal for her carafe and glasses with cut decorations. As a designer, she has collaborated with many glassworks: Škrdlovice, Crystalex of Nový Bor, Karlovarské sklo of Karlovy Vary, and Bohemia of Poděbrady. She has used multiple techniques, but her preference for cut or engraved decorations and heat-shaped forms (Škrdlovice) is evident.

She began to focus on sculpture in the 1970s. At first she elaborated blown forms of geometric inspiration ordered in compositions recalling building games, and then evolved towards a more and more spontaneous expression. She often used blown pieces in irregular forms of monumental character in conjunction with other materials, like metal. Her present work is the result of innovative experimentation in which painting plays an important role. In her most recent works, Žertová joins Vladimír Kopecký and the Expressionist current widespread among young glass-makers.

JÁN ZORIČÁK

Ždiar 1944 - lives in France.
1959-1963: trained at the Specialized School of Glassmaking in Železný Brod.
1963-1969: Academy of Applied Arts in Prague,
Professor Stanislav Libenský's studio.
1970: established himself in France and, since the late seventies,
has been included in the French selections for major international exhibitions.

At the end of his studies in Stanislav Libenský's studio, Ján Zoričák concentrated on his original version of prismatic sculpture. Along with Marian Karel and Aleš Vašiček, he was one of the main representatives of the current in Czech glassmaking that, oriented towards clear and precise forms, attempted to define the relationship between the interior space of the sculpture and surrounding spaces, by linking them through biases in the play of light. Though he maintains privileged contacts with Czechoslovakia and has greatly facilitated the circulation of Czech glass in France, Zoričák, since 1980, has been considered part of the very cosmopolitan French School.

208. EQUILIBRIUM, 1973.
Cut optical glass.
H. 27 cm.
Moravian Gallery, Brno
(Inv. 22 024).

Historical synopsis

600 Empire of Samo (623-659).

800 State of Great Moravia.

900 Fall of Great Moravia (c. 906).
Creation of a first feudal Czech state under the Přemyslides (10th century-1306).
Prince Wenceslas (921-929), assassinated by his successor Boleslav the First, is canonized and becomes the patron saint of Bohemia.
Under Boleslav II, Creation of the Bishopric (Diocese) of Prague (975).

1000 Vratislav II, prince of Bohemia, obtains the royal crown (1085).
Přemysl Otakar the First (1197-1230) recognized as hereditary and autonomous sovereign.

1200 Economic boom during the 13th century (colonization, urban development, silver mining).
Přemysl Otakar the Second (1253-1278): conquest of the Alpine provinces.
Great power of the Kingdom of Bohemia.
Wenceslas II (1278-1305) joins the crowns of Poland and Hungary to his own.

1300 Extinction of the Přemyslides (1306).
Luxembourg Dynasty (1310-1437).
Reign of John the First (1310-1346): incorporation of Silesia and Lusacia within the State of Bohemia.
Charles IV (1346-1378) elected Holy Roman Emperor.
Foundation of the University of Prague (1348).
General development of Czech literature and Gothic art.
Prague becomes one of the first great cities of Europe.

1400 Reign of Wenceslas IV (1378-1419).
Dissemination of the ideas of Jan Hus (deceased in 1415).
Revolutionary Hussite Movement (1419-1434).
Reign of Sigismund of Luxembourg (1436-1437).
Polish Dynasty of the Jagellons (1471-1526).
Formation of the National Confederation of Bohemia and Hungary: 1490.
Beginnings of Czech Humanism.

1500 Influence of the seigneurial oligarchy under the Jagellons (1471-1526).
Hapsburg Dynasty accedes to the throne of Bohemia (1526-1918).
1547: Municipal Anti-Hapsburg Revolt.
Expansion of Lutheranism.
Development of Humanism and influence of the Italian Renaissance.

1600 Emperor of the Holy Roman Empire Rudolph II (1576-1612) moves the court to Prague.
Opposition movement of the Protestant nobility.
Royal letters on the liberty of confession (1609).
Anti-Hapsburg insurrection by the States of Bohemia (1618-1620); defeat at the Battle of the White Mountain (1620).
Thirty Years' War (1618-1648).
Catholicism imposed by force.
Emigration of Protestants: Jan Amos Komenský (Comenius, deceased in 1670).
Installation of a foreign aristocracy by the Hapsbourgs.
Appearance of Baroque art connected with the advent of the Jesuits.

1700 Reign of Maria-Teresa (1740-1780) and Joseph II (1780-1790).
Creation of an absolute monarchy.
Development of textile and glass manufacturing in Bohemia.
Loss of Silesia, annexed by Prussia (1742).
Abolition of serfdom in 1781.
Germanization by the Hapsburgs.
National movements in Bohemia and Slovakia.

1800 Wars against Napoleon I (1801-1813).
Metternich's reactionary absolutism.
Beginnings of the Industrial Revolution.
Progress of the national movement in the Czech countries and in Slovakia.
Revolution of 1848.
Reign of Franz-Joseph I (1848-1916): installation of the absolutist regime.
Beginning of the constitutional regime in 1860.
Flourishing of Czech civilization and especially literature and music (Smetana and Dvořák).

1900 World War I (1914-1918)
Disintegration of Austria-Hungry and birth of the Republic of Czechoslovakia (28 October 1918).
Repercussions of the world economic crisis (1929-1934).
Appearance of the Nazi movement (Konrad Henlein) and his manoeuvres to detach the border regions from the Republic.
1939: Occupation of the Czech countries by Nazi Germany (protector of Bohemia-Moravia).
World War II (1939-1945).
1945: Liberation of Czechoslovakia by the Soviet Army; Edvard Beneš, president.
1948: Communist putsch; Klement Gottwald, president.
1968: Occupation by the Soviet army.
1989: Fall of the Communist government.

Bibliography

When no author is mentioned, we have listed entries by city names (for catalogues) or review titles (for articles).

PUBLICATIONS OF GENERAL INTEREST ON BOHEMIAN GLASS FROM THE MIDDLE AGES TO TODAY

A.H.I.V. (Association Internationale pour l'Histoire du Verre, ex-Journées Internationales du Verre), Comité National Tchécoslovaque des Journées Internationales du Verre, *Le Verre en Tchécoslovaquie*, Bulletin des Journées Internationales du Verre, n. 4, Liège, 1965-1966.

Beard, G., *International Modern Glass*, London, 1976.

Czihak, E. von, *Schlesische Gläser*, Breslau, 1891.

Drahotová, O., *L'Art du verre en Europe*, Paris, 1983.

Drahotová, O. -Langhamer, A., *Bohemian Glass*, Crystalex, Nový Bor, 1985.

Hetteš, K., *La verrerie en Tchécoslovaquie*, Prague, 1958.

Jiřík, F.X., *České sklo* [Bohemian Glass], Prague, 1934.

Jubiläumsbericht *anlässlich des 80 jährigen Bestandes der deutschen Staatsfachschule fur Glasindustrie in Steinschönau*, Steinschönau, 1936.

Klesse, B. -Mayr, H., *Veredelte Gläser aus Renaissance und Barock, Sammlung Ernesto Wolf*, Vienna, 1987.

Mareš, F., České sklo [Bohemian Glass], Prague, 1893.

Mitscherlich, A., Die böhmische Glasindustrie der Vergangenheit und Gegenwart, Aussig, 1930.

Pazaurek, G.E., *Die Gläsersammlung des Nordböhmischen Gewerbemuseums in Reichenberg*, Leipzig, 1902.

Pazaurek, G.E., *Deutsche Fayence- und Porzellan-Hausmaler*, vol. I, Leipzig, 1925.

Pešatova, Z., *Bohemian Engraved Glass*, London, 1968.

Poche, E., *Le verre de Bohême*, Cahier de l'Histoire Mondiale, Paris, Unesco, 1959.

Schebek, E., *Böhmens Glasindustrie und Glashandel*, Prague, 1878.

Schmidt, R., *Das Glas*, Berlin-Leipzig, 1922.

Schmidt, R., *100 Jahre österreichische Glaskunst, Lobmeyr 1823-1923*, Vienna, 1925.

Strasser, R. von-Siegl, W., *Dekoriertes Glas. Renaissance bis Biedermeier*, Munich, 1989.

Tomek, W.W., *Dějepis města Prahy* [History of the City of Prague], vol. I, Prague, 1855, vol. II, Prague, 1871.

Vávra, J., *Pět tisic let sklářského díla* [Five thousand years of glass], Prague, 1953.

Catalogues

Adlerová, A. -Drahotová, O., *300 Years of Czechoslovakian Glass and Costume Jewellery*, Tokyo, 1983.

Adlerová, A. -Brožová, J. -Drahotová, O. -Hejdová, D., *Czechoslovakian Glass 1350-1980*, Corning, 1981.

Poche, E., *Sklo a výtvarník* [Glass and the designer], Prague, 1950.

Urbancová, J. -Svatoňová, J., *Sklárna Harrachov 1712-1987* [The Harrach Glassworks 1712-1987], Nový Bor, 1987.

Urešová, L., *Bohemian Glass*, London, 1965.

Articles

Hetteš, K., "O tradici šeského skla a jeho puvodnosti" ["On the Czech glass tradition and its originality"], *Tvar*, 1962, n. 13, p. 2-28.

Hetteš, K., "O umění našeho řezaného skla" ["On the art of our engraved glass"], *Vytvarné umení*, 1963, n. 13, p. 245-259. (Summary in German.)

Hetteš, K., "Úvaha nad osudem harrachovské sklárny" ["Some reflections on the fate of the Harrachov Glassworks"], *Tvar*, 1963, n. 14, p. 267-287. (Summary in French.)

THE MIDDLE AGES AND THE RENAISSANCE

Baumgartner, S., *Sächsisches Glas - Die Glashütten und ihre Erzeugnisse*, Wiesbaden, 1977.

Losos, L., *Počátky české gotické sklomalby* [Beginnings of Stained-Glass Windows in Bohemia], (Thesis at the Faculty of Letters of Charles University), Prague, 1967.

Mathesius, J., *Sarepta oder Bergpostill*, Nuremburg, 1592, re-ed., Prague, 1975.

Matouš, F., *Mittelalterliche Glasmalerei in der Tschechoslowakei. Corpusvitrearum medii aevi, Tschechoslowakei*, Prague, 1975.

Poche, E., «*Umělecké řemeslo*» [Decorative Arts], *in České umění gotické 1350-1420* [Gothic Art in Bohemia 1350-1420], Prague, 1970.

Rademacher, F., *Deutsche Gläser des Mittelalters*, Berlin, 1933.

Saldern, A. von, *German Enameled Glass, The Edwin J. Beinecke Collection and Related Pieces*, Corning, 1965.

Catalogues

Baumgartner, E. -Krueger, I., *Phoenix aus Sand und Asche, Glas des Mittelalters*, Bonn, Basel, 1988.

Articles

Chrzanowska, A., "Slaskie szkla ryte diamantem z XVI i XVII wieku w zbiorach polskich" ["Diamond-engraved Silesian Glasses from the sixteenth and seventeenth centuries in the Polish Collections"], *Roczniki Sztuki Slaskiej III*, Wroclaw, 1965, p. 147-155. (Summary in French.)

Drahotová, O., "Schürerové a Preusslerové jako výrobci kobaltového skla" [Cobalt-blue Glass from the Schürer and Preussler Glassworks], *Acta UPM*, XV, Prague, 1980. (Summary in German.)

Drahotová, O., "Identifying glass from the Buquoy glass factory at the Nové Hrady Estate (Gratzen, in the seventeenth century"), *Journal of Glass Studies*, vol. 23, 1981, p. 46-55.

Frýda, F., "Le verre médiéval de Plzeň", XXXIV, 1979, n. 8, p. 24-27.

Hejdová, D., "La verrerie moyenageuse de Sklenařice dans la Bohème du Nord", XVIII, 1963, n. 12, p. 360-364.

Hejdová, D., "Recherches archéologiques du four de verrerie de Sklenařice" *Ars Vitraria*, 1966, n. 1, p. 11-26. (Summary in French.)

Hejdová, D., "Types of Medieval Glass Vessels in Bohemia", *Journal of Glass Studies*, 1975, n. XVII, p. 145-150.

Hejdová, D. -Nechvatal, B., "Late 14th to Mid. 15th century medieval glass from a well in Plzen Western Bohemia", *Journal of Glass Studies*, 1970, n. 12, p. 84-101.

Hetteš, K., "De l'origine du verre de la mosaïque de la cathédrale Saint-Guy de Prague", *Revue du Verre*, XIII, 1958, n. 5, p. 3-7.

Hetteš, K., "Le verre de Bohème au Moyen Age", *Revue du Verre*, XIII, 1958, n. 7, p. 4-9, n. 9, p. 2-6.

Hetteš, K., "A significant contribution to the history of Bohemian glass-making of the 14th century", *Czechoslovak Glass Review*, XIV, 1959, n. 5, p. 15-18.

Hetteš, K., "Středověké skleněné číše z Benediktské ulice v Praze" ["The medieval glasses of Benediktská Street in Prague"], *Umění*, 1959, n. 7, p. 44-49.

Hetteš, K., "Venetian trends in Bohemian glassmaking in the sixteenth and seventeenth centuries", *Journal of Glass Studies*, 1963, n. 5, p. 39-53.

Lehečková, E., "Nové nálezy středověkého skla z Kutné Hory" ["New discoveries of medieval glass from Kutná Hora"], *Památky archeologické*, 1975, LXVI, p. 450-485. (Summary in German.)

Olmerová, H., "Découverte du verre du Moyen Age dans la vieille ville de Prague", *Revue du Verre*, XXXII, 1977, n. 5, p. 24-27.

THE BAROQUE PERIOD

Catalogues

Blažíček, O.J. -Hejdová, D. - Neumann, J. -Preiss, P., *Le Baroque en Bohème*, Grand Palais, Paris, 1981.

Drahotová, O., *Barokní Řezané sklo 1600-1760* [Baroque Engraved Glass 1600-1760], Prague, 1989.

Poche, E., *České sklo 17 a 18. století* [Bohemian glass in the seventeenth and eighteenth centuries], Prague, 1970.

Articles

Brožová, J., "České dvojstěnné sklo a jeho autoři" ["Double- walled glass and its creators"], *Acta UPM*, 8 C., Commentationes 1, Prague, 1973, p. 60-77. (Summary in German.)

Drahotová, O., "The circle of the master of the so-called Koula's goblet, a contribution to the problems of the development of engraved glass in the Bohemian-Silesian region", *Czechoslovak Glass Review*, XX, 1965, n. 11, p. 340-343.

Drahotová, O., "Bohemian glass decor in the style of Jean Berain", *Annales pour l'Histoire du Verre*, Ravenne et Venise, 1967, Liège, 1969, p. 193-199.

Drahotová, O., "Medaile a mince jako předlohy pro řezané barokní sklo v Uměleckoprumyslovém muzeu v Praze" ["Coins and Medals as Models for Baroque engraved glass at the Prague Museum of Decorative Arts"], *Ars Vitraria*, 1971, n. 3 Jablonec nad Nisou, p. 17-29. (Summary in French.)

Drahotová, O., "Le verre rubis tchèque à l'intersection des XVIIe et XVIIIe siècles", *Revue du Verre*, XXVIII, 1973, n. 4, p. 8-11.

Drahotová, O., "Severočeské barokní řezané sklo ve světle historicky lokalizovaných památek" ["Engraved glass of Northern Bohemia from the point of view of historical and local documents"], *Ars Vitraria*, 1973, n. 4, p. 20-35. (Summary in English.)

Drahotová, O., "K problematice českého skla v benátském stylu" ["On the problems of Venetian-style Czech Glass"], *Ars Vitraria*, 1979, n. 6, p. 11-22. (Summary in French.)

Drahotová, O., "Bohemian Baroque engraved Glass of the 17th and 18th centuries', Glass review, XXXVI, 1981, n. 10, p. 2-4.

Drahotová, O., "Comments on Caspar Lehmann, central European glass and hard stone engraving", *Journal of Glass Studies*, vol. 23, 1981, p. 34-45.

Drahotová, O., "Le verre gravé de la région de Nové Hrady dans la seconde moitié du XVIIIe siècle", *Revue du Verre*, XXXVII, 1982, n. 12, p. 13-17.

Drahotová, O., "Bohemian glass trade to Spain in the 18th century", *Annales du 10*[e] *congrès de l'Association pour l'Histoire du Verre*, Madrid, Segovie, 1985, Amsterdam, 1987.

Dreier, F.A., "Stichvorlagen und Zeichnungen zu Gläsern Christian Gottfried Schneiders", *Journal of Glass Studies*, vol. VII, 1965, p. 66-78.

Hirsch, E., "Die Erfindung des böhmischen Kristallglases", Mitteilungen des Vereins für Geschichte der Deutschen in Böhmen, 1936, 74, p. 42-66.

Holzhausen, W., "Dresden-Prager Glas- und Steinschnitt um 1600", *Neues Archiv für sächsische Geschichte und Altertumskunde*, 1934, 55.

Jiřík, F.X., "Ignatius Preissler, domácký malíř skla a porcelánu" ["Ignatius Preissler, In-house painter of glass and porcelain"], *Zprávy Kuratoria Uměleckoprumyslového muzea v Praze za rok 1923*, Prague, 1924, p. 4-20.

Meyer-Heisig, E., "Caspar Lehmann, ein Beitrag zur Frühgeschichte des deutschen Glasschnittes", *Anzeiger des Germanischen National-Museums 1963, Festschrift Ludwig Grote*, p. 116-131.

Müller-Hofstede, A., "Der schlesisch-böhmische Hausmaler Ignaz Preissler", *Keramos*, 1983, 100, p. 3-50.

Pazaurek, G.E., "Die Anfänge des deutschen Glasschnittes", *Glastechnische Berichte*. 1934, n. 12, p. 203-204.

Röver, F., "Caspar Lehmann von Uelzen, zur Biographie und Herkunft des ersten europäischen Glasschneiders der Neuzeit", *Niederdeutsche Beiträge-zur Kunstgeschichte*, 1965, n. 4, p.251.

Ryneš, V., "Z galerie zušlechtovatelu českého skla v Kamenickém Šenově na někdejším českokamenickém panství" ["New Names in the pleiad of Bohemian glass-makers and glass-refiners from Kamenický Šenov in the ex-domain of Česká Kamenice"], *Ars Vitraria*, 1966, n. 1, p. 121-125. (Summary in French.)

Schmidt, R. "Deutsche Hochschnittpokale" *Die Weltkunst 19*, June, 1949, issue 8, p. 2-4.

Strasser, R. von, "Twelve Preissler Glasses", *Journal of Glass Studies*, 1973, n. XV, p. 135-142.

Strasser, R. von, "Ignaz Preissler: frühe Arbeiten, weniger bekannte Meisterwerke und die Nachfolge", *Journal of Glass Studies*. 1987, n. 29, p. 81-109.

Urban, S., "Edelsteinschneider am Rudolphinischen Hofe in Prag und deren Einfluss auf die Entwicklung des böhmischen Barockglases", *Annales du 6e congrès de l'Association pour l'Histoire du Verre, Cologne, 1973*, Liège, 1974, p. 177-186.

Urban, S., "Řezáči drahých kamenu v Čechách v 16. a v 17. století" ["Fine stone-cutters in Bohemia in the sixteenth and seventeenth centuries"], *Acta UPM*, IX, D, 1976, Supplementa 2, Prague, p. 11-18. (Summary in German.)

FROM THE NEO-CLASSICAL TO HISTORICISM

Pazaurek, G.E., *Gläser der Empire-und Biedermeierzeit*, Leipzig, 1923.

Pazaurek, G.E. -Philippowitch, E. von, *Gläser der Empire-und Biedermeierzeit*, Braunschweig, 1976.

Catalogues

Brok, J. -Brožová, J. -Lukáš, V., *Severočeské sklo 19. století* [Nineteenth century Northern Bohemian Glass], Jablonec nad Nisou, 1970. (Summary in German.)

Brožková, H., *Böhmisches Glas des 19. Jahrhunderts aus dem Kunstgewerbemuseum Prag*, Berlin, 1983.

Brožová, J., *Historismus, Umělecké řemeslo 1860-1900* [Imitations of Past Styles in the Decorative Arts 1860-1900], Prague, 1975. (Summary in German.)

Brožová, J., *Bedřich Egermann (1777-1864) a severočeské sklo jeho doby* [Bedřich Egermann (1777-1864) and Glass of his time in Northern Bohemia], Nový Bor, 1977. (Summary in German.)

Brožová, J., *České sklo 1800-1860* [Bohemian Glass 1800- 1860], Prague, 1977.

Brožová, J., *České sklo století ze sbírek Uměleckoprumyslového muzea v Praze a Moravské galerie v Brně* [Bohemian Glass of the nineteenth century in the collections of the Prague Museum of Decorative Arts and the Moravian Gallery of Brno], Brno, 1979.

Steinschönau, *Die kaiserlich-königliche Fachschule für Glasindustrie, Gegendenkschrift zum vierzigjahrigen Bestande*, Steinschönau, 1896.

Articles

Brozková, H., "Vues de villes et de paysages sur verre de la moitié du XIXe siècle", *Revue du Verre*, XXXVII, 1982, n. 9, p. 2-7.

Brozová, J., "Le verre restauration de Harrachov et son exportation en Italie", *Revue du Verre*, XXVI, 1971, n. 8, p. 236-240.

Brožová, J., "Lithyaliny a Friedrich Egermann" ["Friedrich Egermann's Lithyalins"], *Ars Vitraria*, 1974, n. 5, Jablonec nad Nisou, p. 75-97. (Summary in English.)

Brožová, J., "Les lithyalines tchèques et Friedrich Egermann", *Revue du Verre*, XXXI, 1976, n. 7, p. 15-18.

Brožová, J., "Harrachovské sklo se zatavenými pastami z 2.čtvrti 19. století" ["Harrach glass with inlayed pastes from the second quarter of the nineteenth century"],*Ars Vitraria*, 1979, n. 6, Jablonec nad Nisou, p. 51-66. (Summary in French.)

Brožová, J., "Bohemian engraved glass of the 19th century", *Glass Review*, XXXVI, 1981, n. 10, p. 5-8.

Brožová, J., "L'époque classique du verre taillé en Bohême 1800-1850", *Revue du Verre*, XXXIX, 1984, n. 8, p. 16-21.

Brožová, J., "Le verre de Bor et les glacis de Friedrich Egermann", *Revue du Verre*, XXXXI, 1986, n. 7, p. 16-20.

Pešatová, Z., "Dominik Biemann", *Journal of Glass Studies*, vol VII, 1965, p. 83-106.

Seydel, H., "Beiträge zur Geschichte des Siegelstein-und Glasschnitts und der Glaserzeugung im Riesen-und Isergebirge", *Schlesiens Vorzeit im Bild und Schrift*, 1919, 7/2, p. 248.

Urbancová, J., "Neo-Renaissance and neo-Baroque ornament on North Bohemian engraved Glass", *Journal of Glass Studies*, n. 23, 1981, p. 74-81.

Vydrová, J., "Dva neznámí Biemannové" ["Two unknown Biemanns"], *Ars Vitraria*, 1966, n. 1, Jablonec nad Nisou, p. 73- 82. (Summary in French.)

FROM ART NOUVEAU TO THE END OF THE THIRTIES

Adlerová, A., *České užité umění 1918-1938* [Czech Decorative Arts 1918-1938], Prague, 1983.

Čadík,J., *Dílo Josefa Drahonovského* [The Work of Josef Drahoňovský], Prague, 1933.

Čadík,J., *Josef Drahoňovský*, Prague, 1937.

Janneau, G., *Modern Glass*, London, 1931.

Kotěra, J., *Práce mé mych záku 1898-1901* [My work and that of my students 1898-1901], Vienna, 1901.

Neuwirth, W., *Das Glas des Jugendstils*, Munich, 1973.

Neuwirth, W., *Glass 1905-1925*, Vienna, 1985.

Pazaurek, G.E., *Moderne Gläser*, Leipzig, 1901.

Pazaurek, G.E., *Kunstgläser der Gegenwart*, Leipzig, 1925.

Pešatová, Z. -Urban, S., *Jaroslav Brychta*, Liberec, 1963.

Catalogues

Adlerová, A., *Český funkcionalismus*, catalogue of the Prague Museum of Decorative Arts, vol. 3, Prague, 1978.

Adlerová, A., *Art deco, České sklo kolem roku 1925* [Art Deco, Bohemian Glass around 1925], Jablonec nad Nisou, 1980. (Summary in German.)

Adlerová, A., Česká secese, užité uměni [Art Nouveau in Bohemia, Decorative Arts], Prague, 1981. (Summary in German.)

Adlerová, A. -Mergl, J. -Panenková, D. -Ploil, E. -Ricke, H. -Vlček, T., Lötz, *Böhmisches Glas 1880-1940*, Prestel, 1989.

Darmstadt, *Tschechische Kunst 1878-1914*, Institut Mathildenhöhe, Darmstadt, 1984.

Tschechische Kunst der 20er und 30er Jahre, Institut Mathildenhöhe, Darmstadt, 1988.

Horneková, J., *Jaroslav Horejc, Výběr z díla, Výstava k 85, narozeninám* [Jaroslav Horejc, Selected Works, exhibition on the occasion of the artist's 85th birthday], Prague, 1971.

Poche, E. -Brožová, J., *Česka secese, Umění 1900* [Art Nouveau in Bohemia, Art 1900], Hluboká nad Vltavou-Brno, 1966.

Articles

Adlerová, A., "Sklo Marie Kirschnerové" ["Marie Kirschnerová's Glass"], *Acta UPM*, 8.C., Commentationes 1, Prague, 1973, p. 97-111. (Summary in German.)

Herain, K., "Ozdobné sklo" ["Decorative Glass"], *Umění*, 1929, n. 2, p. 381-406.

Hetteš, K., "Po stopách zapomenuté historie, Příspěvek k dějinám českého sklářství z let před první světovou válkou" ["Contribution to the history of the Bohemian Glass Industry in the years preceding World War I"], *Ars Vitraria*, 1966, n. 1, Jablonec nad Nisou, p. 83-95. (Summary in French.)

CONTEMPORARY CREATORS

Czech glass-makers took part in large international shows like the Universal Expositions of Brussels in 1958, Montreal in 1967 and Osaka in 1970, or the Milan Triennales in 1957 and 1960. They also displayed at large international glass exhibitions like the Corning in 1959 and 1979, the Coburg in 1977 and 1985, Kassel in 1981 and Sapporo in 1982, 1985 and 1988. A catalogue exists for each of these shows.

COLLECTIVE STUDIES

Adlerová, A., *Contemporary Bohemian Glass*, Prague, 1979.

Buechner, T.S. -Warmus, W., *Czechoslovakian Diary 1980*, Corning, 1980.

Grover, R. & L., *Contemporary Art Glass*, New York, 1975.

Raban, J., *Verre moderne de Bohème*, Prague, 1963.

Šindelář, D. *Současné umělecké sklo v Československu* [Contemporary Glass in Czechoslovakia], Prague, 1970.

Catalogues

Adlerová, A., *Tchechoslowakisches Glas*, Leipzig, 1964.

Adlerová, A., *Sklo severočeských výtvarníku* [Works by Northern Bohemian glass-makers], Prague, 1969.

Adlerová, A., *Böhmisches Glas der Gegenwart*, Hamburg, 1973.

Adlerová, A., *Moderne Tjekkoslovakisk Glas*, Copenhagen, 1983.

Adlerová, A., *Masters of Czech Glass 1945-1965*, London, 1983.

Adlerová, A., *Contemporary Czechoslovak Glass in Architecture*, University of London Institute of Education, London, 1986.

Adlerová, A. - Ebbinge Wubben, J.C., *Objecten van glas en ceramiek uit Tsjechoslowakije*, Rotterdam, 1970.

Adlerová, A. - Wacquez-Ermel C., *Artistes verriers de Tchécoslovakie* [Glass-making Artists of Czechoslovakia], Transparence Gallery, Brussels, 1988.

Barten, S.R., *Transparente For men, 4 Glasmacher aus Prag*, Zürich, 1977.

Bay Harbor, *Contemporary Czechoslovakian Glass*, Bay Harbor Islands, Florida, 1983-1985.

Berlin, *Kunsthandwerk aus der Tschechoslowakei*, Berlin- Erfurt, 1985.

Boca Raton, *Contemporary Glass Art*, Boca Raton, 1985.

Bràme, *Modernes Glas aus der Tschechoslowakei*, Bràme, 1980.

Couren, J.P., *Sculptures et volumes de verre*, Annecy, 1979.

Drdácká-Rossini, P., *Amsterdam Chamber Symposium*, Amsterdam, 1986.

Eisenbeis, C., *Glaskunst der Gegenwart, Kassel*, 1977.

Gotthelf, F., *1982 Jugend gestaltet*, Munich, 1982.
Gotthelf, F., *1983 Jugend gestaltet*, Munich, 1983.
Habatat Gallery, Czech Glass, Lathrup Village, 1984.
Hetteš K., *Současné sklo, Deset let práce československých výtvarníku* [Contemporary Glass, ten years of work by Czechoslovakian artists], Liberec, 1955.
Hetteš, K. -Mariacher, G. -Perrot, P.N., *Glass Czechoslovakia and Italy*, New York, 1964.
Horneková, J., *Kulturtage der Tchechoslowakischen Sozialistischen Republik in Österreich*, Vienna, 1986.
Horneková, J. -Petrová S., *Scultura in vetro e ceramica collezione del Museo delle arti decorative di Praga*, Capua, 1987.
Langhamer, A., *Interglass Symposium Československo 82-85*, Nový Bor, 1985. (Czech - English).
Medková, J., *Sklenĕna plastika* [Sculpture in Glass], Brno, 1987.
Melniková-Papoušková, N., *Nové cesty skla* [New Paths of Glass], Prague, 1951.
Mladek, M., *Seven Masters Czechoslovak Glass*, New York, 1983.
Munich, *Exempla '79, Arbeit und Lebensform im Kunsthankwerk*, Munich, 1979.
Munich, *Kunst in Glas aus der Tschechoslowakei*, Munich, 1981.
Munoz, Pilar, *Vidre d'art*, Barcelona, 1987.
Neuwegein, *Architectonische en geometrische glassculpturen*, Neuwegein, 1984.
Nickl, P., *Jugend gestaltet*, Munich, 1985.
Nickl, P., *Jugend gestaltet*, Munich, 1989.
Ohm, A. - Bauer, M., *Modernes Glas aus Amerika, Europa und Japan*, Frankfurt, 1976.
Petrová, S., *New Czech Glass, pupils of Professor Stanislav Libenský*, Riihimäki, 1988.
Petrová, S., *Sovremennaja stekljannaja plastika* [Contemporary Glass Sculpture], Moscow, 1988.
Ricke, H., *Licht - Form - Gestalt. Objekte aus geschliffenem Glas, Düsseldorf*, 1980.
Roztoky, *"4 x 4"*, Roztoky u Prahy, 1984.
Suda, K., *11 Vitraj 1984/1985*, Červenec, 1985.
Suda, K., *Prostor* 1 [Space 1], Prague, 1982.
Suda, K., *Prostor* 2 [Space 2], Prague, 1983.
Suda, K., *Prostor* 3 [Space 3], Prague, 1986.
Toledo, *Contemporary Glass, National-International*, Toledo, 1984.
Washington, *Art in Glass, Glass in Art*, Washington, 1981.

ARTICLES

Adlerová, A., "Sklo, objekty a plastiky" ["Glass, objects and sculptures"], *Umĕnía řemesla*, 1974, n. 4, p. 18-31. (Summary in French.)
Adlerová, A. "Le verre moderne", *Revue du Verre*, XXXXI, 1986, n. 1, p. 34-36.
Adlerová, A., "Tschechoslowakische Glasplastik 1983", *Neues Glas*, 1983, n. 3, p.125.
Adlerová, A., "Les artistes tchécoslovaques du deuxième prix de Cobourg", *Revue du Verre*, XXXXI, 1986, n. 1, p. 18-23.
[Verre d'art], *Revue du Verre*, 1986, n. 2, p. 34-36.
Buechner, T.S. -Warmus, W., *Czechoslovakian Diary: 1980, 23 Glassmakers*, Corning, 1981.
Borrmann, G., "Junge Gestalter", *Kunst + Handwerk*, 1980, n. 2, p. 55.
Candamo, L.G. de, "Los escultores checoslovacos exponen en Madrid" *TG*, 1980, n. 30, p. 52-55.
Drdácká, P. "Unir la pensée loqique à l'intuition créatrice" *Revue du Verre*, XXXVII, 1982, n. 3, p. 18-23.
Drdácká, P., "La recherche d'une nouvelle communication du verre", *Revue du Verre*, XXXVII, 1982, n. 7, p. 2-38.
Drdácká, P., "Premier colloque verrier international à Nový Bor", *Revue du Verre*, XXXIX, 1984, n. 12, p. 17-43.
Drdacka, P. "Glaskunst in der Tschechoslowake", *Neues Glas*, 1984; n. 3, p. 163.
Dracka, P. "La création exclusive d'auteurs en verrerie", Revue de Verre XXXIX, 1984, n. 10, p. 2-13.
Hartmann, A., "Mission actuelle du métier d'art en Tchécoslovquie", *Revue du Verre*, XXXIX, 1984, n. 12, p. 17-43.
Kaplický, J., "Sklo" ["Glass"], *Tvar*, 1953, n. 5, p. 231-235. (Summary in German.)
Klivar, M., "L'exposition World Glass Now 82", *Revue du Verre*, XXXVII, 1982, n. 11, p. 19-21.
Klivar, M., "Anciens élèves de l'atelier du professeur Stanislav Libenský", *Revue du Verre*, XXXIX, 1984, n. 9, p. 14- 15.
Klivar, M., "Deux sculptures de verre", *Revue du Verre*, XXXIX, 1984, n. 9, p. 14-15.
Klivar, M., "Vers une nouvelle expression artistique", *Revue du Verre*, XXXII, 1987, n. 8, p. 20-24.
Kříž, J., "Espace I - 1982", *Revue du Verre*, XXXVIII, 1983, n. 4, p. 13-15.
Langhamer, A., "Gravures sur verre sorties des ateliers d'artistes", *Revue du Verre*, XXXVIII, 1983, n. 2, p. 12-16.
Langhamer, A., "Le verre tchécoslovaque", *Revue du Verre*, XXXX, 1985, n. 9, p. 3-45.
Langhamer, A., "Une haute appréciation des artistes verriers tchécoslovaques", *Revue du Verre*, XXXX, 1985, n. 4, p. 27-28.
Maršiková, J., "Sochařka skla" ["The woman glass sculptor"], Domov, 1977, n. 5, p. 28-31.
Maršiková, J., "Verre de l'atelier de jeunes artistes", *Revue du Verre*, XXXV, 1980, n. 9, p. 2-8.
Mžyková, M., "Les activités créatrices des jeunes verriers", *Revue du Verre*, XXXX, 1985, n. 7, p. 22-24.
Nicola, G., "Junge Glaskünstler aus der CSSR und aus Deutschland", *Neues Glas*, 1984, n. 2, p. 91.
Nicola, G., "Junge Europäische Glasgestalter", *Neues Glas*, 1985, n. 2, p. 73-74.
Petrová, S., "Le verre et la céramique contemporains des collections du musée des Arts décoratifs de Prague", *Revue du Verre*, XXXXII, 1987, n. 7, p. 14-19.
Pohribny, A., "A la recherche d'un nouveau style dans le domaine du verre gravé", *Revue du Verre*, XI, 1963, n. 12, p. 325- 331.
"L'oeuvre plastique de verre 1983", *Revue du Verre*, XXXVIII, 1983, n. 12, p. 12-21.
"Le verre d'art contemporain et la tradition", *Revue du Verre*, XXXV, 1980, n. 2, p. 2.
Ricke, H., "IIIe Quadriennale Erfurt", *Neues Glas*, 1982, n. 4, p. 202.
Schou-Christensen, J., "Der grosse Aufbruch, Europäische Glaskunst seit 1945", *Neues Glas*, 1980, n. 1, p. 9.
Skarlandtová, J., "Trois artistes de Tchécoslovaquie aux galeries Habatat", *Revue du Verre*, XXXXII, 1987, n. 8, p. 16-19.
Sotola, V., "Sculptures de verre", *Revue du Verre*, XXIV, 1969, n. 6, p. 162-164.
Suda, K., "L'espace de jeu, le jeu de l'espace", *Neues Glas*, 1984, n. 4, p. 187-191.
Suda, K. -Ricke, H., "Form und Bedeutung", *Neues Glas*, 1981, n. 3, p. 117.
Vojta, J.M. "Quatre journées d'expérimentation", *Revue du Verre*, XXXV, 1980, n. 4, p. 2-7.

STUDIES BY ARTIST

ILJA BILEK

Hartmann, A., *Sklo - Ilja Bílek* [Glass - Ilja Bílek], Liberec, 1987.

VACLAV CIGLER

Adlerová, A., *Václav Cigler, Glasobjecten*, Rotterdam, 1975.
Klivar, M., "Václav Cigler - Créateur et philosophe", *Revue du Verre*, XXXVII, 1982, n. 9, p. 24-27.
Maršiková, J., "Václav Cigler", *Revue du Verre*, XXXIV, 1979, n. 4, p. 6-9.
Šotola, V., *Josef Hospodka - Václav Cigler*, Vienna, 1969.

BOHUMIL ELIÁŠ

Adlerová, A., "Kapka Toušková et Bohumil Eliáš, le verre dans l'architecture", *Revue du Verre*, XXX, 1975, n. 7, p. 18-21.
Klivar, M., *Bohumil Eliáš, Obrazy a sklo* [Bohumil Eliáš, paintings and glasses], Prague, 1985.
Klivar, M., "Vers une nouvelle expression artistique", *Revue du Verre*. XXXXII, 1987, n. 8, p. 20-23.
Petrová, S., "Bohumil Eliáš. Optik und Kinetik", *Neues Glas*, 1989, n. 2, p. 103-107.

JAN EXNAR

Drdácká, P., *Jan Exnar a František Janák*, Prague, 1984.
Maršiková, J., "Verre de l'atelier de jeunes artistes", *Revue du Verre*, XXXV, 1980, n. 9, p. 2-8.

JAN FIŠAR

Kříž, J., "La série dramatique de Jan Fišar", *Revue du Verre*, XXXXIV, 1989, n. 4, p. 20-23.

MILAN HANDL

Petrová, S., "Une exposition d'oeuvres contemporaines de verre tchèque en Finlande", *Revue du Verre*, XXXXIV, 1989, n. 1, p. 11-13.

JIŘI HARCUBA

Adlerová, A., "Les gravures de portraits de Jirí Harcuba", *Revue du Verre*, XXXVI, 1981, n. 10, p. 12.
Holešovský, K., *Jiří Harcuba, sklo, medaile, mince* [Jiří Harcuba, glass, medals, coins], Brno, 1979.
Holešovský, K., *Jiří Harcuba, sochař, rytec skla, medailer* [Jiří Harcuba, sculptor, glass-engraver, medal-maker], Rychnov nad Kněžnou, 1981.
Holešovský, K., *Tvář, intaglie a medaile Jiřího Harcuby* [The face, intaglio and medals of Jiří Harcuba], Brno, 1988.
Schmitt, E., "Jiří Harcuba - Portatschnitt heute", *Neues Glas*, 1988, n.3, p. 206-210.
Trnková, J., *Jiří Harcuba, sklenené intaglie, lité medaile, ryté a broušené sklo* [Jiří Harcuba, glass intaglio, medals, cut and engraved glass], Semily, 1983.

PAVEL HLAVA

Drdácká, P., "Pavel Hlava, une personnalité du domaine de l'art du verre", XXXIX, 1984, n. 6, p. 14-18.
Hettes, K., "Pavel Hlava, les réflexions", *Revue du Verre*, XXIX, 1974, n. 12, p. 2-4.
Langhamer, A., *Pavel Hlava život a práce* [Pavel Hlava, life and work], Nový Bor, 1986. (Summary in English.)
Langhamer, A., "Une exposition du verre de Pavel Hlava", *Revue du Verre*, XXXXII, 1987, n. 1, p. 25-29.
Poche, E., *Pavel Hlava*, Prague, 1970.
Pohribný, A., "Pavel Hlava", *Revue du Verre*, XVII, 1962, n. 10, p. 203.
Šindelář, D., *Pavel Hlava, Vladimír Jelínek, Adolf Matura*, Prague, 1970.
Šindelář, D., "Nouvelles créations de verre de Pavel Hlava", *Revue du Verre*, XXV, 1970, n. 6, p. 166-169.

IVANA HOUSEROVÁ

Petrová, S., "Une exposition d'oeuvres contemporaines de verre tchèque en Finlande", *Revue du Verre*, XXXXIV, 1989, n. 1, p. 11-13.

FRANTIŠEK JANÁK

Drdácká, P., *Jan Exnar a František Janák*, Prague, 1984.
Drdácká, P., "Le verre taillé de František Janák", *Revue du Verre*, XXXX, 1985, n. 8, p. 16-20.
Horneková, J., *František Janák*, Cheb, 1988.

VLADIMIR JELÍNEK

Klivar, M., *Vladimír Jelínek sklo o brazy kresby grafika*, Prague, 1984.
Klivar, M., "The Glass Art of Vladimír Jelínek", *Glass Review*, XXXIX, 1984, n. 4, p. 10-15.
Šindelář, D., *Pavel Hlava, Vladimír Jelínek, Adolf Matura*, Prague, 1970.

JOSEF KAPLICKÝ

Kaplický, J., "Sklo", *Tvar*, 1953, n. 5, p. 231-235. (Summary in German.)

MARIAN KAREL

Maršíková, J., "Le verre sortant de l'atelier de jeunes artistes. Marian Karel", *Revue du Verre*, XXXV, 1980, n. 7, p. 6-9.
Šindelář, D., *Sklo - Marian Karel, Oldřich Plíva, Aleš Vašíček, Ján Zoričák*, Prague, 1981.
Vondra, V., "Expositions aux Etats-Unis", *Revue du Verre*, XXXXII, 1987, n. 12, p. 23-25.

Vladímir Kopecký

Stará, E., "Vladimír Kopecký et huit autres créateurs", *Revue du Verre*, XXXXIII, 1988, n. 1, p. 15-19.

Trinkewitz, K., "Vladimír Kopecký und das Glas", Im Herzen Europas, 1966, n. 3, p. 20-21.

Jan Kotík

Jan Kotík, Arbeiten aus den Jahren 1980-1985, Figuren, Essen, 1986.

Herman, E., "Glaser von Jan Kotík", Bildende Kunst, 1957, n. 12, p. 841.

Kotík, J., "Vzorovaní hutnického skla" ["Shaped glass"], *Tvar*, 1952, n.5/6, p. 129.

Kotík, J., "Die zeitgenossische tschechische Glasschneidekdunst", *Bildende Kunst*, 1956, p. 553.

Stanislav Libenský - Jaroslava Brychtová

Adlerová, A., "Les débuts créateurs de Stanislav Libenský (verre peint 1945-1948), en commémoration du 65e anniversaire de l'auteur", *Revue du Verre* XXXXI, 1986, p. 9-13.

Chihuly, D., *Libenský - Brychtová, glass, sculpture*, New York, 1988.

Drdácká, P., "The sculptures of Jaroslava Brychtová and Stanislav Libenský in the U.S.A.", *Glass Review*, XXXVI, 1981, n. 1, p. 10-13.

Drdácká, P., "Stanislav Libenský péda-gogue", *Revue du Verre*, XXXVI, 1981, n. 3, p. 23-25.

"Stanislav Libenský, successor to prof. Kaplický at the Academy of Applied Arts", *Glass Review*, XIX, 1964, n. 1, p. 10-15.

Kehlmann, R., "A talk with Stanislav Libenský", *Glass Art Society Journal*, 1981, p. 28-32.

Klein, D. -Stern, N. -Petrová, S., *Stanislav Libensky et Jaroslava Brychtová*, Paris, 1988.

Langhamer, A., "Les oeuvres plastiques fondues de Stanislav Libenský, artiste et péda-gogue", *Revue du Verre*, XXXXI, 1986, n. 11, p. 9-15.

"Derrière le rideau de verre, Libenský, Brychtová, interview", *L'Atelier*, 1989, n. 1, p. 35-40.

Libenský, S., "The 20th Century Revival of Glassmaking in Czechoslovakia", *Glass Art Society Journal*, 1981, p. 33-35.

Libenský, S., "Stanislav Libenský et Jaroslava Brychtová: A 40 Year, Retrospecitive - Czechoslovakian Glass Art", *Neues Glas*, 1982, n. 1, p. 2-10.

Petrová, S., *Stanislav Libenský - Jaroslava Brychtová*, Národní glaerie v Praze, Prague, 1989. (Summary in English.)

Warmus, W., "The Art of Libenský and Brychtová", *Neues Glas*, 1985, n. 2, p. 132-144.

Věra Lišková

Hetteš, K., *Glas von Věra Lišková*, J. und L. Lobmeyr, Vienna, 1973.

Klivar, M., "Le verre de Věra Lišková", *Revue du Verre*, XXXVII, 1982, n. 11, p. 8-13.

Ladýřová, L., *Sklo Věra Liškové* [Věra Lišková's Glass], Pardubice, 1970.

Maršíková, J., "L'atelier de Věra Lišková", *Revue du Verre*, XIII, 1968, n. 10, p. 335-338.

Maršíková, J., "L'exposition de verre de Věra Lišková", *Revue du Verre*, 1972, n. 9, p. 270-274.

Rejl, R., "Une idée de l'artiste Věra Lišková", *Revue du Verre*, XXIII, 1968, n. 2, p. 47-49.

"Les oeuvres plastiques de verre de Věra Lišková", *Revue du Verre*, XXXII, 1977, n. 7, p. 10-14.

Stehlík, Z., "Le monde imaginaire de Věra Lišková", *Revue du Verre*, XXIX, 1974, n. 7, p. 23-25.

Václav Machač

Kříž, J., "Les sculptures de verre de Václav Machač", *Revue du Verre*, XXXX, 1985, n. 2, p. 16-18.

Ivan Mareš

Petrová, S., "Une exposition d'oeuvres contemporaines de verre tchèque en Finlande", *Revue du Verre*, XXXXIV, 1989, n. 1, p. 11-13.

Adolf Matura

Drdácká, P., "Adolf Matura", *Revue du Verre*, XXXV, 1980, n. 1, p. 2-9.

Drdácká, P., "Glasgestalter Adolf Matura", *Fur Sie aus der Tschechoslowakei*, 1979.

Hlava, P., "Adolf Matura", *Revue du Verre*, XVI, 1961, p. 206.

Langhamer, A., "A propos des résultats de la coopération avec Adolf Matura", *Revue du Verre*, XXXI, 1976, n. 12, p. 12-16.

Matura, A., "Tři roky práce výt*varn*ého střediska prumyslu skla v Praze", *Tvar 8*, 1956, n. 5, p. 146.

Šindelář, D., *Pavel Hlava, Vladimír Jelínek, Adolf Matura*, Prague, 1970.

Alois Metelák

Adlerová, A., *Alois Metelák, sklo z let 1924-1963* [Alois Metelák, work from the years 1924-1963], Prague, 1963.

Langhamer, A., "Alois Metelák octogénaire", *Revue du Verre*, XXXII, 1977, n. 8, p. 12-15.

Langhamer, A., "Alois Metelák in memo-riam", *Glass Review*, XXXVI, 1981, n. 3, p. 26.

Metelák, A., "Pětadvacet let práce o vývoji nového českého uměleckého skla", *Českoslo-vensko I*, 1948, n. 3, p. 1.

Jiří Nekovař

Petrová, S., "Une exposition d'oeuvres contemporaines de verre tchèque en Finlande", *Revue du Verre*, XXXXIV, 1989, n. 1, p. 11-13.

Ladislav Oliva

Hofmeisterová, J., "Ladislav Oliva", *Revue du Verre*, XVI, 1961, p. 274.

Klivar, M., *Ladislav Oliva sklo* [Ladislav Oliva, Glass], Jablonec nad Nisou, 1987. (Summary in English and German.)

Langhamer, A., "Deux artistes verriers et un créateur de bijoux", *Revue du Verre*, XXXXII, 1987, n. 12, p. 18-22.

Vondra, V., "Collection de Ladislav Oliva á Crystalex", *Revue du Verre*, XXXXIII, 1988, n. 5, p. 6-7.

Oldřich Plíva

Maršíková, J., "Le verre sortant des ateliers de jeunes artistes, Oldřich Plíva", *Revue du Verre*, XXXV, 1980, n. 3, p. 15-16.

Šindelář, D., *Sklo - Marian Karel, Oldřich Plíva, Aleš Vašíček, Ján Zoricák*, Prague, 1981.

Suda, K., *Oldřich Plíva*, Badisches Landesmuseum, Karlsruhe, 1987.

Jaroslav Rona

Zadražil, P., *Jaroslav Róna, paintings 1980-1988*, Prague, 1988.

René Roubíček

Adlerová, A., *René Roubíček Sklo, Miluše Roubíčková-Kytková/Sklo*, Okresni galerie v Ji číne, Březen, 1982.

Adlerová, A. -Hetteš, K. -Kříž, J., *René und Miluše Roubíčk, Arbeiten 1950-1987*, galerie Gottschalk-Betz, Frankfurt, 1987.

Kříž, J., "L'homme et les choses de René Roubíček", *Revue du Verre*, XXXXII, 1987, n. 9, p. 25-28.

Langhamer, A., "Miluše et René Roubíček", *Revue du Verre*, XXXVIII, 1983, n. 1, p. 12-17.

Mašek, V., "Médaille d'or de René Roubíček et Laděna Víznerová à Munich", *Revue du Verre*, XXIV, 1969, p. 309.

Roubíček, R. "L'apport des artistes tchéco-slovaques à la création mondiale du verre", *Revue du Verre*, XVI, 1961, n. 5, p. 143.

Roubíček, R. "Le verre modelé de nos jours", *Revue du Verre*, XVI, 1961, n. 11, p. 312.

Miluše Roubíčková

Adlerová, A., *René Roubíček/Sklo, Miluše Roubíčková- Kytková/Sklo*, Okresni galerie v Jičíně, Březen, 1982.

Adlerová, A. -Hetteš, K. -Kříž, J., *René und Miluše Roubíček, Arbeiten 1950-1987*, galerie Gottschalk-Betz, Frankfurt, 1987.

Hetteš, K., "Miluše Roubíčková und ihr Glas", Für Sie aus der Tschechoslowakei, 1975, n. 3, p. 38-40.

Langhamer, A., "Miluše et René Roubíček", *Revue du Verre*, XXXVIII, 1983, n. 1, p. 12-17.

Eliška Rožátová

Klivar, M., "La manière personnelle de voir le verre de Eliška Rožátová", *Revue du Verre*, XXXIX, 1984, p. 16-17.

Ivo Rozsypal

Klivar, M., *Ivo Rozsypal, Luft-Wasser-Erde-Zivilisation*, Frankfurt, 1987.

Langhamer, A., *Ivo Rozsypal, ten years of artistic cooperation with the Crystalex Branch corporation at Nový Bor, New Hall*, Prague, 1984. (Summary in English and German.)

Langhamer, A., "Ivo Rozsypal, six années de coopération avec Crystalex dans le domaine du design", *Revue du Verre*, XXXX, 1985, n. 6, p. 22-27.

Schnitt, P., "Störfaktor Zivilisation Glasskulpturen von Ivo Rozsypal", *Neues Glas*, 1988, n. 3, p. 201-205.

Vamberecká, J., "Le profil de la création d'Ivo Rozsypal", *Revue du Verre*, XXXVI, 1981, n. 1, p. 14-19.

Vojta, M., "Ivo Rozsypal et le verre peint", *Revue du Verre*, XXXI, 1976, n. 1, p. 20-23.

Jaromír Rybák

Petrová, S. *Jaromír Rybák Skulpturen aus Glas*, Essen, 1988.

Rusquec, C. du, "Jaromír Rybák", *La Revue de la Céramique et du Verre*, 1986, n. 26, p. 29-30.

Suda, K., "The Glass Object - The Space of Drawings", *Neues Glas*, 1985, n. 4, p. 258-261.

Gizela Šaboková

Adlerová, A., "Les objets et les tableaux de verre de Gizela Šabóková", *Revue du Verre*, XXXXII, 1987, n. 7, p. 20-24.

Klivar, m., "Les oeuvres de Gizela Šabó-ková", *Revue du Verre*, XXXXII, 1987, n. 1, p. 9.

Schránilová, E., *Gizela Šabóková, sklo*, Prague, 1986.

Ludvika Smrčková

Adlerová, A., "Le double jubilé de Ludvika Smrčková", *Revue du Verre*, XXVIII, 1973, n. 2, p. 3-7.

Adlerová, A., *Czechoslovak Exhibition of Glass Works of Art by Mrs Ludvika Smrčková*, Coventry, 1974.

Adlerova, A., *Ludvika Smrčkova, Sklařske dílo 1923-1978* [Ludvika Smrčkova, Glassworks 1923-1978], Prague, 1978.

Adlerová, A., "A l'occasion du soixante-quinzième anniversaire de Ludvika Smrčková", *Revue du Verre*, XXXIII, 1978, n. 2, p. 5-10.

Adlerová, A., *Ludvika Smrčková, sklárské dilo 1923-1983* [Ludvika Smrčková, glass-making work 1923-1983], Prague, 1983.

Drdácká, P., "Une vie consacrée au verre", *Revue du Verre*, XXXVIII, 1983, n. 6, p. 21-27.

Drdácká, P., "Revue de la création de toute une vie", *Revue du Verre*, XXXIX, 1984, n. 4, p. 24-26.

Hetteš, K., *Sklo Ludviky Smrčkové* [Ludvika Smrčková's Glass], Pardubice, 1959.

Hofmeisterová, J., "Le nouveau verre de Ludvika Smrčková", *Revue du Verre*, XXV, 1970, n. 7, p. 197-202.

Holuborá, M., *Ludvika Smrčková*, Prague, 1961.

Výstava skla Ludviky Smrčkové 1923-1958 [Ludvika Smrčková's Glass Exhibit], Jablonec nad Nisou, 1958.

Langhamer, A., "L'oeuvre de la vie de Ludvika Smrčková", *Revue du Verre*, XXXXIII, 1988, n. 2, p. 22-27.

Melniková-Papoušková, N., *Skleněný sen Ludviky Smrčkové* [Dream in glass by Ludvika Smrčková], Prague, 1948.

Pešatová, Z., "Honneur au 65e anniversaire de Ludvika Smrčková", *Revue du Verre*, XXIII, 1968, n. 5, p. 150-159.

Plátek, V., *Ludvika Smrčková, sklo 1945-1960*, Prague, 1960.

Smrčková, L., "New Czechoslovak Engraved Glassware", *Revue du Verre*, VI, 1951, n. 4, p. 7.

Smrčková, L., "Nové *tvary* českého broušeného křišťálového skla" ["New forms of cut Czechoslovakian glass"], *Tvar 4*, 1951, p. 208.

Urbancová, J., *Ludvika Smrčková, Vyběr ze sklářského díla 1945-1983*, [Ludvika Smrčková, retrospective 1945-1983], Jablonec nad Nisou, 1983.

IVANA ŠRÁMKOVÁ-ŠOLCOVÁ

Petrová, S., "Une exposition d'oeuvres contemporaines de verre tchèque en Finlande", *Revue du Verre*, XXXXIV, 1989, n. 1, p. 11-13.

VRATISLAV ŠOTOLA

Adlerová, A., *Vratislav Šotola, sklo*, Prague, 1981.

"Le verre utilitaire moulé de Jiří Brabec et Vratislav Šotola", *Revue du Verre*, XXXVII, 1982, n. 12, p. 18.

Drdácká, P., "Vratislav Šotola, interview avec un artist verrier", *Revue du Verre*, XXX-VII, 1982, n. 10, p. 26-27.

Klivar, M. "Le verre de Vratislav Šotola", *Revue du Verre* , XXXVII, 1982, n. 10, p. 26-27.

Šotola, L., "Um die Gestaltung sandgestrahlten Kristallglases", *Glaswelt*, 7, 1963, p. 48.

JIŘÍ ŠUHÁJEK

Adlerová, A., "Jiří Šuhájek", *Revue du Verre*, XXXVII, 1982, n. 4, p. 12-17.

Klivar, M., "L'oeuvre plastique de verre vitalisite de Jiří Šuhájek", *Revue du Verre*, XXXIX, 1984, n. 7, p. 17-20.

Klivar, M., *Jiří Šuhájek, eighteen years of cooperation with the Crystalex State Corporation*, Nový Bor, 1989. (Summary in Czech.)

Sherman, E., "Jiří Šuhájek's Viscous Humor", New Work, 1987, n. 28, p. 10-11.

JAROSLAV SVOBODA

Čubrda, Z., *Jaroslav Svoboda, sklo* [Jaroslav Svoboda, Glass], Brno, 1972.

Čubrda, Z., *Jaroslav Svoboda, skleněná plastika* [Jaroslav Svoboda, sculpture in glass], Prague, 1979.

Holešovský, K. *Jaroslav Svoboda, vyběr ze sklářského díla 1970-1984* [Jaroslav Svoboda, selected works from 1970-1984], Brno, 1985.

Medková, J., *Jaroslav Svoboda*, Prague, 1974.

Valoch, J., *Jaroslav Svoboda*, Brno, 1978.

Černý, B., "Jaroslav Svoboda, artiste et pédagogue", *Revue du Verre*, XXXIII, 1988, n. 5, p. 21-25.

Maršíková, J., "Les objets de verre de Jaroslav Svoboda", *Revue du Verre*, XXXIV, 1979, n. 3, p. 16-20.

FRANTIŠEK TEJML

Raban, J., *Le verre moderne de Bohême*, Prague, 1963.

DALIBOR TICHÝ

Adlerová, A., "In Remembrance of Dalibor Tichý", *Neues Glas*, 1985, n. 4, p. 269.

Adlerová, A., "Dalibor Tichý in memoriam", *Umění a řemesla*, 1986, n. 3, p. 56. (Summary in English).

Drdácká, P., "Méditations poétiques de Dalibor Tichý", *Revue du Verre*, XXXVI, 1981, n. 8, p. 20-23.

Drdácká, P.,"Dalibor Tichý, un jeune artiste verrier tchécoslovaque", *Revue du Verre*, XXXVIII, 1983, n. 4, p. 19-23.

Skarlandtová, J., "Le legs de verre de Dalibor Tichý", *Revue du Verre*, XXXXI, 1986, n. 8, p. 9-13.

PAVEL TRNKA

Adlerová, A., "Pavel Trnka", *Umění a řemesla*, 1989, n. 2, p. 38-39. (Summary in English.)

Mžyková, M., *Trnka, Budíková*, Mělník, 1982.

Mžyková, M., "Les objets de verre de Pavel Trnka", *Revue du Verre*, XXXX, 1985, n. 3, p. 23-25.

Scremini, C., "L'Art de désobéir, une voie pour continuer fidèlement", *La Revue de la Céramique et du Verre*, 1987, n. 35, p. 48-49.

Trnka, P., *Pavel Trnka, Glasobjekte*, Hanover, 1988.

Vondra, V., "Les oeuvres de Pavel Trnka", *Revue du Verre*, XXXXIV, 1989, n. 1, p. 18.

DANA VACHTOVÁ

Kříž, J., *Dana Vachtová, skleněná plastika - Jaroslava Severová, grafika* [Dana Vachtová, sculpture in glass - Jaroslava Severová, engravings], Prague, 1984.

Maršíková, J., "La femme-sculpteur Dana Vachtová", *Revue du Verre*, XXXVI, 1981, n. 8, p. 11-14.

KAREL VANURA

Petrová, S., "Karel Vaňura, Peintre, graveur, pédagogue, artiste-verrier", *Revue du Verre*, XXXXIII, 1988, n. 6, p. 22-27.

MILENA VELÍŠKOVÁ

Digrin, I., "Milena Velíšková", *Tvar*, VIII, 1957, n. 8, p. 242-249.

FRANTIŠEK VÍZNER

Holešovský, K., *František Vízner*, 1962-1982, Brno, 1983.

Holešovský, K., "Le verre de Vízner á la galerie Moravian", *Revue du Verre*, XXXIX, 1984, n. 2, p. 17-21.

Kreps, M., *František Vízner, sklo*, 1980.

Maršíková, J., "Les trois types de la création verrière de František Vízner", *Revue du Verre*, XXIV, 1969, n. 8, p. 231-235.

Maršíková, J., "Le verre de František Vízner en architecture", *Revue du Verre*, XXXI, 1976, n. 6, p. 12-16.

Warmus, W., "František Vízner", New Work, 1988, n. 33, p. 26-27.

KAREL WÜNSCH

Adlerová, A., "Karel Wünsch, le verre dans l'intérieur", *Revue du Verre*, XXXI, 1976, n. 6, p. 2-6.

Adlerová, A., "Karel Wünsch, 25 années d'activité créatrice", *Revue du Verre*, XXXX, 1985, n. 10, p. 22-26.

Dolejš, *Eva Brodská, gobelíny - Karel Wünsch, sklo* [Eva Brodská, tapestries - Karel Wünsch, glass], Litomerice, 1977.

Stehlík, Z., "Karel Wünsch", *Revue du Verre*, XXIV, 1969, n. 9, p. 264-268.

ASKOLD ŽÁČKO

Adlerová, A., "Askold Žáčko, Prinzip Vielseitgkeit", *Neues Glas*, 1987, n. 4, p. 271-275.

Klivar, M., "Askold Žáčko, artiste et pédagogue", *Revue du Verre*, XXXVIII, 1983, n. 2, p. 17-19.

Lovíšková, D., *Askold Žáčko, sklenené objekty* [Askold Žáčko, glass objects], Trenčin, 1986.

DANA ZÁMEČNÍKOVÁ

Chambers, K.S., "Dana Zámečníková: Artist and Magician", Craft International, 1985, January - March, p. 20.

Suda, K., *Dana Zámečníková, Objects*, Prague, 1980.

Suda, K., "L'espace de jeu, le jeu de l'espace, oeuvres de verre de Dana Zámečníková", *Revue du Verre*, XXXVII, 1982, n. 5, p. 24-27.

Suda, K., "Play of Space, Space of Play", *Neues Glas*, 1984, n. 4, p. 187-191.

Vondra, V., "Exposition aux Etats-Unis", *Revue du Verre*, XXXXII, 1987, n. 12, p. 23-25.

JIŘINA ŽERTOVÁ

Maršíková, J., "Le verre de Jiřina Žertová", *Revue du Verre*, XXXV, 1980, n. 6, p. 18-21.

JÁN ZORITČÁK

Adlerová, A., "Skleněné plastiky Jána Zoričáka" ["Ján Zoritčák's Sculptures in Glass"], *Umění a řemesla*, 1972, n. 4, p. 16-18. (Summary in French.)

Girard, S., "Ján Zoritčák", *Revue de la Céramique et du Verre*, 1982, n. 4, p. 26-29.

"Interview mit Ján Zoritčák", *Neues Glas*, 1987, n. 4, p. 290-291.

Rusquec, C. du, "Réalité du verre au Japon, interview de Ján Zoritčák", *La Revue de la Céramique et du Verre*, 1986, n. 27, p. 27-30.

Save, C., "Le verrier du froid", *L'Atelier des Métiers d'Art*, 1980, n. 45, p. 8-10.

Šindelář, D., *Sklo - Marian Karel, Oldřich Plíva, Aleš Vašíček, Ján Zoričák*, Prague, 1981.

Zinz, D., "Ján Zoritčák - The 4th Dimension", *Neues Glas*, 1989, n. 1, p. 17-21.

INDEX

Only the principal artists, glassmakers and glassworks are indexed.